Transitional Justice Archives

Latin America has amassed comprehensive expertise in generating, managing, and providing access to archives documenting widespread human rights violations. This book explores and traces the multiple pathways that led to the creation and production of transitional justice archives in selected Latin American countries. Examining how transitional justice mechanisms have gathered and organised evidence by way of comparing traditional methods used in previous cases with the innovations introduced by digital technologies, the work also shows that the methods used to produce and create transitional justice archives will significantly affect their future utilisation. Presenting the viewpoints of archivists, scholars, and professionals engaged in truth commissions and trials, it incorporates perspectives from diverse fields such as law, human rights, archival studies, history, anthropology, and criminology. The volume is divided into two parts. The first focuses on case studies from Argentina, Chile, and Peru. Argentina and Chile have played a leading role in the development, management, and accessibility of extensive records documenting human rights abuses that occurred during the dictatorships in both countries. In the second part, academics and professionals of the Integrated System for Peace, Colombia's most recent transitional justice framework, discuss current challenges and developments in building the archives of the ongoing transitional justice process.

This book will be of significant interest to researchers and academics of transitional justice and human rights, as well as archivists and historians specialising in human rights.

Anita Ferrara is an assistant professor at the Irish Centre for Human Rights (ICHR), University of Galway.

Beatrice Canossi is a research fellow at Queen's University Belfast, School of Law.

Routledge Research in Human Rights Law

Defamation and the Right to Freedom of Speech
The UK in Comparative Perspective
Mariette Jones

Bulk Surveillance, Democracy and Human Rights Law in Europe
A Comparative Perspective
Marcin Rojszczak

Surveillance Law, Data Retention and Human Rights
A Risk to Democracy
Matthew White

Domestic Abuse and the European Court of Human Rights
Ronagh J.A. McQuigg

Human Rights Law and Corporate Regulation
A Neo-Concession Approach
Jonathan Barrett

Refugee Displacement, Disability and Human Rights
The Production, Processing and Power of Data
Philippa Duell-Piening

Detention and the Right to Liberty
Addressing Gaps in Protection at the European Court of Human Rights
Sabina Garahan

Transitional Justice Archives
Documenting Human Rights Violations in Latin America
Edited by Anita Ferrara and Beatrice Canossi

For more information about this series, please visit: www.routledge.com/Routledge-Research-in-Human-Rights-Law/book-series/HUMRIGHTSLAW

Transitional Justice Archives

Documenting Human Rights Violations in Latin America

Edited by Anita Ferrara and Beatrice Canossi

Routledge
Taylor & Francis Group
LONDON AND NEW YORK

First published 2025
by Routledge
4 Park Square, Milton Park, Abingdon, Oxon OX14 4RN

and by Routledge
605 Third Avenue, New York, NY 10158

Routledge is an imprint of the Taylor & Francis Group, an informa business

British Library Cataloguing-in-Publication Data
A catalogue record for this book is available from the British Library

Library of Congress Cataloging-in-Publication Data
Names: Ferrara, Anita, editor. | Canossi, Beatrice, editor.
Title: Transitional justice archives : documenting human rights violations in Latin America / edited by Anita Ferrara and Beatrice Canossi.
Description: Abingdon, Oxon [UK] ; New York, NY : Routledge, 2025. | Series: Routledge research in human rights law | Includes bibliographical references and index.
Identifiers: LCCN 2025003449 (print) | LCCN 2025003450 (ebook) | ISBN 9781041003397 (hardback) | ISBN 9781041003403 (paperback) | ISBN 9781003609322 (ebook)
Subjects: LCSH: Transitional justice—Latin America. | Justice, Administration of—Latin America. | Political crimes and offenses—Law and legislation—Latin America. | Violence (Law)—Latin America. | International law and human rights.
Classification: LCC KG495 .T73 2025 (print) | LCC KG495 (ebook) | DDC 026/.323044098—dc23/eng/20250128
LC record available at https://lccn.loc.gov/2025003449
LC ebook record available at https://lccn.loc.gov/2025003450

ISBN: 978-1-041-00339-7 (hbk)
ISBN: 978-1-041-00340-3 (pbk)
ISBN: 978-1-003-60932-2 (ebk)

DOI: 10.4324/9781003609322

Typeset in ITC Galliard Pro
by Apex CoVantage, LLC

This book is dedicated to all who devote their lives to collecting, gathering, and preserving evidence of human rights violations to protect the memory of what happened against oblivion, lies, and fear.

Contents

About the Editors

Anita Ferrara is an assistant professor at the Irish Centre for Human Rights (ICHR), University of Galway. Her research focuses on transitional justice and human rights, integrating memory studies, archival studies, and peace building. She leads the Transitional Justice and Peace Building Research Cluster (TJPR) at the ICHR and has previously worked with UN agencies and NGOs in Africa and Latin America.

Beatrice Canossi is a research fellow at Queen's University Belfast. She is a lawyer who specialises in criminal law and human rights. Beatrice received a prestigious award from the Irish Research Council and completed her PhD in law at the Irish Centre for Human Rights. Her research examines the relationship between judicial and extrajudicial bodies in transitional contexts, specifically focusing on the Colombian Integrated System for Peace.

Contributors

Aurora Yezzenia Ávila-Quintero is a political scientist and lawyer specialising in constitutional law from the National University of Colombia. She has participated in various university research groups and co-authored several academic articles. Since 2019, she has been working in Colombia's Special Jurisdiction for Peace in the office of Magistrate Oscar Parra-Vera.

Fernanda Barbosa Dos Santos is a journalist, historian, PhD candidate in human and social sciences at Universidad Nacional de Colombia, and a member of the media outlet Rutas del Conflicto. She has also been a consultant to the Colombian Truth Commission, a professor at Universidad del Rosario, and a reporter on local and international affairs.

Ruth Elena Borja Santa Cruz is a professor at Universidad Nacional Mayor de San Marcos, Perú. She worked at the General Archive of the Nation, the Truth and Reconciliation Commission from 2002 to 2003, and the Ombudsman's Office from 2004 to 2012. She also served as the Director of the Historical Archive between 2022 and 2024.

Emilio Crenzel is a principal researcher at the National Council of Scientific Research (CONICET) and a professor at the University of Buenos Aires, Argentina. He has extensively published on transitional justice, human rights, and social memories of political violence and dictatorships in the Southern Cone of Latin America.

Courtney Curran is an Australian-qualified lawyer with domestic and international investigative and prosecutorial practice experience in government and the private sector. Her doctoral research focuses on the intersectionality of transitional justice, archival science, and domestic legal efforts to address atrocity crimes. She is currently working for the Australian federal government.

Natalia Andrea Herrera Gálvez is a lawyer specialising in justice, victims, peacebuilding, and human rights defence. She has experience representing and supporting victims of serious human rights violations and conducting socio-legal investigations.

Andrés Medina Valencia served as the Coordinator for the Mission Information System of the Colombian Truth Commission. He is interested in connecting the natural and human sciences and has focused on designing and implementing transdisciplinary research and knowledge management methodologies, specifically focusing on the Colombian armed conflict.

Oscar Parra-Vera is a magistrate for Colombia's Special Jurisdiction for Peace (JEP). He holds an MSc in criminology and criminal justice from the University of Oxford and lectures at the National University of Colombia. Previously, he served as a senior legal officer at the Inter-American Court of Human Rights and has contributed as an expert for various international human rights bodies.

Trudy Huskamp Peterson worked at the U.S. National Archives (more than two years as Acting Archivist of the United States), the Open Society Archives (Budapest), and the UN High Commissioner for Refugees. She consults with police archives, truth commissions, and international tribunals and publishes extensively on archives and human rights.

Maria Prada Ramírez served as a permanent advisor to Francisco de Roux, the president of the Colombian Truth Commission. In this role, she led the institution's Legacy Strategy. She has been actively involved in peacebuilding and transitional justice efforts, focusing on policy and project implementation, facilitating dialogue and building strategic networks for political engagement and social ownership.

Flor Alba Romero Medina is an anthropologist specialising in human rights and holds a PhD in education. She is currently a professor and researcher at the National University of Colombia, where she teaches in the master's program on Human Rights, Transition, and Post-conflict.

Folco Zaffalon graduated in International Relations from the University of Bologna (Italy) and holds a master's degree in defence of Human Rights from the University of Santo Tomas in Bogota. In Colombia, he worked as an advisor to the Colombian Truth Commission, co-coordinator of the project "Traces of Disappearance" (2018–2022), and researcher for the Special Jurisdiction for Peace (2023–2024).

Introduction

Transitional Justice Archives: Documenting Human Rights Violations in Latin America

Anita Ferrara and Beatrice Canossi

Introduction

The concept for this book originated from an online international conference organised by the Irish Centre for Human Rights, University of Galway, in 2022. During this conference, scholars specialising in transitional justice (TJ), archivists, and professionals in the field discussed the significance and impact of records and documentation created by transitional justice mechanisms in various Latin American countries. Transitional justice is the process through which states and societies confront the consequences of serious and widespread human rights violations. This approach supports transitions from authoritarian regimes and conflict to democracy and peace. Key mechanisms to achieve these goals include truth commissions, trials, reparations, memorialisation initiatives, grassroots restorative practices, and guarantees to prevent future violations. Transitional justice institutions gather evidence of past crimes to address violations and repair harm done to victims and society.

This book defines transitional justice archives as "all records and documentary collections produced and left behind by transitional justice mechanisms, including truth commissions, judicial mechanisms established or specially dedicated to investigating mass atrocity crimes, places of memory, and institutions that provide reparations".[1] The book addresses a research gap by defining and outlining the characteristics of this specific group of archives. While the archives of human rights organisations and civil society groups have received considerable attention over the past 20 years, the archives related to transitional justice mechanisms have not been studied thoroughly and do not have the recognition they deserve. This introduction highlights several key characteristics of transitional justice archives that distinguish them from other types, such as human rights or state/repressive archives, which have primarily been the focus of existing literature. Previous literature has examined the instrumental role of archives in helping societies come to terms with

1 Anita Ferrara, "Archives and Transitional Justice in Chile: A Crucial Relationship," *Human Rights Review* 22 (2021): 253–78, https://doi.org/10.1007/s12142-021-00626-0.

DOI: 10.4324/9781003609322-1

widespread human rights violations.[2] Scholars and practitioners have focused on archives as human rights protection and accountability tools,[3] vehicles for preserving collective memory, and mechanisms for promoting social justice.[4] Quintana's report emphasises the vital importance of human rights archives in achieving both collective and individual rights.[5] The UN Principles to Combat Impunity also assert that archives are essential for realising the rights to truth, justice, and reparation.[6] The experiences of many transitional countries further demonstrate that the demands for truth, justice, and memory are closely linked to people's ability to access documents and records. As a result, several international organisations have conducted significant research on archives preservation, access, and safekeeping.[7] Viebach, Dagmar, and Luhe's special issue introduces conceptual advancements regarding the relationship between archives and transitional justice, drawing insights from critical archival scholarship applicable to transitional justice.[8]

Bell, Bernasconi, Hernández García, and Sosa analyse three specific sets of archives called "archives of violence". Their study discusses the Vicariate of Solidarity Archives in Chile, Open Memory in Argentina, and the National Commission of Historical Memory in Colombia. The authors examine how

2 Ramon Alberch I. Fugueras, *Archivos y Derechos Humanos* (Gijón: Trea, 2008); Elisabeth Baumgartner, Brandon Hamber, Briony Jones, Gráinne Kelly, and Ingrid Oliveira, *Documentation, Human Rights and Transitional Justice* (Baden-Baden: Nomos Verlagsgesellschaft, 2016); Kirsten Weld, *Paper Cadavers: The Archives of Dictatorship in Guatemala* (Durham, NC: Duke University Press, 2014).

3 Joel A. Blanco-Rivera, "Archives as Agents of Accountability and Justice: An Examination of the National Security Archive in the Context of Transitional Justice in Latin America" (PhD diss., University of Pittsburgh, 2012); Ferrara, "Archives and Transitional Justice in Chile."; Francesca Lessa, "Remnants of Truth: The Role of Archives in Human Rights Trials for Operation Condor," *Latin American Research Review* 56, no. 1 (2021): 183–99, https://doi.org/10.25222/larr.769.

4 Wendy M. Duff, Andrew Flinn, Karen Emily Suurtamm, David A. Wallace, "Social justice impact of archives: a preliminary investigation", *Archival Science*, no. 4 (2013): 317–348.; Randall C. Jimerson, "Archives for All: Professional Responsibility and Social Justice," *The American Archivist* 70, no. 2 (2007): 252–81, http://www.jstor.org/stable/40294571; Amanda Strauss, "Treading the Ground of Contested Memory: Archivists and the Human Rights Movement in Chile," *Archival Science* 15 (2015): 369–97, https://doi.org/10.1007/s10502-014-9223-3.

5 Antonio González Quintana, *Archival Policies in the Protection of Human Rights* (Paris: International Council on Archives, 2009), https://www.ica.org/app/uploads/2023/12/Report_Gonzalez-Quintana_EN.pdf.

6 UNHCHR, *Updated Set of Principles for the Protection and Promotion of Human Rights through Action to Combat Impunity* (E/CN.4/2005/102/Add.1, 2005).

7 Swisspeace Archives and Dealing with the Past Project, http://archivesproject.swisspeace.ch; International Council on Archives, *Principles of Access to Archives*, Committee on Best Practices and Standards Working Group on Access, 2012, https://www.ica.org/resource/principles-of-access-to-archives/; CNMH, *Política Pública de Archivos de Derechos Humanos, Memoria Histórica y Conflicto Armado* (Bogotá: Centro Nacional de Memoria Histórica, 2017), https://centrodememoriahistorica.gov.co/politica-publica-de-archivos-de-derechos-humanos-memoria-historica-y-conflicto-armado/.

8 Julia Viebach, Dagmar Hovestädt, and Ulrike Lühe, eds., "Beyond Evidence: The Use of Archives in Transitional Justice," *International Journal of Human Rights* 23 (2021): 381.

these archives were developed and used, particularly as judicial evidence in trials. Moreover, they emphasise several themes across the cases, including the reasons for their establishment, their intended purposes, and issues of autonomy and ownership. In their reflections, the authors also consider how new technologies may shape the future dissemination of these archives.[9] In addition to protecting human rights and ensuring accountability, archives are increasingly recognised for their role in shaping a nation's collective memory. They are often seen as independent "memory spaces".[10] According to Nora, archives are essential for creating memory about recent events. They interact with various objects and artefacts, providing spaces for contesting the past through dynamic and limitless processes.[11] A wide range of scholarship in Latin America has been dedicated to the relationship between archives and memory, and the topic is currently at the centre of a very active and lively debate.[12]

However, since the early publication of Peterson's works, "Final Acts" and "Temporary Courts, Permanent Records", very few studies have examined the role and impact of the archives and records left behind by truth commissions and trials.[13] In her in-depth analysis of Chile's case, Ferrara examined the various and often unexpected ways human rights archives and truth commissions' archives have contributed to and interacted with subsequent transitional justice mechanisms throughout the long transitional period.[14] Jones and Oliveira highlighted the potential of truth commissions' archives as democratic spaces.[15] One of the latest works on truth commissions' documentation is the edited book by Proscovia Svärd and Bonny Ibhawoh. The book addresses the many challenges of TRC archives' location and access policies. It argues that the truth commissions' archives remain largely unavailable and inaccessible

9 Vikki Bell, Oriana Bernasconi, Jaime Hernandez Garcia, and Cecilia Sosa, *Archives of Violence: Case Studies from South America* (Goldsmiths, University of London, 2021), https://www.memoriayderechoshumanosuah.org/publicaciones/archives-of-violence-case-studies-from-south-america/.

10 Maria Graciela Acuña et al., *Archivos y memoria de la represión en América Latina (1973–1990)* (Santiago: LOM Ediciones, 2016).

11 Eric Ketelaar, "Archives as Spaces of Memory," *Journal of the Society of Archivists* 29, no. 1 (2008): 9–27; Pierre Nora, "Between Memory and History: Les Lieux de Mémoire," *Representations* 26 (1989): 7–24.

12 Comité Nacional de la Memoria del Mundo, Archivos en Chile: Miradas, Experiencias y Desafíos (2016), https://museoquillota.cl/wp-content/uploads/2023/06/libro.pdf; Ludmila Da Silva Catela, "El mundo de los archivos," in *Los archivos de la represión: Documentos, memoria y verdad*, eds. Ludmila Da Silva Catela and Elizabeth Jelin (Madrid: Siglo XXI, 2002), 1–18; Archivo Nacional de Chile, *Derecho a la Memoria: Archivos de Derechos Humanos*, 2020, https://www.archivonacional.gob.cl/sites/www.archivonacional.gob.cl/files/2022-09/Derecho%20a%20la%20memoria%201.%20Archivos%20y%20derechos%20humanos.pdf.

13 Trudy Huskamp Peterson, *Final Acts: A Guide to Preserving the Records of Truth Commissions* (Washington, DC: United States Institute of Peace, 2005).

14 Ferrara, "Archives and Transitional Justice in Chile."

15 Briony Jones and Ingrid Oliveira, "Truth Commission Archives as 'New Democratic Spaces'," *Journal of Human Rights Practice* 8, no. 1 (February 2016): 6–24, https://doi.org/10.1093/jhuman/huv016.

in the post-conflict societies where truth commissions are established. The authors claim that: "Despite their mandates and objectives of accessible public interest documentation, TRC documentation is often politicised and out of reach for the victims and the post-conflict societies at large".[16]

Even fewer studies have focused on the archives left behind by international courts and tribunals and the archives from domestic trials prosecuting international crimes. Vukušić emphasises the extensive material produced by the International Criminal Tribunal for the former Yugoslavia (ICTY). She discusses how the nature and purpose of the institution shaped these archives. Her article illustrates that the contents of these archives are essential for understanding the various aspects of the violence that occurred during the disintegration of Yugoslavia. Vukušić argues that these archives are crucial for combating denial and for preserving the memory of the brutal violence that claimed over 100,000 lives and traumatised many more. She argues for accessibility to the greatest extent possible without jeopardising legal proceedings or the safety of witnesses.[17] Redwood's book is one of the few in-depth studies of the archives of the International Criminal Tribunal for Rwanda. It presents a critical analysis of the knowledge production processes within international courts. It examines the type of international community envisioned in these archives. It highlights the significance of archives' physical nature in understanding how knowledge is generated and contested in the international sphere.[18]

Redwood also highlights the close association between archives and justice, claiming that "the archive plays two clear roles in this search for justice. The first is a perhaps less glamorous role of facilitating a justice to come. The second is acting as a site of justice, in and of itself".[19] Nevertheless, Redwood raises critical questions about the relationship between archives, transitional justice, and the community. He claims that TJ archives might become tools of nationalist governance and selective in their evidence collection. The author argues that TJ discourses shape the testimonies collected, including privileging divisive victim/victimiser binaries and narratives. To counter this, the authors call for scholars and practitioners to fight for the inclusion of the "counter-archive" within transitional justice practice and, indeed, to challenge what is imagined as transitional justice.[20]

16 Proscovia Svärd and Bonny Ibhawoh, eds., *Documentation from Truth and Reconciliation Commissions*, 1st ed. (London: Routledge, 2024) p. 4.
17 Iva Vukušić, "Archives of Mass Violence: Understanding and Using ICTY Trial Records," *Comparative Southeast European Studies* 70, no. 4 (2022): 585–607, https://doi.org/10.1515/soeu-2021-0050.
18 Henry Redwood, *The Archival Politics of International Courts* (Cambridge: Cambridge University Press, 2021).
19 Henry Redwood, "Archiving Justice," in *The Oxford Handbook of Transitional Justice*, eds. Jens Meierhenrich, Alexander Laban Hinton, and Lawrence Douglas (Oxford: Oxford University Press, 2023).
20 Redwood, "Archiving Justice."

Although there is increasing acknowledgement of archives' various roles in transitional contexts and their intricate relationship with transitional justice, the challenges regarding how transitional justice mechanisms develop their archives have not been adequately addressed. This encompasses understanding the methods used to gather evidence, the approaches to data collection and analysis, the contexts in which these archives are established, and how they are utilised over time. The chapters of this book are designed to provoke dialogue on these critical areas. They provide a distinct perspective on transitional justice archives, differentiating them from other archival records and documentary collections. This distinction is based on five main aspects: 1) the timing of their creation, 2) the role of the institutions that construct these archives, 3) their permanent and official status, 4) the variety of sources that make them up, and 5) the diverse uses over the longer-term.

The book examines these aspects by analysing four case studies from Latin America: Argentina, Chile, Peru, and Colombia. The Latin American region has developed most transitional justice mechanisms, including truth commissions, domestic and transnational trials, reparations, memorialisation initiatives, and institutional reforms.[21] Consequently, the countries examined have developed significant expertise in the creation, assembly, organisation, management, and access policies of archives that record widespread human rights violations.[22]

The book is divided into two parts. The first part analyses the cases of Chile, Argentina, and Peru. Chile and Argentina have taken the lead in documenting and collecting evidence of human rights abuses. They have received significant international recognition for their efforts in organising and classifying documents related to the atrocities committed during their dictatorships.[23] Bernasconi's work examines how the Vicariate of Solitary in Chile constructed its archives and, along with many other civil society organisations, pioneered evidence collection while abuses occurred.[24] Their painstaking work in evidence collection produced two significant impacts: 1) it significantly expanded the culture of human rights since the 1970s, and 2) the evidence collected activated most of the contemporary international and regional human rights mechanisms, including the Inter-American System of Human Rights and various United Nations bodies and mechanisms responsible for human rights protection and monitoring.[25]

21 Elin Skaar, Jemima García-Godos, and Cath Collins, *Transitional Justice in Latin America: The Uneven Road from Impunity towards Accountability* (London: Routledge, 2016).

22 Oriana Bernasconi and Elizabeth Lira, "Making State Violence Visible: Documenting, Investigating and Denouncing Atrocities," in *Resistance to Political Violence in Latin America: Documenting Atrocity*, ed. Oriana Bernasconi (Cham: Springer, 2019), 1–30.

23 Louis Bickford, "The Archival Imperative: Human Rights and Historical Memory in Latin America's Southern Cone," *Human Rights Quarterly* 21, no. 4 (1999): 1097–122, http://www.jstor.org/stable/762757.

24 Oriana Bernasconi, ed., *Resistance to Political Violence in Latin America: Documenting Atrocity* (Cham: Springer, 2019).

25 Darren G. Hawkins, *International Human Rights and Authoritarian Rule in Chile* (Lincoln: University of Nebraska Press, 2002).

When democracy was restored, the truth commissions established in Chile and Argentina after the brutal dictatorships of Pinochet and the military junta accomplished a monumental work in a short time. They collected existing records and heard thousands of testimonies despite facing hostility and non-cooperation from the military and armed forces.[26] As shown in the respective chapters, the truth commissions in these two countries have set a global precedent for information gathering and classification methods that have been emulated worldwide. Additionally, Chile is the only country in the world that has created a second truth commission specifically focused on the survivors of torture and political imprisonment that occurred during the dictatorship.

A few years later, the Truth Commission's final report in Peru represented an enormous achievement in the search for truth and justice in Peru.[27] Even before it was released, many implicated in the abuses drew harsh criticism. Peru's Truth Commission archives were an innovative development in Latin America. It was the first truth commission in the region to hold public hearings and promoted extensive accessibility to the records collected by the TRC.[28] Before the Peruvian Truth Commissions, most TRC archives in Latin America were kept confidential except for the judges and lawyers investigating the human rights cases. Finally, the cases of Chile, Argentina, and Peru provide insight into how their transitional justice archives have been utilised following the dismantling of the institutions that produced them.

The second part of the book focuses entirely on the case of Colombia, which is implementing a complex transitional justice system known as the *Sistema Integral para la Paz* (Integrated System for Peace – SIP). This system consists of several components: a judicial body called the Special Jurisdiction for Peace (JEP), a Truth Commission (CEV), and a Unit for the Search of Missing Persons (UBPD). These mechanisms were preceded by a range of judicial and non-judicial bodies aimed at addressing the crimes committed during more than 50 years of armed conflict. Consequently, the current TJ mechanisms have gathered substantial information from multiple sources. Academics and professionals engaged in the system provide invaluable insights into the ongoing processes of archival creation, examining current challenges, developments, and innovations in creating both the Truth Commission

26 Anita Ferrara, *Assessing the Long-Term Impact of Truth Commissions: The Chilean Truth and Reconciliation Commission in Historical Perspective* (Routledge, Taylor & Francis Group, 2015); Emilio Crenzel, "Between the Voices of the State and the Human Rights Movement: Never Again and the Memories of the Disappeared in Argentina," *Journal of Social History* 44, no. 4 (Summer 2011): 1063–76.

27 Lisa J. Laplante, "The Peruvian Truth Commission's Historical Memory Project: Empowering Truth-Tellers to Confront Truth Deniers," *Journal of Human Rights* 6, no. 4 (2007): 433–52, https://doi.org/10.1080/14754830701692989.

28 Eduardo González Cueva, "The Peruvian Truth and Reconciliation Commission and the Challenge of Impunity," in *Transitional Justice in the Twenty-First Century: Beyond Truth versus Justice*, eds. Naomi Roht-Arriaza and Javier Mariezcurrena (Cambridge: Cambridge University Press, 2012), 70–91.

archives and the judicial archives of the JEP. Colombia has developed innovative methods for collecting information, preserving evidence, and disseminating findings. The Colombian Truth Commission is recognised as the world's first fully digital truth commission.[29] Colombia is a unique and significant case in discussions of transitional justice and archives, particularly regarding their timing and transitional momentum within its context and the broader Latin American landscape. The country has experienced a prolonged internal conflict while functioning as a liberal democracy. It has initiated various efforts to address its past and has made some progress in resolving the conflict. According to Alberch I Fugueras, archives in Colombia have been essential in promoting peace. However, this role also brings specific challenges, especially concerning archives documenting human rights violations. The author highlights two primary areas of concern: access to these archives and preservation of the documentary legacy related to the conflict.[30] The challenges discussed in this book's chapters about Colombia and the innovative practices developed by the TJ personnel to address them are significant contributions to this field.

Finally, the chapters of this book can be seen as a progressive history of archives and transitional justice mechanisms. The book highlights a significant shift in archival knowledge and awareness that has occurred since the early establishment of truth commissions in Latin America. The early commissions had limited powers and focused on fact-finding for future trials. Since the 1990s, there have been numerous developments, including advancements in human rights law and a growing recognition of the importance of archives in safeguarding individuals' rights. Additionally, there have been improvements in archival protection laws and access to public information. This book discusses how these developments have contributed to meaningful progress and innovations in the field. The book's chapters feature contributions from academics, archivists, and professionals with diverse backgrounds. It showcases the perspectives of local scholars and practitioners from various fields, such as law, human rights, archival studies, history, anthropology, and criminology. It draws on the wealth of experience from some contributors while also considering the voices of emerging scholars and professionals.

The Conceptualisation of TJ Archives

The literature often categorises various types of archives that document human rights violations under the umbrella term "human rights archives". Caswell went so far as to argue that records documenting violations everywhere are all

29 "Colombia Tiene la Primera Comisión de la Verdad Nativa Digital del Mundo," *Hacemos Memoria*, July 12, 2021, accessed December 21, 2024, https://hacemosmemoria.org/2021/07/12/colombia-tiene-la-primera-comision-de-la-verdad-nativa-digital-del-mundo/.

30 Ramon Alberch I. Fugueras, "Archives for Memory and Justice in Colombia after the Peace Agreements," in *Archives and Human Rights*, eds. Jens Boel, Perrine Canavaggio, and Antonio González Quintana (Abingdon: Routledge, 2021), 273–74.

human rights archives.[31] Jelin and Da Silva Catela have grouped human rights archives into three main categories: archives of repressive institutions, such as secret agencies, police, and military services; archives of human rights organisations and victims' organisations that opposed and resisted the repressive regimes; and finally, the archives of courts, truth commissions, and memory sites created to deal with the legacy of past violations.[32] Balcells and Sullivan have defined another category of archives as "conflict archives" to refer to "written material systematically produced as part of a political contest between a government force and an armed challenger (either domestic or international) and later collected and preserved for public access".[33] Conflict archives typically contain memos, investigative reports, communiqués, and other documents produced by government or rebel forces. Such records are inherent to and contemporaneous with the conflict.[34]

This book argues that there needs to be clearer definitions regarding the different categories of archives that record violent and systemic abuses of power. Although human rights archives, conflict archives, state secret archives, and transitional justice archives all record human rights violations, it is crucial to emphasise their differences. Understanding these distinctions is essential for appreciating their unique roles and impacts within their societies. This understanding also has significant implications for future dissemination, access, and management policies related to these archives.

The TJ archives are distinctive for several reasons:

1. First, there is a temporal factor: human rights, repressive, and conflict archives are typically assembled while violations occur. Human rights archives are created by civil society groups that oppose human rights violations as a form of documentation and resistance. Repressive archives are bureaucratic records maintained by the state and its secret agencies and intelligence services responsible for the atrocities. In contrast, transitional justice archives are established after violations occur. By the time evidence, documents, and testimonies are discovered and organised into a new archival collection, a perspective of time has developed.
2. Secondly, the role of the institutions that build TJ archives: TJ mechanisms are official bodies, usually authorised and/or funded by states, to overcome complex transitions while at the same time guaranteeing the rights of the victims to truth, reparation, justice, memory, and non-repetition.

31 Michelle Caswell, "Defining Human Rights Archives: Introduction to the Special Double Issue on Archives and Human Rights," *Archival Science* 14, no. 3–4 (2014): 207–13.

32 Ludmila Da Silva Catela and Elizabeth Jelin, eds., *Los Archivos de la Represión: Documentos, Memoria y Verdad*, vol. 4 (Madrid: Siglo XXI de España Editores, 2002).

33 Laia Balcells and Christopher M. Sullivan, "New Findings from Conflict Archives: An Introduction and Methodological Framework," *Journal of Peace Research* 55, no. 2 (2018): 137–46, https://www.jstor.org/stable/48596161.

34 Balcells and Sullivan, "New Findings from Conflict Archives."

Despite having different objectives and mandates, all TJ bodies utilise a vast amount of existing information; in doing so, they also generate and maintain their own archives. These bodies strive to find a balance between competing interests, to protect and promote the rights of the victims while at the same time rebuilding the foundation of the social texture divided and traumatised by years of conflict and oppression. While providing victims and their families with a platform to share their stories, TJ mechanisms also verify and cross-check the reliability of the information gathered. In this way, transitional justice mechanisms transform previously denied, undisclosed, unknown, or hidden stories and information into public and official knowledge about the past. Furthermore, the significance of the TJ archive is enhanced by the state's recognition of the crimes committed in the past, along with its acceptance of responsibility and occasional delivery of an apology, which establishes an obligation to act and provide reparations. For example, Niezen notes that in relation to the digital evidence collected by civil society and those exiled in the Syrian Archives, the relationship between digital evidence databases and transitional justice has become complex in contexts of ongoing violence. In such situations, perpetrators are typically absent from the process, which means there are no apologies or acknowledgements of responsibility. Transitional justice archives can potentially include the perspectives of these individuals because of the unique conditions under which they are created. The involvement of perpetrators is crucial for addressing the unanswered questions of victims. While developing a digital evidence database is an incredibly valuable and essential effort that can contribute to accountability, it is important to recognise that, as he claims, perpetrators often remain unknown and unknowable.[35]

3. Thirdly, TJ archives are permanent official records: TJ institutions are temporary bodies of justice and have a limited amount of time to fulfil their functions and mandates; their archives, however, are permanent and constitute one of their most important legacies. As Adler notes, truth commissions do not conclude with their mandates and reports; instead, their archives serve as a living record of these mechanisms.[36] In connection with court archives, the UN established the International Residual Mechanism for Criminal Tribunals (IRMCT) to preserve the records of the Tribunal for the former Yugoslavia and the International Tribunal for Rwanda. Redwood

35 Ronald Niezen, "Open-Source Justice: Digital Archives and the Criminal State," in *Narratives of Mass Atrocity* (2022): 247–78.

36 Cited in Daniel Ospina-Celis, "*Archives and Transitional Justice: Lessons from Colombia's Truth Commission*," in *Documentation from Truth and Reconciliation Commissions*, eds. Proscovia Svärd and Bonny Ibhawoh, 1st ed. (London: Routledge, 2024), 20, https://doi.org/10.4324/9781032618623; Nanci Adler, "Introduction: On History, Historians, and Transitional Justice," in *Understanding the Age of Transitional Justice: Crimes, Courts, Commissions, and Chronicling*, ed. Nanci Adler (New Brunswick: Rutgers University Press, 2018), 1–18.

argues that the significance of these archives was so profound that the UN decided to construct a new facility for follow-on mechanisms, recognising the need for an upgraded archive capable of permanently storing the tribunal's records. The archives were seen as a means for the tribunal's work to endure into the future.[37]

4. Fourthly, transitional justice archives are extremely diverse and rich in content: they include a wide variety of records from numerous public and private sources. These archives encompass documents from human rights organisations, religious groups, private organisations, victims' and relatives' groups, community archives, opposition groups, trade unions, and political parties. Additionally, they contain documentation from international and regional organisations. The TJ archives also have access to state records from most public agencies, including ministerial records, civil registries, regional and local archives, as well as archives from repressive agencies and secret intelligence files. They collect declassified documents from international agencies and institutions as well. Furthermore, the archives include direct testimonies from thousands of victims, their families, witnesses, exiles, and even perpetrators. This wide range of sources gives the TJ archives significant historiographical value, enabling them to impact societies over the long term, as demonstrated by the cases discussed in this book.
5. Fifthly, TJ archives are dynamic and continue to be relevant many years after their creation: these archives have the potential to be used and re-used multiple times to advance transitional justice objectives, preserve the collective memory, challenge denial and historical revisionism, and uncover new sources of information. As demonstrated in the chapters of this book, these records take on a life of their own and will be adapted to various contexts over time.

The Construction and Legacy of the TJ Archives

This volume is organised around three main themes: 1) the methods used by transitional justice mechanisms to gather evidence and create their archives; 2) the challenges of accessing different sources of evidence, especially records from secret and intelligence agencies; and 3) the various ways transitional justice archives have been utilised and repurposed over time. The chapters in this book explore how transitional justice mechanisms gather evidence from various sources to document human rights violations committed by past regimes or during armed conflicts. They provide a comprehensive analysis of how truth commissions and courts evaluate and utilise the material gathered during their existence and their role in organising and archiving this evidence for future use and dissemination. The cases presented in this book highlight the importance of making informed decisions about the organisation of collected evidence,

37 Redwood, "Archiving Justice."

the creation of databases, the methods used to gather and analyse statements, and the application of information science. These factors play a critical role in determining how the archives will be constructed and utilised. Even more critical are the choices related to access, confidentiality, and the preservation of these archives. The chapters in this book also stress the importance of creating specific institutions to preserve, manage, and utilise transitional justice archives. Examples include the National Archive of Memory in Argentina, the Information Centre in Peru, and the National Commission for Historical Memory in Colombia.

A recurring theme throughout the chapters is the increasing importance of archival legacies over time. The cases of Argentina, Peru, and Chile illustrate how truth commission archives have been utilised multiple times to fulfil states' obligations, assist victims, and contribute to forming a nation's collective memory. From a temporal perspective, these cases offer an opportunity to retrospectively examine the diverse and often unexpected ways in which these archives have been used and the roles they have played in revealing and documenting the histories of conflicts and dictatorships over the years. The diverse composition of transitional justice archives make them dynamic and vital records, continually evolving to meet various needs and purposes. Earlier cases demonstrate that TJ archives gained significance over time through practical experience. However, the recent situation in Colombia highlights that the legacy of the Truth Commission and the archives of the Special Jurisdiction for Peace have been significant concerns for professionals and researchers from the beginning of the process. Colombia stands out as one of the few examples where preserving records and ensuring access were central functions of the Colombian Truth Commission right from the outset.[38]

Trudy Huskamp Peterson's chapter introduces the book by emphasising how transitional justice institutions create remarkable records that comprise a unique collection of materials that can never be replicated. Peterson notes that the records generated during transitional justice processes can be utilised in future litigation unless the establishing act explicitly prohibits their use in subsequent prosecutions. However, the records of transitional justice institutions provide much more than that; she shows how these records can support societies in many additional ways unrelated to litigation.

The chapter by Emilio Crenzel explores the creation and reconstruction of archives related to the system of disappearances in Argentina from the military dictatorship to the present day. The chapter discusses the vital role of the *Comisión Nacional sobre la Desaparición de Personas* (National Commission on the Disappearance of Persons – CONADEP) in investigating and documenting the disappearances in Argentina. The information collected by CONADEP was sourced from both local and international human rights organisations that had documented these events during the period of repression, as well as from

38 Ospina-Celis, *Archives and Transitional Justice*, 17–19 and 26.

the archives of the repressive forces that were uncovered during its investigation. The CONADEP archive was created in conjunction with its investigation, and it became an active instrument for understanding human rights violations, which was essential in challenging the prevailing narrative of the armed forces in the public sphere. The Commission collected thousands of testimonies from survivors of disappearances and thousands of photos documenting the existence of clandestine centres. The CONADEP archive was essential evidence for the 1985 trial of the military junta, and this information became a valuable tool in the legal cases that reopened in the country many years later. While other archives have complemented years later the information provided by the CONADEP, its archive has continued to be a source of evidence over time for the search for the children of the disappeared who were kidnapped, for the location of the secret burials and remains an irreplaceable source of historical knowledge in the reconstruction of those events. Crenzel claims that these archives have been shaped by political struggles to give meaning to this dark period of history, and their formation, along with their collection and classification strategies, have been influenced by these struggles. The records of the military junta trials, all human rights prosecutions, and the CONADEP are currently stored in the *Archivo Nacional de la Memoria* (National Archive of Memory). While this archive represents a progressive step towards nearly universal access to these documents, it increasingly employs discretionary criteria for accessing them.

Anita Ferrara's chapter explores the impact of the Truth Commissions' archives in Chile on subsequent efforts related to reparation, justice, and memory. The aim is to enhance our understanding of the various roles that the Truth and Reconciliation Commissions' (TRCs) archives have played as tools for achieving truth, justice, and reparation throughout Chile's long transitional period. The Rettig Commission marked the first public acknowledgement of the human rights violations committed during the brutal dictatorship of Pinochet and sparked a public debate about these events. The Truth Commission collected thousands of testimonies nationwide and gathered all available evidence regarding human rights violations. This monumental effort was primarily possible due to the previous work of human rights organisations, especially the Vicariate of Solidarity, which had meticulously compiled data on every reported case of disappearance. Although the impact of the Rettig Commission was short-lived, its archives served several important purposes. First, they were used to provide reparations to the thousands of relatives of victims recognised by the Commission. Later, these archives served as crucial evidence in trials. In the following years, the Commission's archives became one of the most reliable sources of evidence in subsequent legal proceedings. This chapter argues that the methods employed for collecting statements and documents, along with the legal backgrounds of the commissioners, were key factors in enhancing the judicial utility of the archives. While the archives of the first Truth and Reconciliation Commission (TRC) were utilised in trials and for reparations, the archives of the second Truth Commission, known as the Valech Commission, were sealed for 50 years. This situation has sparked intense debate and initiated a lengthy judicial battle to open these archives. The chapter discusses some of these issues and reflects on their implications for the future of the country's historical memory.

Courtney Curran explores the role of court archives in the contemporary Chilean memory landscape. These records were left behind by the famous trial of the Chilean military junta in France held in 2010, also known as the French Pinochet case. Against the theoretical framing of "law as memory", the use of audio-visual recordings from the French-Pinochet trial in the exhibition called *Juzgar y Filmar* (Judging and Filming) showcased by the Museum of Memory and Human Rights (MMDH) in Santiago, between September 6 and December 10, 2023, demonstrates how judicial archives can contribute to constructing a collective memory of atrocity. This piece by Curran provides a novel methodology to better understand the uses of archives in transitional justice processes by tracing court-derived files as they travel through space-time, accruing new meanings with each activation. The legal archive created by the French Pinochet trial consists of court files and audio-visual recordings, posters and press releases, sketches and speeches. This vast repository stored files containing French, Spanish, English, and German languages with imbued cultural and legal system nuances, with some original documentation, photographs, and other artefacts transferred from various continents for the French judiciary by relatives of the victims and by judges in other jurisdictions working on similar or related cases. The anthropologically inspired method of following objects in motion as they accrue meaning with each use or activation is posited in the chapter as an effective way to understand how these legal archives have been used in later and ongoing memory processes.

In her chapter, Ruth Elena Borja Santa Cruz, having worked in the Peruvian Truth Commission's Documentation Centre, discusses the construction and utilisation of the Truth Commission's archives. Since she played a vital role in managing these archives, the author offers an inside perspective on how the Truth and Reconciliation Commission's (TRC) Documentation Unit collected evidence from various public and private organisations. The TRC's most significant accomplishment was the creation of a comprehensive database that recorded the names of victims, their relatives, locations, and instances of violence. This database included testimonies from victims, their families, witnesses, and, in some cases, perpetrators from across the country. Gathering these accounts enabled the TRC to build numerous cases for prosecution and reparations while also raising public awareness about the human rights violations that occurred during the 20 years of internal armed conflict. This documentation was transferred to the Ombudsman's Office, which established a dedicated Information Centre. In 2004, a transparency law empowered the Information Centre to disclose the TRC's information while ensuring the security and privacy of individuals. This law allowed the public to access information regarding the country's experiences over the previous two decades. Borja Santa Cruz's chapter highlights various ways the Information Centre disseminates information, including organising school visits for students and providing access to relatives searching for details about their disappeared or murdered loved ones. The Information Centre also supplies information from its databases to public agencies for the payment of reparations to victims and offers support to courts investigating related cases. Preserving this legacy is essential for future generations, who must learn from these painful chapters to help build a country's collective memory of the past.

Moving to the second part of the book, the chapters will discuss important innovations introduced by the case of Colombia in terms of how the current transitional justice mechanisms are building their archives and preserving them for future uses. Colombia has certainly benefited from the experiences of other countries. Still, it is important to recognise the extensive experience accumulated within the country in relation to documenting human rights violations over many years. While Colombian law classifies all archives documenting human rights violations as human rights archives, the archives discussed in this book are identified as transitional justice archives.[39] The most remarkable aspect of Colombia's case is that the TJ mechanisms implemented after the 2016 Peace Agreement included in their respective mandates specific clauses containing instructions on the preservation, safekeeping, and access policies for the archives they would produce, in accordance with Colombian archival laws, national security laws, transparency laws, and data protection laws.

As the chapter by Flor Alba Romero Medina shows, Colombia has experienced an armed conflict for over 50 years, resulting in a vast amount of documentation and evidence. Given the abundance of existing archives surviving TJ mechanisms established even before the transition, her chapter gives us an overview of the different types of TJ archives gathered in the country since 2005. The Justice and Peace Law provided the framework for how the Colombian State addressed the members of Colombia's United Self-Defense Forces. These trials left behind judicial archives by the courts that dealt with demobilised paramilitary in the country. The trials played a crucial role in helping the country understand the phenomenon of paramilitarism and its criminal methods of social and territorial control. Beyond court archives, the chapter also highlights the importance of establishing the National Center for Historical Memory in 2011, whose archives are critical for constructing historical and collective memory. Romero Medina examines the role and potential impact of the archives associated with the current mechanisms of the Integrated System, which include the Jurisdiction for Peace (JEP), the Truth Commission, and

39 Presidency of the Republic of Colombia, *Decree 1081/2015 (full version with modifications)*, Bogotá, May 26, 2015, art. 21.1.5.4.7; Human rights documents and archives. Human rights archives correspond to documents that broadly refer to violations of human rights and infractions of International Humanitarian Law. Human rights archives must be subject to the preservation, protection, and access measures defined in the international human rights framework, jurisprudence, domestic legislation, and in particular, the final paragraph of article 21 of Law 1712 of 2014.

the Unit for the Search for the Missing. These archives contain crucial information about the contexts of structural violence and the individuals responsible for it. They hold significant legal, historical, political, and cultural value, making them an essential resource for the historical memory of the country and its society. In summary, Romero Medina argues that these archives are vital for the reconciliation of Colombian society.

The chapter by Andrés Medina Valencia and Maria Prada Ramírez explores the innovative methodology the Truth Commission of Colombia employed in constructing its archives. The authors provide valuable insider knowledge, having directly contributed to establishing the Documentary Fund of the Truth Commission. The chapter is the first in-depth account of how the archives of the truth commissions were built, becoming the first fully digital commission worldwide. They highlight the decision to rely on modern digital information systems and platforms, combining traditional and innovative archival methodology with the help of information science and big data equipment. As the authors claim, this methodology has also been an experiment in transparency, accountability, and reliability of the data collected. The documents are fully accessible online and open source, offering a unique opportunity for archives' accessibility. The Commission focused on active listening, collecting thousands of testimonies and reports, and encouraging social dialogue throughout its three-year mandate. It also developed a legacy strategy aimed at integrating the results of its efforts within a social and political framework for the medium and long term. This strategy seeks to make meaningful contributions to coexistence and prevent future conflicts. The Truth Commission presented a transmedia report that provides permanent access to society, enabling a more immersive exploration of the stories, experiences, testimonies, cases, and files collected and lived during the armed conflict in Colombia. The Commission's experience emphasises the importance of an interdisciplinary approach to understanding and managing documentary collections that include diverse resources. The chapter discusses the most substantial aspects of the Truth Commission and the lessons learnt. The Documentary Fund of the Truth Commission is considered an essential historical legacy for Colombia and has recently been recognized by UNESCO's Memory of the World Program (MoWLAC).

The chapter by Oscar Parra-Vera, Aurora Yezzenia Ávila-Quintero, and Natalia Andrea Herrera Gálvez provides a comprehensive examination of how the Special Jurisdiction for Peace is gaining access to intelligence and security archives of the Security's Administrative Department (DAS). This state agency operated until 2011, when it was discovered that it illegally used intelligence to persecute political opponents and critics of the government, committing human rights violations and having links to paramilitary groups. This chapter discusses how the Special Jurisdiction for Peace safeguards and obtains access to these secret archives using precautionary measures. These archives can potentially shed light on serious human rights violations, violations of international humanitarian law, and facts related to the armed conflict. The most relevant aspects discussed in the chapter are the debates and public conversations regarding securing access to and protecting the DAS archives. Entities involved in these discussions included many Colombian state agencies, the United Nations, civil society organisations, academic experts, victims, judicial representatives, and other stakeholders. These roundtables collected the views of civil society and victims on the importance of disclosing these archives and led to establishing protocols with the National Archive to organise, classify, and preserve these documents that remain hidden and under challenging conditions of access. In this regard, the chapter also highlights the constant tension between the principle of legal reserve and the right to access information, showing how the JEP is taking steps to resolve these issues.

Fernanda Barbosa Dos Santos and Folco Zaffalon, two researchers of the Colombian Truth Commission, discuss their experience of creating, developing, and publishing a novel archive of transitional justice called "Traces of Disappearance". The exhibition project is based on investigations by the Colombian Truth Commission, in collaboration with Forensic Architecture, focusing on three episodes of violence: 1) the forced disappearances during the retaking of the Palace of Justice, 2) the dispossession of the land in a region of Colombia (Urabá Antioquia), and 3) the effects of the conflict on the territory and the Nukak indigenous people. The chapter delves into the challenges faced while collecting information, including the abundance of materials of different types, the lack of institutional response, access to reserved documents, and the discovery of previously unknown archives. It also explains how new archives were created using tools and technologies typical of Forensic Architecture's work and the choice of the final narrative that emerged in the exhibition. Finally, the chapter discusses how these new archives were circulated through physical exhibitions in some of Colombia's leading museums and online platforms. Throughout the text, the authors reflect on several questions, such as how the ability (or inability) to access archives impacts investigations into human rights violations, what the decision not to make all the material public tells us, the challenges of circulating new transitional justice files, and what opportunities for knowledge and research are opened up by the public exhibition of archives. Their chapter also examines the difficulties in balancing the principle of maximum openness of the records and the protection of witnesses and victims whose lives could be at risk if exposed. Those dilemmas will continue to represent important aspects of the debate in relation to the opening of the archives of truth commissions and other mechanisms where confessions and testimonies were obtained under confidentiality.

Conclusions

As the chapters of this book demonstrate, significant strides have been made in recent decades regarding the management, systematisation, preservation, and accessibility of transitional justice archives. Just in 2015, De Greiff identified an inconsistency in archives management related to transitional justice mechanisms, such as truth commissions. To address this issue, the then Special Rapporteur formulated a set of general recommendations based on the right to know.[40] However, many archives from truth commissions and temporary national and international court archives remain largely unknown and difficult to access. Recent research indicates that most Truth and Reconciliation Commission (TRC) documentation is hard to access and citizens are not adequately informed about the findings.[41] Additionally, despite significant information technology advancements, ongoing challenges are related to the long-term preservation of digital information.[42] Overcoming these challenges requires substantial resources and a proactive approach, particularly in countries with underdeveloped information management systems.[43]

Despite that, the cases discussed in the book present a more hopeful perspective and highlight the increasing significance that transitional justice mechanisms' archives have acquired in the public space. Although the countries analysed in this book still present significant challenges in ensuring safe storage, proper funding, and increased access to these archives, several efforts have been made in all the examined countries to acknowledge the importance of these archives and their role and impact on the respective society. Except for the Chilean case, which has the most restrictive access to its Truth Commission archives and a widely dispersed system for storing these documents, Colombia, Argentina, and Peru are among the leading examples of advancements in transparency laws and accessibility to transitional justice archives. In relation to the preservation of the TJ archives, it remains uncertain whether the institutions created to protect these archives, such as the National Memory Archive in Argentina and the Information Centre in Peru, will secure sustainable funding over the years. It is also uncertain whether the states will fulfil their responsibility to properly preserve and manage these archives. Nevertheless, the cases presented in this book highlight two significant trends.

First, transitional justice archives increasingly play a significant role in public debates. For instance, the collaborative effort involving various stakeholders to preserve and access the DAS's repressive archives in Colombia through precautionary measures highlights this trend. On December 30, 2024, the Special Jurisdiction for Peace (JEP) received a comprehensive evaluation of

40 Jens Boel, Perrine Canavaggio, and Antonio González Quintana, "Records and Archives Documenting Gross Human Rights Violations," in *Archives and Human Rights*, eds. Jens Boel, Perrine Canavaggio, and Antonio González Quintana (Abingdon: Routledge, 2021), https://doi.org/10.4324/9780429054624.

41 Proscovia Svärd and Bonny Ibhawoh, "Introduction: Truth Commissions and Challenges of Documentation," in *Documentation from Truth and Reconciliation Commissions*, eds. Proscovia Svärd and Bonny Ibhawoh, 1st ed. (London: Routledge, 2024), 5, https://doi.org/10.4324/9781032618623

42 Svärd and Ibhawoh, "Introduction: Truth Commissions and Challenges of Documentation," 5; Fugueras, "Archives for Memory and Justice in Colombia."

43 Svärd and Ibhawoh, "Introduction: Truth Commissions and Challenges of Documentation."

the documentary collection of the archives of the now-defunct Administrative Department of Security (DAS). This evaluation aims to assess the declassification of these documents and facilitate access for victims of the armed conflict in Colombia.[44] According to Judge Oscar Parra-Vera of the JEP, this is a crucial step toward granting access to the files, which are essential for addressing impunity related to serious human rights violations committed during the conflict. The evaluation, prepared by the General Archive of the Nation, will enable the JEP to determine how to make public various intelligence and counterintelligence files, reserved expenses, and other documents in this collection, ensuring that victims can access this information.

In a similar way, the discussion in Chile about the sealed archives of the Valech Commissions and their impact on the country's historical memory demonstrates the growing public attention that archives are receiving, even amid their silence. The secrecy surrounding these archives has fuelled debates within Chilean society regarding the role and importance of archives and has kept the conversation about the past alive. All the cases in this book show a widespread understanding that archives represent a unique heritage vital for reconstructing countries' historical memory and strengthening democracy. A testament to this significance is the inclusion of transitional justice archives, such as the Documentary Fund of the Colombian Truth Commission and the archives of the Truth Commission in Peru, in UNESCO's Memory of the World Program (MoWLAC).

Second, there has been a substantial change in how transitional justice mechanisms gather and analyse information related to human rights violations. There is a growing recognition that a transdisciplinary approach incorporating various social science methods is essential for effectively understanding and interpreting the large volumes of data these institutions collect. In Chile, the legal backgrounds of the commissioners greatly influenced the evidence-gathering process, utilising a legal methodology that facilitated extensive use in future prosecutions. In contrast, Colombia's Truth Commission employed staff and researchers with different disciplinary backgrounds, allowing for a more inclusive analysis of the interviews and materials collected. This approach goes beyond simply presenting factual evidence; it seeks to understand the context and nature of the violations, the structures of oppression involved, and the levels of complicity and silence within society. Understanding these elements is crucial, as it not only proves guilt but also fosters a more profound comprehension of differences and paves the way for reconciliation. The diverse sources within the transitional justice archives allow multiple voices to be heard. When effectively studied and analysed, these voices can promote mutual understanding and help explain the atrocities that occurred. In summary, the archives of transitional justice are essential for building peace.

44 "Desclasificarían archivos secretos del DAS en Colombia," *La Opinión*, Wednesday, January 1, 2025, https://www.laopinion.co/colombia/desclasificarian-archivos-secretos-del-das-en-colombia.

Bibliography

Acuña, Maria Graciela, Patricia Flier, Myrian González, Bruno Groppo, Evelyn Hevia, Loreto López, Nancy Nicholls, et al. *Archivos y Memoria de la Represión en América Latina (1973–1990)*. Santiago: LOM Ediciones, 2016.

Adler, Nanci. "Introduction: On History, Historians, and Transitional Justice." In *Understanding the Age of Transitional Justice: Crimes, Courts, Commissions, and Chronicling*, edited by Nanci Adler, 1–18. New Brunswick: Rutgers University Press, 2018.

Alberch I Fugueras, Ramon. *Archivos y Derechos Humanos*. Gijón: Trea, 2008.

Baumgartner, Elisabeth, Brandon Hamber, Briony Jones, Gráinne Kelly, and Ingrid Oliveira. *Documentation, Human Rights and Transitional Justice*. Baden-Baden: Nomos Verlagsgesellschaft, 2016.

Bell, Vikki, Oriana Bernasconi, Jaime Hernandez Garcia, and Cecilia Sosa. *Archives of Violence: Case Studies from South America*. Goldsmiths, University of London, 2021. https://www.memoriayderechoshumanosuah.org/publicaciones/archives-of-violence-case-studies-from-south-america/.

Bernasconi, Oriana, ed. *Resistance to Political Violence in Latin America: Documenting Atrocity*. Cham: Springer, 2019.

Blanco-Rivera, Joel A. "Archives as Agents of Accountability and Justice: An Examination of the National Security Archive in the Context of Transitional Justice in Latin America." PhD diss., University of Pittsburgh, 2012.

Boel, Jens, Perrine Canavaggio, and Antonio González Quintana. "Records and Archives Documenting Gross Human Rights Violations." In *Archives and Human Rights*, edited by Jens Boel, Perrine Canavaggio, and Antonio González Quintana, [specific page number]. Abingdon: Routledge, 2021. https://doi.org/10.4324/9780429054624.

CNMH. *Política Pública de Archivos de Derechos Humanos, Memoria Histórica y Conflicto Armado*. Bogotá: Centro Nacional de Memoria Histórica, 2017. https://centrodememoriahistorica.gov.co/politica-publica-de-archivos-de-derechos-humanos-memoria-historica-y-conflicto-armado/.

Crenzel, Emilio. "Between the Voices of the State and the Human Rights Movement: Never Again and the Memories of the Disappeared in Argentina." *Journal of Social History* 44, no. 4 (Summer 2011): 1063–76.

Da Silva Catela, Ludmila, and Elizabeth Jelin, eds. *Los Archivos de la Represión: Documentos, Memoria y Verdad*. Vol. 4. Madrid: Siglo XXI de España Editores, 2002.

Duff, Wendy M, Flinn Andrew, Karen Emily Suurtamm, David A. Wallace, "Social justice impact of archives: a preliminary investigation", *Archival Science*, no. 4 (2013): 317–348.

Ferrara, Anita. *Assessing the Long-Term Impact of Truth Commissions: The Chilean Truth and Reconciliation Commission in Historical Perspective*. Routledge, Taylor & Francis Group, 2015.

Ferrara, Anita. "Archives and Transitional Justice in Chile: A Crucial Relationship." *Human Rights Review* 22 (2021): 253–78. https://doi.org/10.1007/s12142-021-00626-0.

González Cueva, Eduardo. "The Peruvian Truth and Reconciliation Commission and the Challenge of Impunity." In *Transitional Justice in the Twenty-First Century: Beyond Truth versus Justice*, edited by Naomi Roht-Arriaza and Javier Mariezcurrena, 70–91. Cambridge: Cambridge University Press, 2012.

Harris, Verne. "The Archival Sliver: Power, Memory, and Archives in South Africa." *Archival Science* 2 (2002): 63–86. https://doi.org/10.1007/BF02435631.

Harris, Verne. "Imperfect Archives and the Historical Imagination." *Archival Science* 14, no. 3–4 (2014): 295–306. https://doi.org/10.1007/s10502-014-9221-5.

Hawks, Darren G. *International Human Rights and Authoritarian Rule in Chile*. Lincoln: University of Nebraska Press, 2002.

Jimerson, Randall C. "Archives for All: Professional Responsibility and Social Justice." *The American Archivist* 70, no. 2 (2007): 252–81. http://www.jstor.org/stable/40294571.

Jones, Briony, and Ingrid Oliveira. "Truth Commission Archives as 'New Democratic Spaces.'" *Journal of Human Rights Practice* 8, no. 1 (February 2016): 6–24. https://doi.org/10.1093/jhuman/huv016.

Laplante, Lisa J. "The Peruvian Truth Commission's Historical Memory Project: Empowering Truth-Tellers to Confront Truth Deniers." *Journal of Human Rights* 6, no. 4 (2007): 433–52. https://doi.org/10.1080/14754830701692989.

Lessa, Francesca. "Remnants of Truth: The Role of Archives in Human Rights Trials for Operation Condor." *Latin American Research Review* 56, no. 1 (2021): 183–99. https://doi.org/10.25222/larr.769.

Niezen, Ronald. "Open-Source Justice: Digital Archives and the Criminal State." In *Narratives of Mass Atrocity, Victims and Perpetrators in the Aftermath*, edited by Sarah Federman and Ronald Niezen, 247–78. Cambridge, UK: Cambridge University Press, 2022.

Ospina-Celis, Daniel. "Archives and Transitional Justice: Lessons from Colombia's Truth Commission." In *Documentation from Truth and Reconciliation Commissions*, edited by Proscovia Svärd and Bonny Ibhawoh, 1st ed., 20. London: Routledge, 2024. https://doi.org/10.4324/9781032618623.

Presidency of the Republic of Colombia. *Decree 1081/2015 (Full Version with Modifications)*. Bogotá, May 26, 2015.

Schwartz, Joan M., and Terry Cook. "Archives, Records, and Power: The Making of Modern Memory." *Archival Science* 2 (2002): 1–19.

Svärd, Proscovia, and Bonny Ibhawoh, eds. *Documentation from Truth and Reconciliation Commissions.* 1st ed. London: Routledge, 2024.

Viebach, Julia, Dagmar Hovestädt, and Ulrike Lühe, eds. "Beyond Evidence: The Use of Archives in Transitional Justice." *International Journal of Human Rights* 23 (2021): 381.

Vukušić, Iva. "Archives of Mass Violence: Understanding and Using ICTY Trial Records." *Comparative Southeast European Studies* 70, no. 4 (2022): 585–607. https://doi.org/10.1515/soeu-2021–0050.

Weld, Kirsten. *Paper Cadavers: The Archives of Dictatorship in Guatemala*. Durham, NC: Duke University Press, 2014.

Part I

1 From a Dangerous to a Usable Past

Trudy Huskamp Peterson

Since the 1980s, a remarkable number of institutions have been created to look at specific past systematic or widespread human rights violations and seek justice for those they have harmed. As they are known, these transitional justice bodies include truth commissions, international criminal courts, commissions to search for missing persons, reparations commissions, vetting tribunals, and more. They generally support one of the four pillars that underlie the transitional justice theory of ways to deal with a troubled past: enacting justice by holding perpetrators accountable, exposing the truth of what happened, guaranteeing non-recurrence of past practices, and adopting reparation and restitution programs. Temporary institutions usually carry out these programs, although some may live on in a permanent successor agency.[1]

These short-lived institutions create extraordinary records, assembling a unique body of material which can never be collected again. These records supply names and dates, identify places, and report harm. Although transitional justice institutions vary in purpose, they usually have investigative materials, case files on individuals or events or types of crime, records of advice from consultants (often medical personnel) on issues of repair and reparation, records of judges or adjudicators, perhaps records of social workers or witness protection services, materials of public relations efforts, as well as the usual administrative records (budgets, personnel, and so on). Most of these institutions will have audio and video materials; while paper persists in most of them, the more recent ones will have the types listed earlier in electronic formats.

Given the transcendent importance of transitional justice institutions, it is obvious that their records need to be preserved. As the UN Updated Set

1 For example, such as Timor Leste's Centro Nacional Chega! was established to promote the implementation of the recommendations made by the nation's truth commission.

DOI: 10.4324/9781003609322-3

of Principles for the Protection and Promotion of Human Rights Through Action to Combat Impunity says:

> The terms of reference of commissions of inquiry should highlight the importance of preserving the commission's archives. At the outset of their work, commissions should clarify the conditions that will govern access to their documents, including conditions aimed at preventing disclosure of confidential information while facilitating public access to their archives.[2]

But it can be – and often is – a struggle to preserve the records of the transitional justice institutions (other than the published report of a commission or the official proceedings in a courtroom). Politically potent actors may not want the full record of investigations to be revealed, not now and not ever. Furthermore, even if the records are saved, they usually are replete with privacy issues that make it unwise to immediately open them all to public research.[3]

If, however, the effort to preserve the records is successful and the records are at least partially available for research, what kinds of inquiry can be supported? Clearly, the records of transitional justice processes can be used in future litigation unless the establishing act forbids their use in future prosecutions. However, the records of transitional justice processes can support many other possible inquiries that are not related to litigation. Here are only a few of them:

1. On the history of the nation or geographic area where the events occurred. The impact of violent events may transcend borders. For example, the former president of Liberia, Charles Taylor, was tried and convicted by the Special Court for Sierra Leone for his role in the Sierra Leone Civil War, and the records of that tribunal are as central to Liberia's history as to Sierra Leone's. For another, records of South American truth commissions have information on Operation Condor, a program that involved a half dozen South American governments and was supported by the United States in a campaign of violent state terrorism.

2 "The Administration of Justice and the Human Rights of Detainees: Questions of the impunity of perpetrators of human rights violations (civil and political). Revised final report prepared by Mr. Joinet pursuant to Sub-Commission decision 1996/119," United Nations Commission on Human Rights, *Sub-Commission on Prevention of Discrimination and Protection of Minorities*, E/CN.4/Sub.2/1997/20/Rev.1, October 2, 1997; updated by E/CN.4/2005/102, February 18, 2005, and E/CN.4/2005/102/Add.1, February 8, 2005, accessed June 30, 2023, https://documents-dds-ny.un.org/doc/UNDOC/GEN/G05/109/00/PDF/G0510900.pdf?OpenElement. I reviewed the principles relating to archives for the 2005 revision.

3 For a discussion of the access issues, see United Nations High Commissioner for Human Rights, *Rule-of-Law Tools for Post-Conflict States: Archives*, accessed October 11, 2023, https://www.ohchr.org/sites/default/files/Documents/Publications/HR_PUB_14_4_Archives_en.pdf.

2. On social relations. Trauma is a key problem for persons and communities recovering from conflict and abuse. The case files on individuals and groups created by a transitional justice institution can provide a benchmark for a longitudinal study of the effects of trauma, especially childhood trauma, on personal, familial, and community relationships. Some of the questions that might be investigated are:

   a. How are succeeding generations affected by an individual's trauma, directly and indirectly, in the second and third generations?
   b. If an individual, such as a child soldier, was both a victim and a perpetrator, how does their trauma manifest itself? Does it differ from that of a person who is solely a victim?
   c. Was there a shift in the patterns of violence (to self or others) after the completion of the transitional justice process? Did the process bring a sense of closure? Did it differ by the severity of the trauma? By gender? By the size (if any) of the compensation?
   d. What has become of the social bonds of the community due to the events investigated? Due to the transitional justice intervention(s)?
   e. Does the trauma differ if the government is the perpetrator by its systematic processes, such as forcing Indigenous children into residential schools, as opposed to trauma inflicted by an individual as the direct perpetrator?

3. On family history. Transitional justice records are a unique source of family history. Often, grandparents will tell grandchildren of events that they were not able to discuss with their children; the grandchildren then seek validation for the story told. The records provide one means of intergenerational validation.

   a. Did the event or practice really happen?
   b. Where was my family living at the time the events investigated took place? Who was living with or near them?
   c. How did the experience documented by the transitional justice institution affect how my mother or grandfather lived out her/his life from the time of the event until the transitional justice staff interviewed her/him? After the interview?
   d. If testimonies were audio recorded, what did my grandmother's voice sound like? My grandfather's?
   e. If testimonies were video recorded, what did my relatives look like? How did they dress for the encounter with the transitional justice institution?

4. On medical topics. The medical information within case files, such as those compiled for reparations claims, are specific to a fixed date and provide a benchmark for longitudinal studies of intergenerational transfer of conditions and inheritable diseases. It is often difficult to obtain clustered medical records for longitudinal studies, but, for example, the records of the

Nuclear Claims Commission of the Marshall Islands are such a research resource. Some of the questions that might be investigated are:

a. Are there clusters of medical conditions of children from the same community distinct from those of other communities? Are there differences based on gender? What biomedical factors appear to play a part in the distinctions?
b. Can medical markers in the children from one group/clan/minority population be identified? What treatment might be developed to ameliorate the condition?
c. Are there clusters of psychological conditions in people from the same community distinct from those of other communities? Are there psychological differences based on gender; if so, what are they?

5. On linguistic topics. The audio records of a transitional justice institution provide a fixed, dated marker for linguistic usage. Most audio records in archives reflect the speech of educated and privileged persons: politicians, civil society leaders, and sports and entertainment figures. It is rare to hear a large quantity of the sound of speech in daily life, as exists in the audio records of testimonies and interviews with transitional justice institutions. Some of the questions that might be investigated are:

a. What are the distinctive word patterns used by persons from an ethnic group? From a community? Who was educated at the same school? Who is male? Who are females? Do they vary by gender?
b. What is the characteristic pitch or tone used in speech by persons from an ethnic group, a community, or a school? Does it vary by gender? Does it change in stressful encounters?

6. On the press. Most transitional justice institutions try to inform the public of the progress of the work. External press reports may echo the institution's press releases, may distort them, may amplify them; they may report accurately on the transitional justice institution's public events, ignore them, or present a biased account. The institution's press office may collect as much press coverage as possible, making comparison possible.

a. How does the press coverage reflect the transitional justice institution's press offerings?
b. Do the characteristics of press coverage vary by media (paper, electronic, audiovisual, television, or radio)?
c. Does the press coverage vary by geographic area of publication? By language group?
d. Does international coverage vary from domestic reporting? If so, how?

7. On the transitional justice process. Understanding administrative actions is essential for the democratic control of institutions, particularly those such

as tribunals and truth commissions whose processes are closed, at least in part, to public oversight.

a. How were adjudications conducted, compared to the stated policies on how they were supposed to be conducted?
b. How fair and consistent was the evaluation of the evidence presented?
c. What documentation did the institution want but NOT get? How did that shape the result?
d. Can the records help a future transitional justice process establish itself? What should a future transitional justice institution avoid?
e. If two transitional justice institutions existed at the same time, for example, a truth commission and a special court such as in Sierra Leone, how did they affect each other?

The archives of transitional justice institutions provide evidence of the institution's origins, structure, functions, and significant transactions and activities; archivists call these "records with evidential value." However, the records of transitional justice institutions provide much more than that: they contain information on the persons, places, things, phenomena, and other matters encountered by and dealt with by the institution as it struggled to discharge its mandate to deal with the past. Certainly, these records can be used to hold persons accountable for past actions. But they are much more than that: they can also be used to explore, to solve open questions, and, perhaps, to heal.

Bibliography

United Nations Commission on Human Rights, Sub-Commission on Prevention of Discrimination and Protection of Minorities. "Revised Final Report Prepared by Mr. Joinet Pursuant to Sub-Commission Decision 1996/119." E/CN.4/Sub.2/1997/20/Rev.1, October 2, 1997. Updated by E/CN.4/2005/102, February 18, 2005, and E/CN.4/2005/102/Add.1, February 8, 2005. https://documents-dds ny.un.org/doc/UNDOC/GEN/G05/109/00/PDF/G0510900.pdf?OpenElement.

United Nations High Commissioner for Human Rights. "Rule-of-Law Tools for Post-Conflict States: Archives." Accessed October 11, 2023. https://www.ohchr.org/sites/default/files/Documents/Publications/HR_PUB_14_4_Archives_en.pdf.

2 The Archives About the System of Forced Disappearance of Persons in Argentina

Emilio Crenzel

Introduction

On March 24, 1976, a military junta conducted a coup d'état in Argentina. Unfortunately, military coups and political violence were not new to the country; in fact, Argentina has a long and turbulent history of such events, beginning in 1930 when the constitutional government of the Radical Civic Union party, led by Hipólito Yrigoyen, was overthrown. This specific military dictatorship marked the beginning of a new era in the use of violence. Unlike previous instances of state repression directed at political or union activists, it implemented a systematic and unprecedented form of political crime: the forced disappearance of people. This reflected a state-sanctioned decision to exterminate them. Disappearances involved both public and secretive phases. They typically started with the detention or kidnapping of individuals by military, police, or security personnel, who could be in uniform or regular clothes. These incidents often occurred before witnesses, on public streets, or at the victims' homes, workplaces, or schools.

The kidnapped persons were kept in illegal captivity in clandestine detention centers, primarily located in military or police facilities, where they were tortured and, in most cases, murdered. Their bodies were buried in anonymous graves, burned, or thrown into the sea, and their property looted. The Armed Forces classified various political groups and social movements under charges of "subversion". Since the end of Peronism in 1955 and the victory of the Cuban Revolution in 1959, their influence was evident in the ideas of the new left, leading to various forms of protest that challenged the established order. Key indicators of this influence included the strengthening of trade unions among the working class, the radicalisation of students, the growth of insurrectional movements, and the emergence of guerrilla groups. The Armed Forces identified these developments as threats that needed to be eliminated.

Many organisations condemned the violations of human rights, including the *Liga Argentina de Derechos Humanos* (Argentine League for Human Rights), the *Servicio Justicia y Paz* (Peace and Justice Service), and the *Asamblea Permanente por los Derechos Humanos* (Permanent Assembly for Human Rights – APDH), which existed before the coup; and the Madres de

DOI: 10.4324/9781003609322-4

la Plaza de Mayo (Mothers of Plaza de Mayo), Relatives of the Detained and Disappeared for Political Reasons, the Grandmothers of Plaza de Mayo, the Ecumenical Movement for Human Rights, and the *Centro de Estudios Legales y Sociales* (Center for Legal and Social Studies – CELS), which were created after the coup. The dictatorship initially denied any responsibility for the disappearances, then minimised the number of the disappearances, identifying them with the guerrillas as justification for their fate because of the "war" that it claimed was being waged in the country.[1]

In this chapter, the author explores the creation and reconstruction of archives related to the system of disappearance in Argentina from the military dictatorship to the present day. It starts by discussing the establishment of various archives within Argentina and beyond, which served as essential tools for raising awareness and denouncing these crimes. It suggests that the uniformity in the content of these archives stems from a consistent approach to collecting, recording, and classifying information. This approach was essential for promoting human rights on a global scale during the 1970s. It then examines the development of the archive of the *Comisión Nacional sobre la Desaparición de Personas* (National Commission on the Disappearance of Persons – CONADEP). This commission was established in 1983 by President Raúl Alfonsín to investigate the fate of individuals who disappeared after the return to democracy. The successful creation of the archive, which is the first official documentation of disappearances, resulted from collaboration between state initiatives and human rights organisations. The chapter analyses how, from 1985 to 2003, the archives on disappearances were expanded and diversified. This development was driven by local and transnational human rights organisations' efforts to uncover existing archives related to the disappearance and the repression, as well as those records established by the repressive forces. This information became a valuable tool in the reopened legal cases concerning human rights violations in the country. The approach to collecting and interpreting these data provided a fresh perspective on a violent past, intending to preserve and pass on the memory of these events to future generations.

Finally, this chapter examines the constitution of the *Archivo Nacional de la Memoria* (National Archive of Memory), which operates under the authority of the state and contains available archives related to acts of repression. It analyses the tensions between the proposals for creating the archive, the drive for academic research, and the need to understand and educate about the past to prevent its recurrence. Additionally, it discusses the political influences that establish discretionary access criteria, which hinder the ability to address crucial questions regarding the disappeared and the circumstances of their disappearance. The chapter examines the history of related archives to reconstruct the hidden reality surrounding forced disappearances. It shows how

1 Raúl Veiga, *Las organizaciones de Derechos Humanos* (Buenos Aires: Centro Editor de América Latina, 1985).

knowledge about these disappearances has developed and is reflected in the formation of these archives. Additionally, it emphasises how various political struggles have shaped the strategies for collecting and interpreting the content within them. These factors help explain why there are still significant unanswered questions about disappearances and the individuals who disappeared, which remain to be investigated.

2.1 Archives of a Hidden Crime

The system of forced disappearance of persons implied a hierarchical structure. A chain of command in which orders were issued and subordinates reported back. Lists were circulated among them with the names of the persons already held captive or to be kidnapped, based on the tasks that for decades had been carried out by the various state intelligence agencies, the national and provincial police, and branches of the Armed Forces. At the operational level, the statements of the abductees obtained through torture enabled new kidnappings and guided the intelligence community on the course to follow in the "anti-subversive struggle". Based on documentary and photographic information found in the archives and files of public agencies, civil servants, employees, and teachers at all levels of education were kidnapped or dismissed. The network of clandestine repression was not, however, exclusively state-run. Various companies made their personnel files available to the authorities, identifying union militants suspected of subversion.[2] The Catholic Church, for its part, replaced or relegated priests and lay people committed to these developing world trends.[3] Among those who denounced the disappearances, their knowledge about the characteristics of the perpetrators and the nature of the events was extremely diverse due to the fragmentation between the public repression (kidnappings and detentions) and the clandestine one (the captivity of the disappeared, their torture and their murder), and the incredulity produced by the experiences of extreme violence.

The relatives of those who disappeared made multiple appeals both within the country and internationally to police authorities, through tens of thousands of habeas corpus filed with the courts seeking to establish the whereabouts of the disappeared and by submitting claims that extended to local human rights organisations such as the Permanent Assembly for Human Rights (APDH) and to transnational human rights organisations and networks such as the Inter-American Commission on Human Rights (IACHR), the United Nations human rights bodies, and the bodies of various public

2 Victoria Basualdo, *Complicidad patronal-militar en la última dictadura argentina: Los casos de Acindar, Astarsa, Dálmine Siderca, Ford, Ledesma y Mercedes Benz* (Buenos Aires: CTA-FETIA, 1996).

3 See Martín Obregón, *Entre la cruz y la espada: La Iglesia católica durante los primeros años del "Proceso"* (Quilmes: Universidad Nacional de Quilmes, 2005).

and private agencies. Due to the increasing number of instances to which the claims were addressed, several archives and collections were established both in the country and abroad. The APDH archive, an organisation created in December 1975, months before the coup d'état, with the participation of political and religious leaders and cultural leaders, gathered nearly 5,500 testimonies on the disappearances, becoming the country's main documentary archive during the dictatorship. It was on the basis of similar denunciations collected by the relatives of the disappeared that the first public appeal was published in October 1977, titled "Mothers and Wives of the Disappeared, we only ask for the truth". It stated, "The truth we ask for is to know if our disappeared are alive or dead and where they are", and it was addressed to the president of the nation, the Chief Commanders of the Armed Forces, the military junta, the ecclesiastical authorities, and the Supreme Court of Justice.[4]

The complaint forms used by APDH and the information classification were based on standardised models previously developed by transnational human rights networks following the military coup of September 11, 1973, in Chile.[5] These forms, as judicial documents, prioritised the detailed description of the circumstances of the kidnappings and, in cases where information was available, the torture suffered, the characteristics of the places of captivity, the names of the victims, and those responsible for the violations. These forms omitted questions about political militancy. Instead, they prioritised recording identity data, such as ages and sexes, nationalities, religious beliefs, occupations, and professions. All these categories restored the humanity that had been denied to those who disappeared and highlighted the broad and indiscriminate nature of state violence.[6] The registration and classification of data and the public dissemination of information based on it challenged the dictatorships' narrative that labelled individuals as "subversives". The text classified and presented the missing individuals without considering the political motives of the repression that occurred. This approach implicitly accepted the boundaries established by the dictatorship, which did not recognise those labelled as "guilty" as legal subjects because of their subversive political beliefs.

The report of the IACHR, which included the figure of 5,580 disappeared persons based on the records of the APDH archive, used these criteria to classify the information it gathered during its on-site inspection in Argentina in September 1979. That same year, Amnesty International published another list of 2,673 missing persons, including the same type of information on the disappeared: their names and surnames, identity documents, nationality, age, whether they had children and how many, the date and place of disappearance,

4 *La Prensa*, October 5, 1977, 9 (capital letters in the original).

5 Keck Margaret and Sikkink Kathryn, *Activists Beyond Borders: Advocacy Networks in international politics* (New York: Cornell University Press, 1998).

6 On the forms used to document human rights violations in Chile but extensible to the Southern Cone, see Oriana Bernasconi, *Documentar la Atrocidad. Resistir al Terrorismo de Estado* (Universidad Alberto Hurtado, 2020).

and their professions or occupations.[7] The APDH archive was created simultaneously to similar archives in other countries of the Region.[8] Since the 1973 coup, the Vicariate of Solidarity in Chile set up an archive on the victims of the dictatorship, which collected and systematised 85,000 documents, including copies of judicial files, reports of torture and forced disappearances.[9] Following the arrival of exiles and political refugees from Argentina, the Archdiocese of Sao Paulo, Brazil, set up the Committee for the Defense of Human Rights for the Countries of the Southern Cone. Its bulletin, called *Clamor*, published its first issue in 1978, which focused on denouncing the repression in Argentina, taking advantage of the media's presence during the World Soccer Championship. *Clamor*, without "any type of classification or archiving technique", between 1978 and 1991, gathered "thousands of photographs, accompanied by notes, letters, and manuscripts with desperate cries for help" sent by relatives of the disappeared from Argentina. All this information supported the denunciations published in its bulletin.[10]

Additionally, information was gathered from those who had been kidnapped and later released, which detailed their experiences during captivity. Most of the victims had cooperated under pressure from their captors. Given their relatively better conditions of confinement, they were able to provide concrete details about the clandestine phases of their captivity, including instances of torture and the murders of the disappeared. On October 12, 1979, at the French National Assembly, Ana Marti, María Milla de Pirles, and Sara Solarz de Osatinsky, survivors of the *Escuela de Mecanica de la Armada* (Navy Mechanics School – ESMA), testified about their clandestine captivity.[11] Their accounts specified the characteristics of ESMA, including sketches and the names and nicknames of the members of the "Task Force" that operated there. In addition, for the first time, they gave an account "from the inside" of the existence of files on the repression to which they had access during their captivity. These files contained the names of the abductees, the place of the kidnapping operations, the personnel involved, the background of the abductee and their condition: "L" (for liberty), or "T" (transfer), a euphemism that concealed their murder. The ESMA archive documented the extermination

7 Amnesty International, *The Disappeared of Argentina: list of cases to Amnesty International. March 1976–February 1979* (New York: Amnesty International, 1979).

8 Ludmila Catela da Silva and Elizabeth Jelin, eds., *Los archivos de la represión: Documentos, memoria y verdad* (Madrid: Siglo XXI, 2002).

9 María Angélica Cruz, "Silencios, Contingencias y Desafíos: El Archivo de la Vicaría de la Solidaridad en Chile," in *Los Archivos de la Represión: Documentos, Memoria y Verdad*, eds. Ludmila Catela da Silva and Elizabeth Jelin (Madrid: Siglo XXI, 2002), 137–78.

10 Samarone Lima, "Clamor: la Colcha de Retazos de la Memoria," in *Los Archivos de la Represión: Documentos, Memoria y Verdad*, eds. Ludmila Catela da Silva and Elizabeth Jelin (Madrid: Siglo XXI, 2002), 120–21.

11 Comisión Argentina para la Defensa de los Derechos Humanos (CADHU), *Testimonios de los sobrevivientes del genocidio en la Argentina* (Barcelona: CADHU, 1979).

and disappearance of individuals. According to their data, 4,726 people had been there, and fewer than 100 remained alive.[12]

The 1980 Amnesty International report was also based on the testimonies of two released *desaparecidos*, Oscar González and Horacio Cid de la Paz, who were held captive in various clandestine centres. It detailed the names, surnames, or nicknames of 330 individuals, as well as the records of the "task forces" that kidnapped them and the date and place where they were held captive, as well as sketches portraying their features. They also reconstructed the forms used by the repressors in the kidnapping operations and interrogations, including those that indicated the "final resolution of each case", stating whether the person was alive or had already been killed.[13] On the one hand, these testimonies uncovered and confirmed the existence of repression files created by the perpetrators. They demonstrated the continuation of earlier classifications, such as those based on the "degree of danger" posed by individuals and the possibilities for the "social readaptation" of detainees, as established by the Argentine prison system.[14] However, they also revealed something new: most of the captives were later murdered. In this way, the recurring use of classificatory criteria in various clandestine centres, such as "transfers", suggests that the records and archives resulted from systematic recording criteria. In this way, those who uncovered the facts began to build up different documentary and testimonial archives in relation to a crime that had been denied, was without responsibility, whose traces had been erased and the bodies of the crime concealed. The archives began to store and categorise information based on human rights principles. The variety and richness of information in these archives have helped to generalise and systematise knowledge about the characteristics and actions of those responsible for disappearances.

2.2 The CONADEP Archive: The State Conducts Investigations Into the Disappearances

When he assumed office on December 10, 1983, Raúl Alfonsín, leader of the Radical Civic Union, ordered the prosecution of the leaders of guerrilla organisations and the chiefs of military juntas that governed during the dictatorship. On December 15, he called for establishing the CONADEP. This commission included prominent figures from civil society and three national deputies and was chaired by the writer Ernesto Sábato. The CONADEP's objectives were to collect complaints and evidence of disappearances and submit them to the courts, investigate the fate of the disappeared persons, identify the location

12 Comisión Argentina para la Defensa de los Derechos Humanos (CADHU), *Testimonios de los sobrevivientes del genocidio en la Argentina*, 30–54.

13 Amnesty International, *Testimonies on the Secret Detention Camps in Argentina* (Barcelona: Amnesty International, 1980), 17, 30 and 31.

14 Lila Caimari, *Apenas un delincuente. Crimen, castigo y cultura en la Argentina 1880–1955* (Buenos Aires: Siglo XXI, 2002), 146–47.

of the abducted children, denounce to the courts any attempt to conceal or destroy evidence of these events, and issue a final report.[15] The CONADEP started gathering information on individuals who had gone missing from the state and military institutions. The military authorities did not provide any information. They even resisted the Commission's access to inspect military facilities, including military schools and barracks, which were denounced as clandestine detention centres. They also refused to provide basic data, such as salary slips or lists of personnel who worked there.

On the other hand, the CONADEP examined records of reassignments and discharges, as well as entries and exits from military service. They found discrepancies that contradicted the military's claims regarding the escape or desertion of the conscripts reported as missing. The documents revealed secret directives from the dictatorship intended to address workers' protests and enforce press censorship. It also recovered operational orders related to kidnappings, along with files of detainees in legal prisons which proved they had been transfered from clandestine centres, such as "La Perla" and "La Rivera", located in the province of Córdoba. It also gathered data from morgues and cemeteries regarding questionable burials of young people who were killed in violent circumstances. It found evidence of official directives to destroy secret documentation related to repressive actions.

While the CONADEP could not confirm compliance with these provisions at the time the documentation was destroyed or what it contained, it did identify an order from the de facto president, General Reynaldo Bignone, who, by Decree 2726/83 on April 28, 1983, months before the presidential elections and the return of democracy, issued directives to "cancel", meaning to destroy, the documentation on persons who had been detained at the disposal of the National Executive Power.[16] The CONADEP focused on centralising the testimonies of disappearances collected nationwide and abroad. Various transnational and regional human rights organisations, including Amnesty International and *Clamor*, among others, gathered these testimonies. To ensure efficiency and avoid duplication, the CONADEP combined the complaints, as many had been submitted to different entities. Consequently, the CONADEP's archive became a centralised state repository for reports of disappearances. A significant number of them, 5,580, were handed over to the Commission by the APDH, which had collected them during the dictatorship and handed them over to the IACHR in 1979. Most of them came from relatives of the disappeared living in the Metropolitan Area of Buenos Aires and in the large cities of the interior of the country where the Commission's offices were

15 National Executive Branch, Decree 187, December 15, 1983, Official Gazette of the Argentine Republic, December 19, 1983, 2.

16 National Commission on the Disappearance of Persons (CONADEP), *Nunca Más. Informe de la Comisión Nacional sobre la Desaparición de Personas* (Buenos Aires: EUDEBA, 1984), 275–79, 322, 361, 365, 367 and 375.

located. A portion of these testimonies provided details about the abductions, those responsible for them, and the actions taken before the justice system, the police, and military authorities.

Human rights organisations provided the Commission with only 70 testimonies from individuals who had disappeared but later survived. This limited the evidence regarding the secret imprisonment, torture, and physical elimination of thousands of disappeared persons, making it difficult to identify those responsible for these actions. To address this issue, the CONADEP, with the assistance of human rights organisations, established local delegations and conducted visits both within the country and abroad to gather testimonies. Many exiles were unwilling to return to the country to testify or to do so at Argentine embassies due to the presence of officials from the dictatorship.[17] The initiatives allowed for a significant expansion of the body of testimony. While the CONADEP received many denunciations already made during the dictatorship, it also collected thousands of new reports that had never been documented. Ultimately, this effort resulted in recording 8,960 missing persons. The Commission requested basic identification information from the relatives of the people involved. This included names, ages, occupations, nationalities, physical descriptions, and photographs to help their identification. Additionally, they sought details regarding the date and location of the abduction.

Using this information, the CONADEP constructed a documentary archive, organising the material according to the aforementioned categories following the model of documenting human rights violations. On the other hand, it built up a photographic archive with the photos of the disappeared, which gathered more than 3,000 photographs.[18] The new testimonies from survivors of disappearances have led to significant changes regarding previous reports. The CONADEP collected around 1,200 testimonies, compared to only 70 that human rights organisations had before the establishment of the Commission.[19] Many individuals confirmed that archives existed in the secret centres, but few could provide evidence gathered during their detention. Victor Basterra was one of the few exceptions. A prisoner at ESMA provided the CONADEP with copies of photographs of individuals who disappeared while held captive at that secret facility. He also supplied images of members of the "task force"

17 CONADEP archive, CONADEP minutes number 7, January 17, 1984, 20; number 19, April 10, 1984, 74; "Convocatoria a la población," *Clarín*, January 21, 1984, 3; "El rabino Meyer recibe denuncias en EE. UU," *Clarín*, January 31, 1984, 8 and "Gestión en el exterior," *Clarín*, August 23, 1984, 10.

18 CONADEP Archive, CONADEP minutes no. 5, January 4, 1984, 13; CONADEP Archive, CONADEP minutes no. 33, July 17, 1984, 134–35 and "Repression in Computers. Como trabajó la CONADEP," *El Periodista de Buenos Aires*, September 22–28, 1984, 8.

19 Anonymous, Interview by the author, Buenos Aires, August 26, 2004, and author's elaboration based on CONADEP minutes.

who operated there, for whom he produced false documents, including passports, identification cards, property titles, and driver's licenses, which were utilised in various clandestine operations.[20]

The CONADEP conducted inspections of the main clandestine centres alongside survivors to verify their testimonies. As a result, 2,020 photographs taken by Enrique Shore, CONADEP's photographer, were added to the Commission's photographic archive. Before this, the archive primarily contained identification photos and family images provided by the relatives of the disappeared. The black-and-white photographs capture the facades and entrance doors of clandestine centres, as well as details such as their cells, walls, stairways, and basements. Many images feature survivors presenting physical evidence to the Commission supporting their testimonies. Some photos document press conferences held by the Commission with the survivors after the investigation, where they informed them of the findings. A dozen testimonies from those responsible for the disappearances were added to CONADEP's file of denunciations.

These individuals were members of the task forces who reported their involvement in the kidnappings, confirmed the use of torture, and provided information on the operation and location of the clandestine centers. They confirmed that thousands of missing persons had gone through their facilities, acknowledging the occurrence of collective executions involving military leaders. There were also reports of anonymous burials or the destruction of the bodies of the disappeared after their murders. There were attempts to depict certain killings as the result of confrontations, supporting the claims made by the relatives and survivors.[21] The Commission gathered a new set of statements from various witnesses, including neighbours who witnessed the abductions, residents from nearby areas who confirmed the presence of military or police at the clandestine centers, doctors and nurses who assisted pregnant women who had disappeared, and cemetery employees who verified the existence of unmarked graves and secret burials. These testimonies shed light on the various ways that civil society interacted with the disappearances and the dictatorship. They included expressions of solidarity with the persecuted, denunciations to the authorities, and the tendency to either overlook or normalise the record of horrors that occurred.

The CONADEP categorised the extensive testimonial material based on the clandestine detention centers. These testimonies acted "like a magnet", attracting accounts from survivors of disappearances who were able to identify both the locations of their captivity and the perpetrators involved. This classification approach was also applied to the children stolen by repressive

20 CONADEP archive, CONADEP minutes number 7, January 174, 1984, 19 and 20 and number 10, February 7, 1984, 29 and 30. On the evidence given by Basterra to CONADEP, see Gerardo Yomal, "Reportaje a Víctor Melchor Basterra, un ex detenido-desaparecido," *Nueva Presencia*, September 28, 1984, 10–12, and 17.

21 "Denuncia de militares sobre desaparecidos," *Clarín*, March 14, 1984, 6; Anonymous, Interview by the author, Buenos Aires, December 3, 2003.

forces, tracing them based on the locations where their mothers were held. This method became the foundation for presenting evidence in court and organising judicial cases. As a result, it was possible to hold those responsible in each clandestine centre accountable for multiple cases while streamlining the evidence presentation. Through this, the CONADEP reversed the nature of the strategic space of the disappearance. The clandestine centres, whose existence was denied by the dictatorship and unknown to the majority of the population, became the axis for reconstructing the fabric of the system of disappearance. Based on the testimonies, the Commission developed a socio-demographic profile of the disappeared individuals, including their sex, age, and nationality. It detailed the circumstances surrounding their abductions and clandestine captivity, specifying the dates and locations of their disappearance and detention. The socioeconomic profiles, including their occupations and professions, were also examined following the classifications used by the human rights organisations during the dictatorship. As in previous classifications, the political affiliations of the disappeared individuals were not included in their profiles.

In summary, over nine months of investigation, the CONADEP, with the assistance of victims and human rights organisations, compiled an archive that brought together all available reports on forced disappearances up to that time. From these reports, they created lists of the disappeared individuals, those who were murdered, the disappeared persons who were later released, and those who were located and seen in clandestine detention centers by other captives. They also recognised the perpetrators named in the testimonies. Additionally, this archive included 25,000 habeas corpus petitions submitted to the courts between 1975 and 1983 and a collection of photographs of the disappeared, along with images of both the interiors and exteriors of the clandestine centers. The entire CONADEP archive was microfilmed. By Decree 3090 of September 20, 1984, the original file remained in the possession of the *Subsecretaria de Derechos Humanos de la Nacion* (Undersecretariat of Human Rights of the Nation), which succeeded the CONADEP as the state entity in charge of collecting complaints of disappearance. A copy was kept in a bank's safe deposit box, and another was stored abroad.

The creation of the CONADEP archive occurred alongside its investigation. Its structure was designed to serve as a tool for uncovering the truth about the system of forced disappearances and for pursuing justice. In this way, it became an active instrument for understanding the human rights violations committed, crucial in challenging the Armed Forces' dominant narrative in the public sphere. The CONADEP archive was essential to developing legal evidence to restore the truth surrounding a hidden crime and identify those responsible.

2.3 The Proliferation of the Archives (1985–2004)

In November 1984, the CONADEP released its report, *Nunca Más* (Never Again), which had significant political and legal impacts in relation to the human rights violations of the past. First, it became an unprecedented publishing success, selling nearly 750,000 copies by 2023 and being translated into German, Hebrew, English, Italian, and Portuguese. Second, the report was introduced in classrooms to educate new generations about the past dictatorship and political violence. Third, together with the CONADEP, it emerged as a model for democratic transitions in Latin America, where various truth commissions publicly revealed the human rights violations that occurred during periods of political violence, civil wars, and dictatorships experienced by these societies from the 1970s to the 2000s. Finally, the *Nunca Más* and the evidence gathered by CONADEP in its archives played a decisive role in the trial of the military juntas.[22]

In the summer of 1985, the State Prosecutor's Office chose cases from the CONADEP archive and new reports collected by the Undersecretary of Human Rights to present allegations against the military junta. Thus, during the trial, which took place between April and December 1985, the body of evidence gathered in the CONADEP archive played a key role in the conviction of those materially responsible for the system of disappearances. The centrality of the CONADEP archive was testified by the frequent attacks and challenges from the Juntas' defence lawyers, who described the testimonies and documents as part of a "subversive strategy" and objected to the number of disappeared persons registered by CONADEP.[23] The ruling that convicted the military juntas established the body of evidence gathered in the CONADEP archive as judicial truth. At the same time, two new archives were created from the CONADEP. The CONADEP sought assistance from the American Association for the Advancement of Science to employ forensic anthropology techniques in cases where it was necessary to identify corpses found in various cemeteries that might belong to missing persons. With guidance from this association, the *Equipo Argentino de Antropología Forense* (Argentine Forensic Anthropology Team – EAAF) was established that year. Since its inception, the team has focused on identifying the remains of missing persons buried in unnamed individual and collective graves and other locations. Although the EAAF has established its archive, the information collected in the CONADEP archive remains crucial for its investigations, such as the location where the person was kidnapped and held captive, their age and physical description, and the specific clandestine centre where they were detained. On the other hand, in 1987, the *Banco Nacional de Datos Geneticos* (National Genetic Data Bank – BNDG) was created. Its objectives focused on guaranteeing the collection, storage, and analysis of genetic information for the clarification of crimes against humanity and, specifically, to assist the justice system in the search and identification of the children of disappeared persons and the identification of the remains of victims of forced disappearance.[24]

22 Emilio Crenzel, *Memory of the Argentina Disappearances: The Political History of Nunca Más* (New York: Routledge, 2011).

23 Crenzel, *Memory of the Argentina Disappearances*, 103–6.

24 "Ministry of Science and Technology," accessed April 8, 2023, http://www.mincyt.gov.ar/ministerio/estructura/org_dependientes/bndg/index.php.

In 1986, under significant military pressure, the Alfonsín government enacted the *Punto Final* (Full Stop) law. This law stipulated that, after 60 days, cases of individuals who had not been summoned to testify would be closed. In June 1987, the *Ley de Obediencia Debida* (Due Obedience Law) was enacted. This law considered all actions taken during the anti-subversive struggle to be executed under coercion and obedience to superior orders, except the abduction of minors and theft of goods. In December 1990, Peronist President Carlos Menem issued pardons that freed the military juntas. In this political climate, the number of reports from relatives of the disappeared to the National Undersecretary of Human Rights began to decline. Subsequently, human rights organisations presented their complaints to the Inter-American Court of Human Rights. The Court declared that the Full Stop and Due Obedience laws and the junta pardons were contrary to international law and recommended reparations for the victims. Under pressure from passing these provisions, President Menem's government passed Law 24.321 in 1994, on the "Absence Due to Forced Disappearance of Persons" and in 1995, enacted Law 24.411, which provided benefits for individuals absent due to forced disappearance and those killed by the Armed Forces.

These laws established economic compensation for the relatives of the disappeared. Both laws recognised the information collected by the CONADEP archive as valid evidence, resulting in the documentation of 3,151 cases of murdered individuals and 8,950 cases of forced disappearances.[25] In this context, the CONADEP archive slowly became the repository for all documentation collected in the country regarding human rights violations and the subsequent initiatives undertaken to address them. This includes records of the trials of the military juntas.[26] On the other hand, the passing of the reparation laws renewed the impetus for correcting the databases containing the lists of the disappeared drawn up by the CONADEP. Due to the fast-paced and hectic nature of the Commission's investigation within its brief nine-month mandate, the list of victims included duplicate names, such as cases of women registered under both their maiden and married names. It also included individuals who had been reported disappeared but were later released without informing the state of their situation and cases with misspelt names and surnames.[27]

In the mid-1990s, the uses, appropriations, and struggles surrounding existing archives on the repression took a new direction, leading to initiatives to create new archives considering the generational changes. In 1998, the Grandmothers of *Plaza de Mayo* created the *Archivo Biografico Familiar* (Family Biographical Archive) to reconstruct the life history of the disappeared whose children, born in captivity or kidnapped with their parents, were stolen

25 On reparations policies in Argentina, see María José Guembe, "Economic Reparations for Grave Human Rights Violations: The Argentinean Experience," in *The Handbook of Reparations*, ed. Pablo de Greiff (Oxford: Oxford University Press, 2006), 21–54.

26 Anonymous, Interview by the Author, Buenos Aires, March 3, 2004.

27 Anonymous, Interview by the Author, Buenos Aires, March 3, 2004.

during the military dictatorship. This archive collects stories from relatives, friends, militants, and fellow captives of the mothers and fathers who were disappeared or murdered. Its purpose is to ensure every grandchild's right to know about their origins and history, in case they would be located and their biological identity restored.[28] Thus, the biographical reconstruction of the disappeared began to transcend the presentation of their basic identity data to integrate their political commitment into reconstructing their life stories. As part of this process, in 1999, various human rights organisations formed the civil association *Memoria Abierta* (Open Memory) with the support of various transnational human rights organisations and US and European foundations.[29]

The establishment of *Memoria Abierta* represented a significant shift in the approach of civil society organisations, which had been hesitant to make their documents publicly accessible due to years of persecution and harassment by repressive forces. *Memoria Abierta* set up several archives. It coordinated the cataloguing of all documents held in the collections and documentation centres of the human rights organizations that are part of the association. Now, 27,366 documents have been catalogued and are available for public consultation through an online database. This initiative greatly enhanced the ease and speed with which researchers can search for and identify these documents. *Memoria Abierta*, on the other hand, has developed several other archives. Among these is an oral archive that collects over 700 interviews with relatives of the disappeared, revolutionary militants from the 1960s and 1970s, human rights organisations, and survivors. These interviews aim to share personal biographies, family backgrounds, and political commitments. Additionally, a documentary archive contains various personal files of leaders from the human rights movement and social organisations. There is also a photographic archive that includes copies of the CONADEP photographic records and photos taken during the mobilisations and actions of the human rights movement. It established the "topography of memory" section, which documents buildings functioning as "clandestine detention centres" through drawings, volumetric representations, models and animation, and materials used in criminal trials for human rights violations.

The creation of the archives of *Memoria Abierta* promoted the professionalisation of archival work through the storage of documents and testimonies under appropriate conditions of temperature, humidity, and security, parameters absent in many of the archives of human rights organisations. It also became part of the "International Coalition of Sites of Conscience", a transnational organisation that actively engages in public debates on memory policies

28 "Abuelas de Plaza de Mayo," accessed April 8, 2023, http://www.abuelas.org.ar/archivo.htm.

29 The organisations in Argentina include Servicio Paz y Justicia, Centro de Estudios Legales y Sociales (CELS), Familiares de Detenidos y Desaparecidos por Razones Políticas, Asamblea Permanente por los Derechos Humanos (APDH), las Madres de Plaza de Mayo Línea Fundadora and the Fundación Memoria Histórica y Social.

to deal with massive human rights violations. To summarise, the biographical archives of the Grandmothers and *Memoria Abierta* are utilised in legal cases related to disappearances, the abduction of minors, and other forms of abuse. These archives strongly convey the importance of imparting to new generations an understanding of the past that emphasises political commitment as a vital element. The establishment of new archives coincided with the discovery of numerous records created by the repressive forces in the Southern Cone, alongside the declassification of official US government archives related to Argentina. On December 22, 1992, at the request of Martin Almada, a former political prisoner and human rights activist, the "archives of terror" were discovered in Paraguay. These contained intelligence documents produced by the dictatorship of Alfredo Stroessner to persecute the political opposition, including documents proving the existence of the so-called Condor Plan, which involved the exchange of information and prisoners in the framework of repressive coordination between the dictatorships of the Southern Cone.[30]

2.4 The National Archive of Memory

Since 2003, when Peronist Néstor Kirchner became president, a new political climate emerged in relation to dealing with the human rights violations of the past. This shift was evident when the National Congress annulled the Full Stop and Due Obedience Law. This measure allowed for the resumption of criminal trials related to human rights violations, which had been closed since the pardons were enacted. In this context, President Kirchner's government formed a strong alliance with most of the human rights movement. As a result, many of their demands were met, including the revival of criminal trials, the official establishment of memory spaces where the main clandestine centres operated, and the designation of a Day of Memory in the national calendar, among other measures.

When the criminal trials resumed, the documents and testimonies collected in the CONADEP archive became crucial evidence to consult once again.[31] The digitisation of the CONADEP archive began in 2000, and this process gained momentum. Its digitisation ended a handmade archive reliant on the archivist's mnemonic skills, facilitating faster information retrieval during the trial resumption. At the same time, the archive was brought into line with international documentation preservation standards.[32] In December 2003, the *Archivo Nacional de la Memoria* (National Archive of Memory) was established under the Secretariat of Human Rights by Decree 1259 of the National

30 Mirian González, "Los Archivos del Terror del Paraguay. La historia Oculta de la Represión," in *Los Archivos de la Represión: Documentos, Memoria y Verdad*, eds. Ludmila Catela da Silva and Elizabeth Jelin (Madrid: Siglo XXI, 2002), 85–114.

31 Anonymous, Interview by the author in Buenos Aires on March 3, 2004.

32 "Informatizan archivos," *Clarín*, February 18, 2000, 25.

Executive Power. This archive brought together the CONADEP archive and other existing records of human rights violations and their prosecution since the return to democracy, including documents collected during the trials of the military juntas. This new collection on repression aims to "preserve the contemporary history of our country along with its lessons and legacies for present and future generations" (Article 3, paragraph a), "to promote the study, research and dissemination of the struggle against impunity and for human rights" (Article 3, paragraph c) and to become a "powerful educational tool to make the Never Again (Article 3, paragraph g) effective (Article 3, paragraph g)".[33]

The creation of the National Archive of Memory received criticism, especially from archival experts, who warned that its powers and functions overlapped with those of the General Archive of the Nation and that, therefore, it "broke with the principles of integrity, original order and, probably, provenance" and its goals exceeded and were alien to the functions of an archive.[34] Articles 5 and 6 of the decree that established the archive grant the authority to directly access and request information from various public administration bodies and agencies. This involves collecting testimonies and documents stored in the Armed Forces' archives. Likewise, the intermediate archive, under the General Archive of the Nation, contains information related to various repressive measures of the state and reports of disappearance, among other documents, which, under the powers of the National Archive of Memory, should be deposited there. The establishment of the National Archive reinforced the separation of the documents and testimonies collected by the state regarding the repression and state crimes from other records of the national history. This creates a dynamic where, on the one hand, the national history is subordinated to the history of human rights violations. On the other hand, a degree of relative autonomy exists between the two collections.

Beyond this, the creation of the National Archive of Memory in 2003 seemed to propose a radical innovation in the access to documents on the repression in general and the disappeared persons in particular since it offered criteria for unprecedented accessibility by making its collection available to those who could prove a "legitimate interest" to access it or, as individuals, could prove a "scientific, research, cultural, historical, or functional interest, whose purpose is to study what happened in the framework of the actions of state repression and State Terrorism as well as the social and institutional responses to it".[35] Despite including previously missing protocols for requesting access to the documentary collection, the actual criteria for accessing the

33 Decree 1259, *Official Gazette*, December 17, 2003.

34 Mariana Nazar, "Archivos, memoria y derechos: reflexiones en torno al caso Argentino," *Comma* 2 (2010): 150.

35 "Protocolo para la consulta pública de los fondos documentales del archivo nacional de la memoria," Ministerio de Justicia y Derechos Humanos, accessed April 8, 2013, http://www.derhuman.jus.gov.ar.

National Archive of Memory are influenced by discretionary criteria. These allow authorities to determine, at their discretion, whether to grant or deny access to the documentary collections. Additionally, there are no regulations in the country that define the conditions for accessing the archives.[36] Restrictions on providing information about disappearances and the disappeared are particularly sensitive and focus on specific political aspects inherent to the struggle for human rights. These restrictions indicate that the social construction of knowledge about this crime arises not just from a lack of information or the suppression of it by the perpetrators. They also emphasise the political dimension that underlie the formation of these archives and the dissemination of information based on or contained within them. In other words, it acknowledges that various actors view "archives as powerful tools for producing political meaning".[37]

The National Archive of Memory does not regularly provide updates on the official number of registered missing persons. The most recent public information available was published in 2015 by the Unified Registry of Victims of State Terrorism. Additionally, the Archive does not disclose information regarding the political affiliations of those who have disappeared. Information regarding survivors of these disappearances is also lacking; there is no data on their numbers, political affiliations, social profiles, or their distribution by location of captivity and year of release. Understanding the political affiliations of the disappeared individuals would allow us to uncover the political rationale behind the extermination. It would help us assess the proportion of militants and their associated organisations, as well as connect these findings to their social class profiles and the specific locations and periods – either before or after the 1976 coup – during which they went missing. This allows us to question arguments that dismiss any radical commitment of the disappeared, particularly the guerrilla fighters, or that suggest the predominance, after the coup d'état, of the disappearances of activists from social movements outside the guerrilla.[38] The universe of survivors also merits examination. On the one hand, as Vezzetti points out, it represents only a fraction of the total number of registered missing persons, which shows the selective nature of the forced disappearances with respect to the processes of genocide, such as those perpetrated by the Nazis, with which it is uncritically compared.[39] Conversely, the lack of information regarding their class profile, political affiliations, or the distribution of their

36 Mariana Nazar, "Dictadura, Archivos y Accesibilidad Documental. A Modo de Agenda," in *Derechos Humanos en la Argentina, informe 2007*, comp. Centro de Estudios Legales y Sociales (Buenos Aires: Siglo XXI, 2007), 421.

37 Graciela Karababikian, "Archivos y Derechos Humanos en Argentina," *Boletín del Archivo General de la Nación* 119 (2007): 619–48.

38 Emilio Crenzel, "De la verdad judicial al conocimiento histórico: La desaparición de personas en Argentina," *Anuario Africano de Retórica* 3 (2012): 53–64.

39 Hugo Vezzetti, "Usos y límites de la figura del genocidio," *Anuario Africano de Retórica* 3 (2012): 53–64.

population by place of captivity and year of liberation could enable a comparison with those still missing. This comparison could provide insights into the factors that influenced the physical elimination or liberation of the disappeared individuals.

In summary, establishing the National Archive of Memory represents a new government initiative to consolidate and centralise existing records related to the repression. Its objectives explicitly provide unprecedented legitimacy for researchers of this period to develop knowledge. However, the political nature of this information, along with its potential uses in the public arena and within the context of the legal and political struggle to interpret this past, greatly influences its accessibility. This, in turn, affects the ability to develop academic knowledge about it. Since December 10, 2023, when the far-right president Javier Milei took office, all state agencies responsible for processing the legacies of human rights violations have suffered substantial budget cuts and staff layoffs, including the National Archive of Memory. This has put its operation and even its very existence at risk. In this way, it is once again evident that the history of the archives is inextricably linked to struggles for memory.

Conclusions

The history of recovering the archives created by those responsible for the system of disappearances, along with the creation of archives on the disappeared, represents a process of reconstructing a long-neglected crime. The victims of this crime were meant to be erased from memory, while those responsible appeared to go unpunished. The archives analyzed offer a thorough understanding of the political and cultural landscape, as seen through the experiences of those who have disappeared. These records were created to document the violence perpetrated by those responsible for these disappearances and to seek accountability for their actions. The archives of intelligence and state bureaucracy, as well as those of certain private companies, played a key role in implementing the system of disappearance. During the dictatorship, local and transnational human rights organisations built up archives based on testimonies and documents that gradually reconstructed the materiality of the crime. After the return to democracy in 1983, the establishment of CONADEP centralised the scattered archives of the disappeared, both within the country and abroad, while also collecting new testimonies. The documentary corpus of the CONADEP archive played an important role in the criminal justice system. It was used in the trial of the military juntas, whose sentences confirmed its validity and evidentiary value. After President Menem's pardons, the archives on repression and the disappeared began to multiply. They all served the judicial cases, which were reopened in 2005 after the annulment of the impunity laws. However, their constitution aimed to contribute to the formation of social memory, focusing on reconstructing the political biographies of the disappeared.

The constitution of the National Archive of Memory has legitimised academic involvement in this archive in unprecedented ways. However, researchers' use of the archive remains regulated by the discretionary decisions of its authorities. use of the archive remains regulated by the discretionary decisions of its.

As a result, knowledge production is limited by the existence of what is considered sensitive data, which is believed to potentially influence the political discourse surrounding interpreting this past. Some precautions taken – such as failing to update the number of registered disappearances and erasing their political commitments – reinforce the dictatorial narrative. This narrative uses the relativisation of the number of victims as an argument to minimise accountability. As if the figures would avoid open condemnation and shift the blame on the disappeared because of their political militancy. Additional archives are likely to be discovered or made public, which could enhance our understanding of the disappearances and those who went missing. State archives from repressive forces, private companies, the Argentine Catholic Church, and relevant countries involved in the political struggles of that era, such as Cuba or the Vatican, probably contain valuable documents. The notion of discovering "the truth" in these archives is a positivist illusion. Nevertheless, these archives can enhance our understanding of this unique crime. However, this understanding does not solely depend on locating one or more key documents. It is also shaped by the political context surrounding the archives, the documents, the testimonies, and the ongoing political struggle over interpreting this past and its key figures. This is evident in the numerous unanswered questions about the disappearances, even though we could now find them in the existing archives.

Bibliography

Amnesty International. *The Disappeared of Argentina: List of Cases to Amnesty International, March 1976–February 1979*. New York: Amnesty International, 1979.

Amnesty International. *Testimonies on the Secret Detention Camps in Argentina*. Barcelona: Amnesty International, 1980.

Basualdo, Victoria. *Complicidad patronal-militar en la última dictadura argentina: Los casos de Acindar, Astarsa, Dálmine Siderca, Ford, Ledesma y Mercedes Benz*. Buenos Aires: CTA-FETIA, 1996.

Bernasconi, Oriana. *Documentar la atrocidad. Resistir al terrorismo de Estado*. Santiago de Chile: Universidad Diego Portales, 2020.

Calandra, Benedetta. "This Is a Part of Our History We Are Not Particularly Proud Of: The U.S. Declassification Projects (1993–2002)." In *The Struggle for Memory in Latin America. Memory Politics and Transitional Justice*, edited by Eugenia Allier and Emilio Crenzel. New York: Palgrave Macmillan, 2015.

Catela da Silva, Ludmila, and Elizabeth Jelin, eds. *Los archivos de la represión: Documentos, memoria y verdad*. Madrid: Siglo XXI, 2002.

Catela da Silva, Ludmila. "Etnografía de los archivos de la represión en la Argentina." In *Historia Reciente. Perspectivas y desafíos para un campo en construcción*, edited by Marina Franco and Florencia Levín, 183–220. Buenos Aires: Paidós, 2007.

Centro de Estudios Legales y Sociales. *Derechos Humanos en la Argentina, Informe 2007*. Buenos Aires: Siglo XXI, 2007.

Comisión Argentina para la Defensa de los Derechos Humanos (CADHU). T*estimonios de los sobrevivientes del genocidio en la Argentina*. Barcelona: CADHU, 1979.

Crenzel, Emilio. *Memory of the Argentina Disappearances: The Political History of Nunca Más*. New York: Routledge, 2011.

Crenzel, Emilio. "From Judicial Truth to Historical Knowledge: The Disappearance of Persons in Argentina." *African Yearbook of Rhetoric* 3 (2012): 53–64.

Funes, Patricia. "Medio siglo de represión: El archivo de Inteligencia de la Policía de la Provincia de Buenos Aires." *Puentes* 11 (2004): 34–43.
González Quintana, Antonio. *Archives of the Security Services of Former Repressive Regimes*. 1998. https://unesdoc.unesco.org/ark:/48223/pf0000140074.
González, Mirian. "The Archives of Terror in Paraguay: The Hidden History of Repression." In *Los archivos de la represión: Documentos, Memoria y Verdad*, edited by Ludmila Catela da Silva and Elizabeth Jelin, 85–114. Madrid: Siglo XXI, 2002.
Guembe, María José. "Reparaciones económicas por graves violaciones de los derechos humanos: La Experiencia Argentina." In *The Handbook of Reparations*, edited by Pablo De Greiff, 21–54. Oxford: Oxford University Press, 2006.
Karababikian, Graciela. "Archives and Human Rights in Argentina." *Boletín del Archivo General de la Nación* 119 (2007): 619–48.
Keck, Margaret, and Kathryn Sikkink. *Activists Beyond Borders: Advocacy Networks in International Politics*. New York: Cornell University Press, 1998.
Lima, Samarone. "Clamor: The Patchwork Quilt of Memory." In *Los archivos de la represión: Documentos, memoria y verdad*, edited by Ludmila Catela da Silva and Elizabeth Jelin, 115–36. Madrid: Siglo XXI, 2002.
National Commission on the Disappearance of Persons (CONADEP). N*unca Más. Informe de la Comisión Nacional sobre la Desaparición de Personas*. Buenos Aires: EUDEBA, 1984.
Nazar, Mariana. "Dictatorship, Archives, and Documentary Accessibility: A Modo de Agenda." In *Derechos Humanos en la Argentina, Informe 2007*, edited by Centro de Estudios Legales y Sociales, 414–24. Buenos Aires: Siglo XXI, 2007.
Nazar, Mariana. "Archives, Memory, and Rights: Reflections on the Argentine Case." *Comma* 2 (2010): 145–58.
Obregón, Martín. *Entre la cruz y la espada: La Iglesia católica durante los primeros años del "Proceso"*. Quilmes: Universidad Nacional de Quilmes, 2005.
Veiga, Raúl. *Las organizaciones de Derechos Humanos*. Buenos Aires: Centro Editor de América Latina, 1985.
Vezzetti, Hugo. "Uses and Limits of the Figure of Genocide." *African Yearbook of Rhetoric* 3 (2012): 53–64.

3 The Impact and Role of the Truth Commission Archives in Chile[1]

Anita Ferrara

3.1 The Rettig Commission's Archives

The Chilean National Truth and Reconciliation Commission, TRC (also known as the Rettig Commission), was created in 1990 through Supreme Decree No. 355 by President Aylwin to investigate and report on the cases of enforced disappearance and political execution committed under the Pinochet dictatorship between 1973 and 1990.[2] The Chilean TRC completed its work one year after it was established and issued its final report in 1991 (known as the Rettig Report), documenting 3,197 persons as victims of enforced disappearance and illegal execution.[3] The Rettig Report is a comprehensive document detailing the dictatorship's main phases, organised by the types of violations committed and the methods of repression employed. The Chilean TRC was established in a restrained political context. Its mandate was restricted, and it did not possess subpoena powers.[4] During the early information-gathering phases, human rights organisations were requested to provide all evidence they had collected regarding cases of individuals who had disappeared and victims of extrajudicial executions between 1973 and 1990. The Chilean TRC had access to the legal archives of the Vicariate of Solidarity, which contained

1 Part of this chapter has already been published in the Human Rights Review. Anita Ferrara, "Archives and Transitional Justice in Chile: A Crucial Relationship," *Human Rights Review* 22 (2021): 253–78, https://doi.org/10.1007/s12142-021-00626-0.

2 *Supreme Decree N.355*, Undersecretary of the Interior, 25 April 1990, Santiago de Chile. The Chilean TRC, commonly known as the Rettig Commission, was named after its President Raul Rettig.

3 Informe de la Comisión Nacional de Verdad y Reconciliación, 1991, http://bibliotecadigital.indh.cl/handle/123456789/170.

4 For a detailed analysis of the Chilean TRC's methodology and work, see Anita Ferrara, *Assessing the Long-term Impact of Truth Commissions: The Chilean Truth and Reconciliation Commission in Historical Perspective* (London: Routledge, 2015); for an analysis of the TRC work in the early political context, see Mark Ensalaco, *Chile under Pinochet: Recovering the Truth* (Philadelphia: University of Pennsylvania Press, 2000).

DOI: 10.4324/9781003609322-5

85,000 documents related to all the individuals the Vicariate had assisted.[5] The Vicariate gathered extensive and detailed information on the individuals who had disappeared or been executed. Each victim assisted by the Vicariate had an individual folder created, which contained comprehensive background information about the circumstances surrounding their disappearance or death. Additionally, these folders documented the efforts made by the victims' relatives and the Vicariate to uncover what had happened.[6] The legal archive included records of individual legal proceedings, such as habeas corpus cases and war council proceedings. It also contained various legal documents, including defence briefs, denunciations, personal accounts, and affidavits concerning instances of human rights violations. The records also included sworn statements from relatives, eyewitness accounts of those who were arrested, and testimonies from witnesses detained in the same locations as the victims. Many individuals who had been arrested went to the Vicariate to provide their testimonies following their release, becoming invaluable witnesses to the detention of victims who later disappeared.[7] It is important to note that these files were created during the time the abuses were occurring. This adds significant value to the documents, as they detail the various detention centres where victims were held or later transferred, the methods of torture they endured, who they were arrested with, the names of the perpetrators, and more. Reconstructing all the factual details about thousands of people many years after the events would have been complicated.[8]

The Chilean Human Rights Commission also provided documentation on cases of political execution and disappearances, including copies of legal actions taken to defend the victims and the corresponding trial records. The Truth Commission cross-checked this information with various sources to verify its accuracy. The Rettig Commission significantly depended on the documentation supplied by human rights organisations, especially the Vicariate of Solidarity.[9] Although the Truth Commission gathered extensive information from various sources, the human rights archives – especially the Vicariate archive – served as an invaluable source of evidence for the Commission's

5 María Paz Vergara Low, "Los Archivos de los Desaparecidos en Chile," *Arch-e: Revista Andaluza de Archivos* 5 (2012): 225–38. See also, Elisabeth Lira, "The Chilean Human Rights Archives and Moral Resistance to Dictatorship," *International. Journal of Transitional Justice* 11, no. 2 (2017): 189–96; Pamela Lowden, *Moral Opposition to Authoritarian Rule in Chile, 1973–90* (Springer, 1995).

6 María Paz Vergara Low, "Los Archivos de los Desaparecidos en Chile"; see also Universidad Alberto Hurtado, *Guía de archivos de memoria y derechos humanos en Chile*, 2017, https://www.memoriayderechoshumanosuah.org/publicaciones/guia-de-archivos-de-memoria-y-derechos-humanos-en-chile/.

7 María Paz Vergara Low, "Los Archivos de los Desaparecidos en Chile."

8 María Paz Vergara Low, "Los Archivos de los Desaparecidos en Chile."

9 *Report of the Chilean National Commission on Truth and Reconciliation* (Notre Dame, IN: Center for Civil and Human Rights, Notre Dame Law School, and University of Notre Dame Press, 1993).

report and its conclusions. In the view of the TRC, human rights organisations have documented and monitored human rights abuses with exceptional accuracy. Beyond the archives of the national and international human rights organisations, the Rettig Commission collected thousands of declarations from victims' relatives, witnesses, and political prisoners who testified before the Commission. The Commission gathered direct testimony on around 3,400 cases.[10] The Commission also solicited information abroad from Chilean exiles.[11]

The armed forces did not cooperate with the Truth Commission, and the only relevant information they provided was about armed forces members killed during military confrontations. However, only a few military officers gave testimony. The TRC cross-checked the records obtained from the civil society organisations with the records of various governmental and public agencies, including the Civil Registry, the Electoral Registry, the National Archives, the General Comptroller's Office and the Chilean Police. Many hospitals provided medical reports, autopsies, and death certificates.[12] The TRC carefully investigated each case in which antecedents existed and opened a file that included all the documentation related to the victim.[13] It also created a database to track cases.[14]

The Truth Commission collected documentary evidence from various sources, collecting 217,000 pages filed in 3,500 folders.[15] Based on the records, testimonies, and documents reviewed, the members of the TRC were able to morally convict thousands of cases involving enforced disappearances or political executions. They employed a detailed methodology that examined each case to qualify the situations. The TRC adopted a classification and systematisation approach similar to that of the Vicariate, which involved compiling all existing documentation, records, and testimonies related to each victim of disappearance and extrajudicial execution into a single file.[16] This practice was highly successful, as it helped restore individual victims' dignity and significantly supported the subsequent provision of symbolic and material reparations. The archives of the Rettig Commission remain confidential to this day, and data protection laws restrict their use. However, they are accessible to

10 Americas Watch, *Human Rights and the 'Politics of Agreements'* (New York: Americas Watch, 1991).

11 *Report of the Chilean National Commission on Truth and Reconciliation*, vol. 1, part 1, 21.

12 *Report of the Chilean National Commission on Truth and Reconciliation*, vol. 1, part 1, 17.

13 Cristina Luz García Gutiérrez, "Fuentes Para El Estudio De La Represión En Iberoamérica: Entre Archivos Y Centros Documentales" (paper presented at the Congreso Internacional 1810–2010: 200 Años de Iberoamérica, Santiago de Compostela, España).

14 Trudy H. Peterson, *Final Acts: A Guide to Preserving the Records of Truth Commissions* (Washington, DC: Woodrow Wilson Center Press with Johns Hopkins University Press, 2005).

15 García Gutiérrez, "Fuentes Para El Estudio De La Represión En Iberoamérica."

16 Jorge Correa, Interview by the author, Executive Secretary of the Rettig Commission, Santiago, 2009.

lawyers and judges who request them for their investigations.[17] For this reason, it is very difficult to determine the exact content of the Rettig archives or how the Commission used all the sources of information it collected.

3.1.1 Impact of Rettig Archives: Reparations and Trials

The most significant direct outcome of the Chilean TRC was the provision of reparations to the relatives of victims it identified. In 1992, a follow-up organisation called the National Corporation for Reparation and Reconciliation (NCRR) was established to continue investigating unresolved cases from the initial TRC. The NCRR also offered legal and social assistance to victims' families and managed a comprehensive reparations programme that included monetary pensions, healthcare, and educational benefits.[18] The Corporation published its final report in 1996, documenting 3,197 people as victims of enforced disappearance and illegal execution.[19] More importantly, the NCRR established an archive and documentation repository to collect and safeguard all the documents and information gathered by the TRC and the Corporation.[20] These records constituted the basis for the payment of different reparation programmes over the long transitional process.[21] The creation of a comprehensive archival record with details about each victim acknowledged by the truth commissions significantly aided the later payment of reparations to the families of the disappeared. When the NCRR completed its work in 1996, all the archives and documents from the TRC, as well as those belonging to the Corporation, were transferred to a new programme established under the Ministry of Interior. This programme, initially called the "Programme for the Continuation of Law 19.123," later became known as the Human Rights Programme. Since 2001, the Human Rights Programme has played a significant role in prosecuting cases related to human rights violations. The organisation became the custodian of the records from the Rettig Commission and its subsequent body, the Corporation. The programme was later transferred to the Ministry of Justice and renamed the Human Rights Programme Unit. As the following paragraphs will illustrate, the significance of preserving and organising these archives under this public body only became clear years later.

17 *Law N. 19.123*, 1992, which creates the National Corporation, states that the archives are confidential, except for the tribunals that need to investigate the cases (art. 2.3).

18 Elizabeth Lira, *Políticas de Reparación: Chile 1990–2004* (Santiago, Chile: Lom Ediciones, 2005), 113–57; see also Elizabeth Lira, "The Reparation Policy for Human Rights Violations in Chile," in *The Handbook of Reparations*, ed. P. de Greiff (New York: Oxford University Press, 2006), 55–101.

19 Corporación Nacional de Reparación y Reconciliación, *Informe sobre Calificación de Víctimas de Violaciones de Derechos Humanos y de la Violencia Política* (Santiago, Chile, 1996).

20 *Law N. 19.123*, 1992, art. 2.3.

21 The TRC archives have been crucial to certifying the status of victims and have been accessed by state agencies to prove the status of the victims' claims for reparations. The topic of reparations, archives, and lists is very broad and contested and requires a separate study.

Although the Chilean TRC did not have any judicial powers, shortly after it concluded its work, it sent to the Chilean courts all the evidence it had collected that seemed new, useful, or relevant to judicial investigations.[22] In the early 1990s, most cases initially submitted by the TRC to the courts had been dismissed by the Chilean tribunals, which had applied the Amnesty Law passed by the Pinochet government in 1978. During the early transition phase, the judiciary was reluctant to investigate human rights violations. Despite numerous attempts by many different actors to obtain justice and accountability, few cases progressed.[23] After Pinochet's arrest in London in 1998, the political context changed dramatically in Chile, and Chilean judges became more inclined to provide justice for victims' families. The Amnesty Law was reinterpreted, allowing new cases to be investigated, and many cases that had previously been dismissed without investigation were reopened.[24] Moreover, special judges were appointed after the creation of the Mesa de Diálogo (Roundtable Dialogue),[25] exclusively dedicated to investigating human rights cases.

These events initiated a new phase for human rights investigations, leading to the advancement of numerous cases.[26] Moreover, a few years later, the Human Rights Programme was empowered to initiate criminal proceedings in the cases of detained-disappeared persons and those extrajudicially executed. This strengthened the programme's role, and it became the main state agency prosecuting human rights cases.[27] In this changed context, investigating judges rediscovered the documentation and records in the Truth Commission's archives. Following Pinochet's arrest, these archives came into focus once again, taking on a new role as the foundation for subsequent prosecutorial efforts in Chile. Two former judges, Juan Guzmán, who first indicted Pinochet in 2001, and Alejandro Solís Muñoz, who played key roles in the significant justice initiatives in Chile, frequently requested access to the Truth Commission's archives and records through the Human Rights Programme. Throughout the years, this body has facilitated access to the Rettig archives from investigative judges.[28] In interviews with the author, both judges stated that their cases largely relied upon documentary evidence from the TRC archives.[29] They both used the records and archives of the TRC as evidence in the human rights trials.[30]

22 *Report of the Chilean National Commission on Truth and Reconciliation.*

23 Ferrara, *Assessing the Long-term Impact of Truth Commissions.*

24 Cath Collins, *Post-Transitional Justice: Human Rights Trials in Chile and El Salvador* (University Park, PA: Pennsylvania State University Press, 2010).

25 *The Mesa de Dialogo* was created in 1999 to facilitate a dialogue between the armed forces, Human Rights lawyers and civil society representatives.

26 Collins, *Post-Transitional Justice.*

27 Observatory for Human Rights, *Annual Human Rights Report* (Santiago, Chile: Centro de Derechos Humanos, UDP, 2010).

28 Francisco Ugas, Interview by the author, Human Rights Lawyer and former Director of the Legal Department of the Human Rights Programme, Santiago, April 2019.

29 Juan Guzman, Interview by the author, Former Appellate Judge, Santiago, 2009.

30 Alejandro Solis Munoz, Interview by the author, Former Special Judge, Santiago, 2009.

In subsequent interviews conducted a few years later, other judges specifically assigned to investigate human rights cases reported that they continued to actively utilise the archives from truth commissions as significant evidence. They emphasised these archives' importance during their proceedings' investigative phases.[31] Judge Carrozza stated that the TRC archives are a valuable asset to his investigations. He noted that the Rettig records include witness statements and declarations from relatives, which provide essential proof for reconstructing the crime being examined.[32] Equally, Judge Cifuentes frequently utilises truth commission records to find witnesses and their relatives or access statements from individuals who can no longer testify.[33] Both judges emphasise the importance of the archives, stating that they consider the archives from the truth commissions to be even more valuable now than in the past. As time passes, evidence diminishes, and both victims and perpetrators are passing away.[34] It is important to note that the Truth Commission archives are just one type of evidence, alongside many other sources, that judges use to build their cases. Investigative judges actively utilise all available archives and records documenting human rights violations, including those from the Vicariate and the armed forces.[35] The Rettig archives hold significant value for advancing current investigations. Francisco Ugas, the former head of the legal department of the Human Rights programme, proposed that all archives from the Rettig Commissions and Corporations be made immediately available to the courts. This would have expedited the proceedings and eliminated the need to request access to the Human Rights programme for each individual case under investigation. Unfortunately, this proposal was never realised, and access to these archives remains fragmented and inconsistent.[36]

3.1.2 The Interaction Between the Rettig Archives and Justice

This study highlights several factors explaining how the Truth Commission's archives in Chile became an unexpected means of accountability years later. Firstly, the records of armed forces and secret agencies have always been largely inaccessible. Many have been destroyed, concealed, or intentionally kept secret by those responsible for past actions. In this context, human rights archives and the archives of truth commissions hold immense value. For example, in Chile, they represent the most significant documentary evidence available, reconstructing the history of repression and providing insights into the functioning of authoritarian state structures.

31 Personal Interviews with several investigative judges: Judge Mario Carrozza, Judge Marianela Cifuentes, Former Supreme Court Judge Milton Juica, Santiago, April 2019.
32 Mario Carrozza, Interview by the author, Judge, Santiago, April 2019.
33 Marianela Cifuentes, Interview by the author, Judge, Santiago, April 2019.
34 Marianela Cifuentes, Interview by the author, Judge, Santiago, April 2019.
35 Personal Interviews with investigative judges: Judge Mario Carrozza, Judge Marianela Cifuentes, Santiago, April 2019.
36 Ugas, Interview by the author, Santiago, April 2019.

Second, in the early transition phase in Chile, victims were eager to testify before the TRC and be heard by a state that had marginalised them and their traumatic experiences for far too long. At the time, they believed nothing more would be done, so they provided all the information they had to the TRC. Former judge Solís pointed out a concerning paradox: after the dictatorship ended, victims' families and other witnesses hurried to share their testimonies with the Truth Commission officers. They provided extensive information about the human rights abuses they had previously kept to themselves. This included names of witnesses, court records, and any relevant documents they possessed. Such contributions enabled the Commission to thoroughly investigate and verify the details of each case under examination.

Third, given the challenging political climate in which the Commission was established, the information received from various sources was collected and systematised meticulously. The commissioners were very thorough and cautious in every case under examination so that the chances of mistakes would be minimal.[37] Ultimately, the fact that most of those who gathered evidence and heard testimonies were lawyers and legal assistants influenced how the evidence was collected and organised. This approach significantly facilitated the use of the evidence in subsequent prosecutions. The combination of these factors resulted in the creation of thousands of documents and files, which, as the ongoing trials are proving, possess a high level of reliability.

3.2 The Valech Commissions' Archives

The second official truth commission, the National Commission on Political Imprisonment and Torture (hereinafter the "Valech I Commission"), was established in November 2003 to investigate the cases of torture and political imprisonment committed during the period between 1973 and 1990. The Valech I Commission produced a massive report divided into seven chapters, which documented 33,221 cases of arbitrary detention and certified 27,255 persons as victims of political imprisonment and torture, in line with its mandate. The Commission's report published in 2004 concluded that throughout the military regime, torture and political imprisonment were systematic and institutional policies of the state, routinely practised by the armed forces and Carabineros, as well as by the intelligence services, especially the DINA and CNI. It stands as the only truth commission in the world to deal exclusively with surviving victims of torture and political imprisonment.

The Valech I Commission followed a work method similar to that used by the Chilean TRC. This process involved several steps, including interviewing victims of torture and political imprisonment. The Commission also collected documents from these victims and corroborated their information with data from various public institutions, human rights organisations, victims' groups,

37 Rafael Otano, *Nueva Conica de la Transicion,* 2nd ed. (Santiago, Chile: LOM Ediciones, 2006).

and eyewitness testimonies.[38] After gathering all the information, the commissioners determined which cases were eligible.[39] The Commission formed agreements to share information with various human rights organisations for access to their archives.[40] Extensive information was also obtained from international organisations, foreign embassies, and the national and international press. As with the Rettig Commission, the archives of the human rights organisations, primarily the Vicariate archives, as well as archives of trade unions, were again extensively used to corroborate the thousands of survivors' testimonies and witness statements.[41] In a significantly different political context compared to that of the earlier Truth Commission, the Valech I Commission had access to much more information from certain branches of the armed forces. These branches provided the Commission with records of detention centre locations, lists of individuals held in these camps, the duration of their detention, and other pertinent information.[42] One of the key advancements of the Valech I Commission was its thorough expansion of information regarding the scope and severity of torture in the country. It documented over a thousand locations that had been used as centres for torture and detention. Similar to the Rettig Commission, the Valech I Commission compiled a single file for each victim of torture and/or political imprisonment who provided testimony before the Commission.

During the dictatorship, human rights organisations systematically engaged in recordkeeping, documenting, and collecting evidence. Their main goal was to meticulously file and preserve archives that documented human rights violations, creating irrefutable evidence of the events that occurred. Civil society organisations quickly engaged with the Valech I Commission to provide all relevant information they had, similar to their involvement with the Rettig Commission. For these organisations, the public and official recognition from the state would signify the most significant achievement of their dedicated efforts in documentation.[43] Some members of the Valech I Commission had a significant history in defending human rights. Like the Rettig Commissioners, they were well aware of the efforts made by human rights organisations during

38 Comisión Nacional sobre Prisión Política y Tortura, *Informe Comisión Nacional sobre Prisión Política y Tortura* (Santiago, Chile: Comisión Nacional sobre Prisión Política y Tortura, 2004), 80.

39 Comisión Nacional sobre Prisión Política y Tortura, *Informe Comisión Nacional sobre Prisión Política y Tortura.*

40 The NGOs were the Vicariate of Solidarity, the Social Aid Foundation of Christian Churches (FASIC), the Committee for the Defence of the Rights of the People (CODEPU), and the Foundation for the Protection of Children Damaged by States of Emergency (PIDEE).

41 Elizabeth Lira, Interview by the author, Professor and Psychologist, Member of the Valech Commission, Santiago, April 2021.

42 Comisión Nacional sobre Prisión Política y Tortura, *Informe Comisión Nacional sobre Prisión Política y Tortura.*

43 Lira, Interview by the author, Santiago, April 2021.

the dictatorship. The Commission President, Bishop Sergio Valech, was the head of the Vicariate of Solidarity during the years of the military regime and later responsible for the archives of the Vicariate. Maria Luisa Sepulveda had worked as a social assistant at the Vicariate of Solidarity; Alvaro Varela was also a human rights lawyer at the Vicariate; and Elisabeth Lira was a renowned psychologist for her extensive work with the victims of repression during the military dictatorship.[44]

Therefore, the combination of a strong civil society mobilisation, the sustained activism of survivors' groups together, and the presence of members of the Valech I Commission closely linked to the human rights organisations enabled good cooperation between the human rights groups, which opened their records to the Valech I Commission. In 2010, the last truth-seeking initiative, the Comisión Asesora para la Calificación de Detenidos Desaparecidos, Ejecutados Políticos y Victimas de Prisión Política y la Tortura (hereinafter "Valech II") was set up to deal with the cases of victims of political imprisonment and torture, and victims of disappearance and political execution, which had either been previously rejected or never presented before a truth commission.[45] The Valech II Commission followed the same criteria and methodology to qualify cases as the Valech I Commission. The Valech II Commission submitted its final report in 2011, documenting a further 9,795 victims of torture and political imprisonment and 30 more cases of enforced disappearance and illegal execution.[46]

All truth commissions in Chile inherited extensive documentation that many civil society organisations had previously collected. In many ways, they adopted the same methods and classification criteria used by the Vicariate of Solidarity. As noted earlier, the Rettig Commission created individual files containing all information related to each victim of enforced disappearance and illegal execution. Similarly, the Valech Commission prepared a file for every alleged victim of torture and political imprisonment. Both truth commissions used this classification method to organise their records to make their findings irrefutable. The reports and archives of the Chilean truth commissions provide a wealth of documentation, testimonies, and evidence regarding the widespread human rights violations that took place during the dictatorship. These accounts have been challenging to dispute. In recent years, the Valech I and II archives have also served as vital tools for justice, reparation, and memory within Chilean society. The following section addresses some of the most contentious debates concerning these archives and their role in promoting the pursuit of truth and justice.

44 Ferrara, *Assessing the Long-term Impact of Truth Commissions*, 168.

45 *Supreme Decree No. 43*, Ministry of Interior, February 5, 2010.

46 Comisión Asesora Presidencial, *Informe de la Comisión Presidencial Asesora para la Calificación de Detenidos Desaparecidos, Ejecutados Políticos y Víctimas de Prisión Política y Tortura*, 2011.

3.2.1 The Legal Saga to Get Access to the Valech Archives

The government initially viewed the Valech I Commission and its reopening in 2011 as the final stages of the Chilean transitional justice process. However, the archives created by the commission have sparked significant controversy and debate since the conclusion of its work in 2004. The Valech I and II archives have led to a national discussion involving various stakeholders around issues such as their opening, access, ownership, and role. Unlike the Rettig archives, a law governing access to the Valech I archives stipulated that all testimonies, documents, and evidence gathered by the Valech I Commission were confidential. This information could not be disclosed to the public for 50 years nor could be used in court.[47] While a draconian secrecy law surrounded the Valech I archives, the law creating the Valech II Commission created a different regime of confidentiality, establishing a reservation rather than a full secrecy clause.[48]

The strict confidentiality of the Valech I archives had two consequences: first, it immediately curtailed the relationship between these archives and the ability to use them to obtain justice. In contrast to the increasingly judicial role of the Rettig archives, the judicial impact of the Valech I archives was severely limited from the start.[49] Second, it slowly sparked a debate within Chilean society on the importance of having access to the records documenting past atrocities to challenge the legacy of authoritarianism still present in Chilean institutions.[50] Several civil society groups, mainly composed of torture survivors, have been involved in a long struggle to access the archives of the Valech I and II Commissions. Other official entities, including the National Institute for Human Rights, the Comptroller General's Office, and the courts, have also contributed to this effort. The state has often stated that the confidentiality clause for the Valech I archives was crucial for the success of the Valech Commission. It also represented a formal commitment by the government to the victims who testified before the Commission. However, according to many survivors of torture, the secrecy surrounding the Valech archives is not there to protect the confidentiality of the victims but to shield the perpetrators from justice.

47 *Law No. 19.992*, December 24, 2004, Title IV, art. 15.

48 Matías G. Meza Lopehandia, "El Caracter Secreto de los Antecedentes de la Comisión Valech," *Biblioteca del Congreso Nacional de Chile* (2016), https://obtienearchivo.bcn.cl/obtienearchivo?id=repositorio/10221/23843/1/FINAL%20-%20COMISI%C3%93N%20-%20El%20secreto%20de%20los%20antecedentes%20de%20la%20Comisi%C3%B3n%20Valech.pdf.

49 The state has, on many occasions, declared that the confidentiality clause established for the Valech I archives was essential for the success of the Valech Commission and represented a formal commitment by the government to the victims who testified before the Commission.

50 Francisco Jara Bustos, "El Secreto de 50 años de los Archivos de la Comisión Nacional de Prisión Política y Tortura (Valech I): Ni Verdad ni Justicia," *Universidad de Chile* (2018): 417–36.

Although the law prevented the use of the Valech I archive in court, a group of torture survivors challenged the secrecy of the archives through the legal avenues open to them. In 2015, Popular Declassification (DP), a political-artistic collective, was created to demand the declassification of the Valech I archives and help survivors who testified before the Valech Commissions gain access to their documents.[51] After a legal battle won by the Declassification Movement, the National Institute of Human Rights (NIHR), currently the legal custodian of the Valech I and II archives, started providing every survivor with a copy of their file, including all the documentation related to their case, on request. In this way, former political prisoners can bring their documentation to the courts and demand the opening of an investigation. However, the NIHR decided to cross out all the information in the individual file related to third parties (victims or witnesses' declarations contained in the same file). While the decision to cross out specific information from the individual folders has been contested, in the words of Leonardo Urrutia, it protects the rights to privacy of those individuals who never agreed to disclose their testimonies publicly. It is relevant to note that the NIHR does not delete any information related to alleged torturers or perpetrators.[52]

The NIHR has frequently expressed concern about the secret nature of the archives and has often requested the government and the National Congress to lift the 50-year secrecy clause, at least for the courts, to respect international standards regarding access to information and the right to truth.[53] Moreover, the courts' lack of access to the Valech I and II archives has been the subject of at least five legal opinions of the Comptroller General Office of the Republic (CGR).[54] Following the interpretation of an opinion from the Comptroller General's Office, the NIHR has decided to grant access to the records of the Valech II Commission when requested by the courts.[55] Nonetheless, the NIHR highlighted that the inconsistency in accessibility to the Truth Commission records violates the principles of equality and non-discrimination, as judges in certain cases do have access to these records (such as the Rettig and

51 Javiera Campos and Luciano Sáez Fuentealba, "Contra el Velo del Secreto y el Silencio: La Demanda por la Desclasificación de los Archivos de la Comisión Valech I en Chile: La Experiencia del Equipo de Desclasificación Popular (2015–2016)," http://conti.derhuman.jus.gov.ar/2016/11/seminario/mesa_24/campos_saezfuentealba_mesa_24.pdf.

52 Leonardo Urrutia, Interview by the author, Head of Memory, Archive and Documentation department, National Institute of Human Rights (NIHR), Santiago, March 2019.

53 Lorena Fries Monleón, "Columna de Opinión: Verdad y Justicia para las Víctimas de Prisión Política y Tortura," *Instituto Nacional de Derechos Humanos*, 2015, https://www.indh.cl/columna-de-opinion-verdad-y-justicia-para-las-victimas-de-prision-politica-y-tortura/.

54 Meza Lopehandia, "El Caracter Secreto de los Antecedentes."

55 Instituto Nacional de Derechos Humanos (INDH), *Informe Anual* (Santiago de Chile, Chile, 2014). The reason behind that decision is that the Valech II archives have a different regime of confidentiality, which does not explicitly establish the prohibition of access to the courts as in the case of the Valech I archives.

the Valech II folders) but not in others (Valech I folders).[56] Judge Carrozza, while investigating cases of torture, declared that the Valech archives could contribute to ongoing investigations in the same way that the Rettig archives contributed to investigations in cases of the detained-disappeared and politically executed. Judge Carroza expressed concern about the uneven criteria for access to the Truth Commission's archives.[57]

The issue surrounding the secrecy of the Valech archives and the different access policies should be resolved by appropriate Congressional legislation and it remains a pending obligation of the Chilean state.[58] The political context of the Valech Commissions was changed compared to the early transition years, and many judicial investigations were already underway. Therefore, the choice to impede the judicial use of the Valech archives has been contested and challenged since the early days of the release of the Valech I report. Thanks to the ongoing efforts of torture survivors, the continuous activism of civil society organisations, and the involvement of various state actors, including the National Institute for Human Rights, the Comptroller General's Office of the Republic (CGR), and the courts, the Valech archives are now partially accessible to the judiciary.

3.3 A Battle for Memory

Civil society organisations have actively campaigned for access to the TRC archives for judicial purposes and to promote democratisation and empower the public in confronting the past. Since 2013, a collective and a site of memory called Londres 38 has conducted a vocal campaign called "No more secret archives," demanding access to all the truth commissions' archives as well as to the military and police archives that remain sealed.[59] This campaign began a much broader movement involving other sectors in society that started to challenge state secrecy as a legacy of authoritarianism still present in contemporary Chile and which continues to shield the state from public accountability and transparency.

The prolonged effort to gain access to the secret archives in Chile has led survivor groups to rally together in their quest to reclaim ownership of their history. Various sectors of society are now challenging the state's exclusive control over what information can be disclosed and when it can be released. The public campaign also testifies to the survivors' current demands for their stories to be made public. While the Valech I and II archives seemed initially to have had a more limited impact than other archives documenting state

56 Instituto Nacional de Derechos Humanos (INDH), *Informe Anual*; Meza Lopehandia, "El Caracter Secreto de los Antecedentes."

57 Carrozza, Interview by the author, Santiago, April 2019.

58 Urrutia, Interview by the author, Santiago, March 2019.

59 "No Más Archivos Secretos," *Londres* 38, 2019, https://www.londres38.cl/1937/w3-article-95544.html.

crimes, the secrecy clauses that sealed them have had quite the opposite effect. Not only has it contributed to fuelling the debates in Chilean society on the role and importance of archives, but it has also kept the issue of the past alive. The battle to make the archives public has now become one to preserve the country's collective memory.[60] Only time will tell what contribution the Valech archives will make in Chile's longstanding battle for truth, justice, and memory.

Truth commissions' archives are currently physically housed in the Museum of Memory and Human Rights, which, since its opening on 11 January 2010, has become the most well-known site of memory in Chile. However, the archives remain sealed to the public. Additionally, while the Museum holds the physical copies of the archives, the legal custodians are different agencies. The Human Rights Programme Unit of the Ministry of Justice manages the Rettig archives. At the same time, the National Institute for Human Rights administers the Valech I and Valeh II archives. This fragmented approach poses challenges for preserving the archives and facilitating public access.

Truth commissions' archives contain critical information on many aspects that remain to be investigated, such as how the truth commissions' members reached their conclusions, how they built the different categories of victims, how they systematised the droves of sources received, what role was played by domestic and external actors, and most importantly what was left out of the official reports and why. All this information will also allow researchers to compare the work methods of the two truth commissions with those of former human rights organisations and how and to what extent their narrative(s) concur or clash.

The archives constitute the legacy left by the truth commissions, and their permanent status makes them fundamental instruments for fulfilling the right to truth. Hence, it is critically important to make the truth commissions' archives accessible and allow Chilean society to engage with its much-contested past. For all the aforementioned reasons, the Rettig Commission and the National Corporation's Archives were declared Historical Monuments in 2022, underlining their fundamental contribution to the transitional justice process during the country's political transition towards democracy. The final inventory reports that the collection of the Rettig Archives comprises 4,785 individual folders containing information about each victim identified by the Commission. These documents detail the circumstances affecting various groups of victims and provide context for the events that took place. This information is invaluable to the collective memory of the country.

60 Oriana Bernasconi Ramírez, Daniela Mansilla Santelices, and Rodrigo Suárez Madariaga, "Las Comisiones de la Verdad en la Batalla de la Memoria: Usos y Efectos Disputados de la Verdad Extrajudicial en Chile," *Colombia Internacional* 97 (2019): 27–55.

Conclusions

This chapter examined the various roles held by truth commission archives throughout Chile's longstanding transition process, serving as tools for truth, justice, and reparations. Chile has witnessed the establishment of two Truth and Reconciliation Commissions. Hundreds of perpetrators have been convicted, and prosecutions are still taking place; different reparation programmes have been implemented and gradually expanded over time; many memorials have been erected, including a Museum of Memory and Human Rights. All the aforementioned measures and processes have strongly benefited from the existence of records and archives that have been adequately preserved and kept. The archives of the truth commissions have been used as essential evidence to obtain reparations for the families of the disappeared and the survivors of torture and political imprisonment recognised by the truth commissions' reports. Moreover, the Rettig archives were used as probative evidence in the belated human rights trials against perpetrators of human rights violations. Furthermore, even though the relationship with justice was initially curtailed, the Valech archives have also been made partially accessible to the courts. Moreover, the Valech archives have been a source of contention within Chilean society for many years, giving rise to intense debates on the role and importance of access to archives and are, hence, playing a crucial role in the battle for memory.

For this reason, the Chilean case illustrates the importance of preserving the archives of truth commissions for future prosecutions, as well as for making reparations and memorialising the past. TC archives can be utilised multiple times over the long term. While the institutions that create these archives are often temporary and have limited duration, the archives and records they produce can serve various purposes in the future, often in unexpected ways.

No one had anticipated that the archives of the Rettig Commission would have been used as judicial evidence in belated human rights trials against those responsible for violations many years after the archives were created. Furthermore, although the connection to justice was initially limited, the Valech archives have also been made partially accessible to the courts over time. Moreover, heated debates around the secrecy of the Valech Commission's archives have provided new opportunities for social and political actors to challenge the issue of the secrecy of state archives as the starting point of a much broader campaign to obtain more transparency and accountability from Chilean institutions. The chapter shows that archives can be activated and re-activated over time to acquire different meanings and purposes.

While the literature has devoted much attention to the archives created by human rights organisations to advance truth commissions, trials, and memory, further research is needed to systematically compare and explore the multiple uses of truth commissions' archives after the truth commissions have completed their work. The use of truth commissions' archives as evidence in prosecution deserves further investigation as it has become a growing practice at both the national and international levels to prosecute international crimes, especially in the Latin American region. It is equally important to investigate further the relationship between truth commissions' archives and "memory building." Truth commissions' archives are crucial in confronting and renegotiating the past, becoming an essential vehicle of memory. Truth commissions' archives uniquely preserve not only victims' voices and their sorrow but also their stories of political struggle and activism, usually omitted from the mainstream narratives on past violence. This makes them essential to integrating multiple and diverse experiences and narratives into society's collective memory and providing safeguards against historical revisionism and future negationism. As such, they play a crucial role in the struggle for memory.

Bibliography

Alberch I Fugueras, Ramón. *Archivos y Derechos Humanos.* Gijón: Trea, 2008.

Americas Watch. *Human Rights and the "Politics of Agreements."* New York: Americas Watch, 1991.

Bernasconi Ramírez, Oriana, Daniela Mansilla Santelices, and Rodrigo Suárez Madariaga. "Las Comisiones de la Verdad en la Batalla de la Memoria: Usos y Efectos Disputados de la Verdad Extrajudicial en Chile." *Colombia Internacional* 97 (2019): 27–55.

Campos, Javiera, and Luciano Sáez Fuentealba. "Contra el Velo del Secreto y el Silencio: La Demanda por la Desclasificación de los Archivos de la Comisión Valech I en Chile: La Experiencia del Equipo de Desclasificación Popular (2015–2016)." http://conti.derhuman.jus.gov.ar/2016/11/seminario/mesa_24/campos_saezfuentealba_mesa_24.pdf.

Collins, Cath. *Post-Transitional Justice: Human Rights Trials in Chile and El Salvador.* University Park, PA: Pennsylvania State University Press, 2010.

Comisión Asesora Presidencial. *Informe de la Comisión Presidencial Asesora para la Calificación de Detenidos Desaparecidos, Ejecutados Políticos y Víctimas de Prisión Política y Tortura.* 2011.

Comisión Nacional sobre Prisión Política y Tortura. *Informe Comisión Nacional sobre Prisión Política y Tortura.* Santiago, Chile: Comisión Nacional sobre Prisión Política y Tortura, 2004.

Corporación Nacional de Reparación y Reconciliación, *Informe sobre Calificación de Víctimas de Violaciones de Derechos Humanos y de la Violencia Política*, 1996.

Correa, Jorge. Interview by the author. Executive Secretary of the Rettig Commission, Santiago, 2009.

Ensalaco, Mark. *Chile under Pinochet: Recovering the Truth.* Philadelphia: University of Pennsylvania Press, 2000.

Ferrara, Anita. *Assessing the Long-term Impact of Truth Commissions: The Chilean Truth and Reconciliation Commission in Historical Perspective.* London: Routledge, 2015.

Ferrara, Anita. "Archives and Transitional Justice in Chile: A Crucial Relationship." *Human Rights Review* 22 (2021): 253–78. https://doi.org/10.1007/s12142-021-00626-0.

Fries Monleón, Lorena. "Columna de Opinión: Verdad y Justicia para las Víctimas de Prisión Política y Tortura." Instituto Nacional de Derechos Humanos, 2015. https://www.indh.cl/columna-de-opinion-verdad-y-justicia-para-las-victimas-de-prision-politica-y-tortura/.

García Gutiérrez, Cristina Luz. "Fuentes Para El Estudio De La Represión En Iberoamérica: Entre Archivos Y Centros Documentales." Paper presented at the *Congreso*

Internacional 1810–2010: 200 Años de Iberoamérica, Santiago de Compostela, España.

Guzman, Juan. Interview by the author. Former Appellate Judge, Santiago, 2009.

Jara Bustos, Francisco. "El Secreto de 50 años de los Archivos de la Comisión Nacional de Prisión Política y Tortura (Valech I): Ni Verdad ni Justicia." Universidad de Chile, 2018, 417–36.

Law N. ° 19.123, 1992.

Law No. 19.992, December 24, 2004.

Lira, Elisabeth. "The Chilean Human Rights Archives and Moral Resistance to Dictatorship." *International Journal of Transitional Justice* 11, no. 2 (2017): 189–96.

Lira, Elizabeth. *Políticas de Reparación: Chile 1990–2004.* Santiago, Chile: Lom Ediciones, 2005.

Lira, Elizabeth. "The Reparation Policy for Human Rights Violations in Chile." *In The Handbook of Reparations*, edited by P. de Greiff, 55–101. New York: Oxford University Press, 2006.

Lowden, Pamela. *Moral Opposition to Authoritarian Rule in Chile, 1973–90.* Springer, 1995.

Meza Lopehandia, Matías G. "El Caracter Secreto de los Antecedentes de la Comisión Valech." Biblioteca del Congreso Nacional de Chile, 2016. https://obtienearchivo.bcn.cl/obtienearchivo?id=repositorio/10221/23843/1/FINAL%20-%20COMISI%C3%93N%20-%20El%20secreto%20de%20los%20antecedentes%20de%20la%20Comisi%C3%B3n%20Valech.pdf.

Observatory for Human Rights. *Annual Human Rights Report.* Santiago, Chile: Centro de Derechos Humanos, UDP, 2010.

Otano Rafael, Nueva. *Conica de la Transicion.* 2nd ed. Santiago Chile: LOM Ediciones, 2006.

Peterson, Trudy H. *Final Acts: A Guide to Preserving the Records of Truth Commissions.* Washington, DC: Woodrow Wilson Center Press with Johns Hopkins University Press, 2005.

Supreme Decree No. 355, Undersecretary of the Interior, April 25, 1990.

Supreme Decree No. 43, Ministry of Interior, February 5, 2010.

Universidad Alberto Hurtado. "Guía de archivos de memoria y derechos humanos en Chile." 2017. https://www.memoriayderechoshumanosuah.org/publicaciones/guia-de-archivos-de-memoria-y-derechos-humanos-en-chile/.

University of NotreDame. *Report of the Chilean National Commission on Truth and Reconciliation.* Notre Dame, IN: Center for Civil and Human Rights, Notre Dame Law School, and University of Notre Dame Press, 1993.

Vergara Low, María Paz. "Los Archivos de los Desaparecidos en Chile." *Arch-e: Revista Andaluza de Archivos* 5 (2012): 225–38.

4 The Exhibition of Court Records at the Museum of Memory in Chile

When Law Meets Memory

Courtney Curran

Introduction

Following periods of State-sanctioned repression and widespread, systematic human rights violations, legal forms of justice routinely feature as integral pillars of the truth and justice-seeking endeavour. As countries confront endemic administrative brutality and transition toward a more democratic system of government, truth-seeking bodies have sometimes been preferred to criminal trials in the immediate aftermath. Third-party countries, in response, have conducted domestic investigations and prosecutions of individuals accused of committing atrocity crimes elsewhere, premised on expansive, extraterritorial jurisdictional grounds to counter otherwise persisting impunity. Such trials have been observed to operate as "monumental didactic spectacles" with a propensity for influencing national narratives as collective memory.[1] The "dramaturgical" nature of these proceedings is imbued into the culminating archival compendium, which remains anything but "dead".[2]

These living archival artefacts wait passively until becoming "activated" by societies continuing to deal with legacies of mass atrocity.[3] Using Chile as a case study, this chapter explores the uses of court archives from the French Pinochet trial in the contemporary Chilean memory landscape as part of the transitional justice (TJ) journey. Against the theoretical framing of "law as memory",[4] the use of audio-visual recordings from the French-Pinochet trial in the exhibition called *Juzgar y Filmar* (Judging and Filming Trials for Crimes Against Humanity), showcased by the Museum of Memory and Human

1 Mark Osiel, *Mass Atrocity, Collective Memory, and the Law* (First paperback printing; Transaction Publishers, 2000).

2 Kirsten Campbell, "The Laws of Memory: The ICTY, the Archive, and Transitional Justice," *Social & Legal Studies* 22 (2013): 247, 247 and 249.

3 Eric Ketelaar, "Tacit Narratives: The Meanings of Archives," *Archival Science* 1 (2001): 131, 138–39; Jacques Derrida, *Archive Fever* (Chicago: University of Chicago Press, 1996), 17.

4 Osiel, *Mass Atrocity*, Osiel frames this discourse in his seminal work to understand the purposeful construction of the memory of administrative massacre with "legal blueprints."

DOI: 10.4324/9781003609322-6

Rights (MMDH)[5] in Santiago, between September 6 and December 10, 2023, demonstrates how legal archives can contribute to constructing a collective memory of atrocity along the TJ continuum.[6] As a corollary contribution, this piece also uses a novel methodology to better understand the uses of archives in TJ processes by tracing court-derived files as they travel through spacetime, accruing new meanings with each activation.[7]

Collective memory comprises the stories societies tell about momentous events in their histories.[8] Historical artefacts help tell the stories by giving credence to the storytellers and purported proof to the audiences. At an individual level, tangible remnants of a brutal past can act as an *aide-mémoire*, recalling visceral memories of the past almost as if they were being experienced again in the present. An excerpt from Marcel Proust's famous poem, "Remembrance of Things Past", illustrates the capacity of an object to mobilise memory long after its creation in unanticipated ways.[9] Societies confronting histories of endemic human rights abuses inflicted by State forces often remain deeply divided.[10] Curating a shared recollection of the administrative repression can improve social solidarity and reinstate respect for the rule of law as a pillar of any democratic society. It is understood that employing law as a mnemonic theatre[11] can help prevent reoccurrence by fostering a shared, enduring memory of State-sponsored brutality.[12] In parallel, investigations and prosecutions concerning the commission of atrocity crimes, including by third-party countries in instances of inability or unwillingness of implicated States, drive public discourse about those processes and public reckonings with national identities. The legal narratives thereby presented add, rewrite or re-orient aspects of a nation's history; these stories thus become

5 Given its immensely positive reception, a second part of the exhibition was curated and available between March 20 and July 28, 2024. This exhibition was a collaboration between the MMDH of Chile and the National Archives of France and is an adaptation of the exhibition organised by the National Archives of France showcased in 2020–2021 in Paris.

6 Anita Ferrara, "Bottom-Up and Thought-Provoking Sites of Memory," in *Localising Memory in Transitional Justice: The Dynamics and Informal Practices of Memorialisation after Mass Violence and Dictatorship*, eds. Mina Rauschenbach, Julia Viebach, and Stephan Parmentier, 1st ed. (Routledge, 2022), 188–222, https://www.taylorfrancis.com/books/9780429330841.

7 Ulrike Lühe and Romain Ledauphin, "From the Forerunners of Document Collection to the Trial of Klaus Barbie and Beyond: The Transitional Justice Journey of the Izieu Telegram," *The International Journal of Human Rights* 25 (2021): 440–41.

8 Osiel, *Mass Atrocity*, 18–19.

9 Marcel Proust, *Remembrance of Things Past*, trans. C. K. Scott-Moncrieff and Stephen Hudson (Penguin Classics, 2022).

10 Osiel, *Mass Atrocity*, 39.

11 Campbell, "The Laws of Memory," 248–49.

12 Ferrara, "Bottom-Up and Thought-Provoking Sites of Memory," 122; see also Mark Coen, Katherine O'Donnell, and Maeve O'Rourke, eds., *A Dublin Magdalene Laundry: Donnybrook and Church-State Power in Ireland* (Bloomsbury Academic), 237–38, accessed November 13, 2024, https://www.bloomsburycollections.com/monograph?docid=b-9781350279087.

woven into the collective memory of the repression and the trial itself as a historically significant spectacle.[13]

Courts, not without strong contestation, are drawn into the construction of collective memory.[14] There is conjecture as to whether key actors involved in such legal events – be they judges, lawyers, witnesses, victims/survivors or "memory militants"[15] – addressing atrocity crimes can ever deliberately influence shared memories of past repression.[16] Despite that proposition's ontological sentiment, the law's effect on collective memory as a characteristically unwitting byproduct is plain. More specifically, there is crafty positioning in trial proceedings to highlight certain aspects of respective sides and downplay others. Some witnesses are more proficient in the witness box than others and better able to articulate their versions clearly and consistently.[17] The order of witness testimony in the trial is another effective tool for reconstructing contextual settings. It is a clever, subtle device that places versions and events in the contended chronological plots. Trials as theatre nonetheless produce authoritative verdicts that garner local and international attention and debate. Given the law's insistence, by design and in the public psyche, on fairness and impartiality, these verdicts over time become synonymous with "truths". Conversely, and central to critiques of trials addressing widespread human rights violations, is the enduring political influence on the trials themselves and the resulting versions of justice they create.[18] It would be naïve to think otherwise; some countries explicitly allow for political involvement,

13 Osiel, *Mass Atrocity*, 293; Walter Benjamin, *The Work of Art in the Age of Mechanical Reproduction: An Influential Essay of Cultural Criticism*, 1st ed. (Penguin Press, 2008); Richard Ashby Wilson, *Writing History in International Criminal Trials* (Cambridge University Press, 2011).

14 Benjamin Thorne, *The Figure of the Witness in International Criminal Tribunals: Memory, Atrocities and Transitional Justice* (Routledge, Taylor & Francis Group, 2023); Kerstin Bree Carlson, *Model (Ing) Justice: Perfecting the Promise of International Criminal Law*, 1st ed. (Cambridge University Press, 2018).

15 The term memory militant has been used by Ferrara in "Bottom-Up and Thought-Provoking Sites of Memory," 117.

16 For example, William Schabas' critique of the Nuremberg trials as anything but fair provides helpful insights into how the law can be used selectively to shape memory at the behest of the respective victors; William Schabas, *Unimaginable Atrocities: Justice, Politics, and Rights at the War Crimes Tribunals* (Oxford University Press, 2012), accessed November 22, 2024, http://www.oxfordscholarship.com/view/10.1093/acprof:oso/9780199653072.001.0001/acprof-9780199653072.

17 Thorne, The Figure of the Witness in International Criminal Tribunals, 2023; Nancy A. Combs, *Fact-Finding without Facts: The Uncertain Evidentiary Foundations of International Criminal Convictions*, 1st ed. (Cambridge University Press, 2010), accessed October 22, 2024, https://www.cambridge.org/core/product/identifier/9780511760259/type/book.

18 Phil Clark's book *Distant Justice: The Impact of the International Criminal Court on African Politics* (Cambridge University Press, 2018) challenges these assumptions, namely the assumption that courts can and do effectively produce justice and are free from external political influence.

requiring authorities to obtain the consent of the attorney-general to permit the prosecution of atrocity crimes under national law.[19] It is largely accepted amongst scholars that deterrence and retribution as conventional legal objectives feature less prominently and, at times, need to be compromised in trials addressing administrative massacre. When effective as a public spectacle, such trials become self-acknowledging, pedagogical tools that can generate public discourses fundamentally about the virtues of liberal legality.[20]

This potentiality is seemingly not lost on key legal protagonists in cases of this kind. The lawyer of one of the families of the four Franco-Chileans disappeared by the Chile secret police Dirección Nacional de Inteligencia (National Intelligence Directorate) described the French prosecutions as "the posthumous trial of Pinochet".[21] Knowing that such a trial would be a legal absurdity, a human rights lawyer had nonetheless successfully conjured a persuasive imaginary that lodged itself into the collective psyche of affected groups, the French polity and the international community. Thus, a new phenomenon was born: international criminal justice was not only possible but incredibly agile.[22] The largely lauded conceptualisation of the French Pinochet trial in this way is central to defending the proposition that such trials, including those in operation in third-party countries, forgo at times traditional objectives of conventional courts of law, corralling public reckoning to ensure against repetition, and restoring civic unity and trust in government institutions to enshrine fundamental liberal values in societies transitioning toward a more democratic system of government.[23]

This eventuality might have underpinned the decision by the respective French authorities to record the French trial proceedings subject of this chapter, as well as other highly publicised hearings, including the trial of Klaus Barbie and other trials involving former Nazis[24] who were ultimately convicted by French courts of committing atrocity crimes in foreign countries. The capacity to shape collective memory by the legal audio-visual archive seems pre-empted

19 In Australia, the current bill is before parliament seeking to amend this.

20 Namely, the respect for the rule of law, moderation, tolerance and honesty. Michael Curtis, "Introduction," in *Mass Atrocity, Collective Memory, and the Law*, by Mark Osiel (First paperback printing; Transaction Publishers, 2000), 1–10.

21 International Federation for Human Rights, "A Historic Trial in France on International Crimes Committed under the Chilean Dictatorship," accessed November 22, 2024, https://www.fidh.org/en/issues/litigation/litigation-against-individuals/Pinochet-and-others-Case/A-Historic-Trial-in-France-on.

22 Interview with human rights lawyer, January 16, 2023.

23 It is important to note that other scholarly groups critique this liberal ideology underpinning trials, highlighting instead the harm caused by the law's construction of collective memory to serve some agendas and silence others.

24 The hearings of the trials of Klaus Barbie (1987), contaminated blood (1992–1993), Paul Touvier (1994), Maurice Papon (1997–1998), and the Badinter-Faurisson trial (2007), the "AZF trial" (2009), the trial of the Chilean dictatorship (2010), the Pascal Simbikangwa trial (2014) were recorded and transcribed.

or, at its highest, though without exaggeration, highly anticipated given that the Audiovisual Archives of Justice was established by French law precisely to create "historical archives of justice".[25] Explicitly linking history, archives and justice into law gives credence to the "Law as a Memory" framework on which this chapter is posited.[26]

This chapter examines the use of the audio-visual archive of the French Pinochet trial by the MMDH as a commemorative, artistic, educative installation and its impact on shaping collective memory. Recalling "transitional justice" is a range of processes implemented by societies coming to terms with histories of widespread human rights abuses. The TJ continuum is used here to present the ongoing endeavour towards accountability, justice, truth, and reconciliation. The method by which this qualitative analysis has been conducted is through an anthropologically derived tracing methodology;[27] following the archives as they become activated along the TJ continuum demonstrates 1) their capacity to accrue different meanings to different audiences in different spaces, 2) the use of legal archives in downstream TJ initiatives has the potential to augment/expand present demarcations of TJ theory and practice as it pertains to archives documenting atrocity, and 3) supports the ongoing reflexivity and creativity, emboldened by "memory militants" and other groups coming to terms with widespread atrocity situations, to access and draw from such archival repositories to continue the transitional journey.

4.1 The French Pinochet Trial

The Chilean citizenry, decades later, continues the struggle to confront Pinochet-era crimes. During Augusto Pinochet's 17-year authoritarian rule, enforced disappearances, systematic torture, illegal political imprisonment and extra-judicial killings were systematically committed by the State against its

25 The French Heritage Code permits sound or audio-visual recordings of judicial or administrative court (public) hearings be made, with a qualification that the recording be considered pertinent to "the creation of historical archives of justice" [author's translation to English of French text], as per articles L.221–1 to L.222–3.

26 This approach also adopts and hopes to contribute to the "Judicial evidence and transitional justice" research project developed at the Universidad Austral de Chile. The author understands this project has dual aims of exploring how judicial proceedings addressing dictatorship-era crimes are reconstructed using varied compilations of evidence types and reflecting on how these trials influence public debate about the past to inform the construction of collective memory: "Historia Del Proyecto," *Expedientes de la Represión*, accessed November 22, 2024, https://expedientesdelarepresion.cl/nuestro-proyecto/.

27 Arjun Appadurai, ed., *The Social Life of Things: Commodities in Cultural Perspective*, 1st ed. (Cambridge University Press, 1986), accessed September 9, 2024, https://www.cambridge.org/core/product/identifier/9780511819582/type/book; Sue McKemmish, Eric Upward, and Graham Reed, "Records Continuum Model," in *Encyclopedia of Library and Information Sciences*, 3rd ed. (Taylor & Francis, 2010), 4447–8.

people.[28] This was done in the name of countering the spread of Communism during the Cold War period, and with the now-known avid support and inculcation by the US and other Western allies' intelligence services.[29] As the country came out of repression and moved toward a more democratic system of government, two official truth commissions were conducted that spanned the years 1990, 2003 and 2010, which first began unravelling the true extent of the institutionalised, State-sponsored crimes committed during the dictatorship.[30] Truth commissions' records were made available (albeit to different degrees)[31] to the judicial system in Chile, bolstering investigations and prosecutions of individuals charged with committing gross human rights abuses as accountability became more favoured over the otherwise persisting impunity.[32] Prosecutors and judges in foreign countries faced with allegations concerning atrocity crimes also began accessing evidence produced by truth commissions[33] and other documents from various archival repositories[34] in support of extradition requests, arrest warrant applications, investigations and prosecutions premised on expansive extraterritorial jurisdictional permissibilities.[35]

28 As verified by the 1991 Chilean National Truth and Reconciliation Commission (Rettig Commission), subsequent truth commissions, namely the 2003 National Commission on Political Imprisonment and Torture (Valech I) and the 2010 Advisory Commission for the Classification of Disappeared Detainees, Politically Executed Persona and Victims of Political Imprisonment and Torture (Valech II).

29 Albeit to lesser extent, though full understanding remains cloaked in secrecy, namely in relation to the involvement of Australia, Canada and France; Peter Kornbluh, ed., *The Pinochet File: A Declassified Dossier on Atrocity and Accountability*, rev. and updated ed., 40th anniversary edition (The New Press, 2013).

30 The official numbers of the crimes committed include 1,100 victims of enforced disappearance, 2,116 victims of political executions and 38,256 victims of political imprisonment and torture.

31 Noting the accessibility limitations associated with the Valech Commission archives: see Francisco Jara Bustos, "El Secreto de 50 años de los Archivos de la Comisión Nacional de Prisión Política y Tortura (Valech I): Ni Verdad ni Justicia," *Universidad de Chile* (2018): 417–36.

32 Anita Ferrara, *Assessing the Long-Term Impact of Truth Commissions: The Chilean Truth and Reconciliation Commission in Historical Perspective* (Routledge, Taylor & Francis Group, 2015), 122–39.

33 Spanish judge Baltasar Garzón pioneered using archives from the Paraguayan "Terror Archive" and Chilean Truth Commission findings to ground the arrest warrants for Pinochet in Spain.

34 For example, records held by immigration, police files and documents preserved by families of the missing and compiled systematically by the Vicariate of Solidarity and other human rights organisations contemporaneous to the conflict or repression.

35 Kathryn Sikkink, The *Justice Cascade: How Human Rights Prosecutions Are Changing World Politics*, 1st ed. (Norton, 2011); Naomi Roht-Arriaza, *The Pinochet Effect: Transnational Justice in the Age of Human Rights* (University of Pennsylvania Press, 2005); Francesca Lessa, *The Condor Trials: Transnational Repression and Human Rights in South America* (Yale University Press, 2022), accessed September 9, 2024, http://www.jstor.org/stable/10.2307/j.ctv2g591p5. The author confirmed this practice by multiple legal practitioners who had worked on transnational cases addressing international crimes emanating from the Latin American dictatorial region conducted during her PhD fieldwork.

The London arrest of Augusto Pinochet in 1998, under an international arrest warrant issued by Spanish judge Baltasar Garzón, galvanised the international criminal justice ecosystem. Heralding a new era in the pursuit of accountability cross-continentally for gross human rights abusers, exiled victim/survivor communities rushed to foreign courts to make private complaints.[36] In France, days after Pinochet's UK arrest, the families of four French Chilean victims successfully lodged private complaints with the assistance of specially experienced lawyers[37] based on the dual nationalities of their still missing loved ones. Georges Klein, a doctor and close adviser to Allende, and Etienne Pesle, priest and land reform convener in Temuco, disappeared in the days immediately following September 11, 1973. Alfonso René Chanfreau Oyarce, a leader of the Revolutionary Left Movement (MIR),[38] and Jean-Yves Claudet-Fernández, a chemist and MIR member with international relations responsibilities, were disappeared during the period 1974 to 1977, which was a particularly brutal period aimed to spread fear and destroy the perceived communist threat.

Over 12 years, investigating Magistrate Roger Le Loire, drawing on his experience working on cross-jurisdictional terrorism matters connected to the Basque separatist region, including with Judge Garzón himself, investigated the circumstances of the four disappearances. After the investigation by a different magistrate, Sophie Clemént, 17 former DINA operatives spanning the hierarchical spectrum of the DINA's security apparatus were charged with criminal offences related to the aggravated kidnapping and torture of Chanfreau, Claudet, Pesle and Klein as ongoing crimes under French law. These findings were endorsed by France's chief prosecutorial body, with a trial set for Paris' highest criminal court in December 2010. Purported international subject matter experts opened the eight-day trial[39] to explain to the court and the public more broadly, to local and international audiences, the Chilean context and the crescendo of conditions that had come together to give rise to the military overthrow of Salvador Allende's former, democratically elected government. Oral evidence was presented in support of the documentary evidence concerning the gross and systemic human rights abuses perpetrated by Pinochet and his regime during the period of his reign. This evidence gave

36 Roht-Arriaza, *The Pinochet Effect*, 118–49.

37 Interview with Human rights lawyer, January 16, 2023.

38 According to its foundation declaration of its principles, the MIR was the "Marxist-Leninist vanguard of the working class and the oppressed layers of Chile," Biblioteca Nacional de Chile, "El Movimiento de Izquierda Revolucionaria (MIR, 1965–1990)," 2023, accessed November 22, 2022, https://www.memoriachilena.gob.cl/602/w3-article-31553.html.

39 On 9 December 2010, Louis Joinet, a former magistrate, former president, member of the UN Sub-Commission on Human Rights, and UN Special Rapporteur on the fight against impunity, gave evidence, as did Stéphane Hessel, a former resistance fighter, member of the National Council of the Resistance and diplomat co-editor of the Universal Declaration of Human Rights (1948).

credence to diagrammatic representations of chain-of-command structures developed during the investigation phase to assist the magistrates. The next four hearing days were devoted to canvassing the circumstances of the disappearances of each of the four victims, with the president allocating one day for each victim.[40]

Structuring the hearing schedule in such a way also allowed for the chronological telling of different phases of the repression, specifically, how it was engineered to repress different classes of Chilean society in various parts of the country over time. Relatives and friends of the missing gave harrowing evidence of how their loved ones were kidnapped, which was highly reflective and symbolic of the Chilean polity's individual and collective grief. Lawyers and other professionals with specialised knowledge also testified, including Chilean human rights lawyer Carmen Hertz; Spanish lawyer Juan Garces, who was pivotal in grounding Pinochet's arrest warrant; Dr Martin Almada, who found the Archives of Terror in Paraguay; John Dinges and Zelma Michelini drawing on their journalistic investigations and exposés concerning the cross-border terror network, Operation Condor; as did the legal representatives of the civil parties International Federation for Human Rights (FIDH) and the Committee for the Defense of People's Rights (CODEPU). At the culmination of the trial, 14 defendants were convicted in absentia, with three having died just before the proceedings and life imprisonment sentences imposed. Although not one of the defendants saw the inside of a French prison, the Chilean judicial process eventually caught up with them.[41]

The documentary universe collated during the French investigative and prosecutorial phases was vast and incredibly diverse in size, type and insofar as cultural specificities are concerned.[42] The legal archive thereby created in France comprised Chilean Truth Commission archives and findings from the Rettig Commission and subsequent Valech I and Valech II commissions. Witness statements gathered in France and various other countries were also drawn into the French legal compendium, together with Chilean and other

40 The author viewed these at the MMDH exhibition, which is now permanently accessible on level 3 of the facility.

41 The final procedure was finalised in Chile in 2024 to conclude decades of accountability efforts to hold Alfonso Chanfreau's abusers to account, an endeavour that was spearheaded by his wife, Erika Hennings. The final verdict was described by Henning's lawyer [as the plaintiff] as very good news to ensure against deniability; "Corte Suprema Confirma Sentencia Contra Ex Coronel de Carabineros y Funcionario Del Ejército Por Desaparición de Alfonso Chanfreau," *Radio Universidad de Chile*, July 23, 2024, accessed November 22, 2024, https://radio.uchile.cl/2024/07/23/corte-suprema-confirma-sentencia-contra-ex-coronel-de-carabineros-y-funcionario-del-ejercito-por-desaparicion-de-alfonso-chanfreau/.

42 The author identified varied archival categories during her doctoral studies in this case file, including records created by the Vicariate of Solidarity, truth commission documents, declassified United States government documents [predominantly made accessible by the efforts of the National Security Archive (NSA) in Washington] and legal case files from third-party countries adjudicating related matters.

Latin American police files, immigration records and judicial determinations handed down in Italy, the US, Argentina and Chile. It also collated swathes of (then recently) declassified US government communicative cables between the CIA, DINA and respective leadership heads that had been made available as a result of intense international pressure mobilised by Garzon's investigations in France and by the UK arrest of Pinochet.[43] The legal archive is complemented by the audio-visual trial recordings, which gave new life to the paper records; the audio-visual representation of the documentary evidentiary matrices operated as a performative synecdoche within the archive itself.

4.2 Archival Activation

The legal archive created by the French Pinochet trial consists of court files and audio-visual recordings, posters and press releases, sketches and speeches. This vast repository stored files containing French, Spanish, English and German languages with imbued cultural and legal system nuances, with some original documentation, photographs and other artefacts transferred from various continents for the French judiciary by relatives of the victims and by judges in other jurisdictions working on similar or related cases.[44] The anthropologically inspired method of following objects in motion as they accrue meaning with each use or activation is posited here as an effective way to understand how these legal archives have been used in later and ongoing TJ processes.[45]

The records continuum model by Upward and McKemmish explains that records are "captured" as evidence by regime systems, they become "organised" into institutional archives for broader uses, and then are "recontextualised" and "pluralised" by interested groups.[46] The inherent pliability of the meanings of archives as they are accessed, interrogated and (re)interpreted indicates their dynamism – this lucid, multifarious quality signals record tracing as a highly suitable methodological vehicle to explore archival uses. This adaptive, interrogatory prism encourages ongoing reflexivity to adequately explore the journeys of archives as they transform with, for and by communities, scholars and industry practitioners seeking to reckon with atrocity situations.[47]

43 This documentary universe was revealed after years of litigation by the National Security Archive (NSA) under Freedom of Information legislation to declassify US government records of intelligence activities connected to Chile and the Latin American region more broadly during the dictatorial period.

44 The Head of the Collections and Research Area of the MMDH, Maria Luisa Ortiz Rojas, explained this to the author.

45 This is still the preferred base model in archival science: McKemmish, Upward, and Reed, "Records Continuum Model," 4447.

46 Ketelaar, "Tacit Narratives," 137–39.

47 Joan M. Schwartz and Terry Cook, "Archives, Records, and Power: The Making of Modern Memory," *Archival Science* 2 (2002): 1.

Record-keeping as an agile process accords with the notion that records are created and understood as the byproduct of human activity.[48] Repressive regimes document their administrative massacre with clerical clarity contemporaneous to the criminal activity.[49] Scrupulous reporting ensures that orders to identify, interrogate and eliminate dissidents are allocated and carried out. Communication is thereby recorded and affirmed through chain-of-command structures that (ironically) then help establish high-level individual criminal culpability. Cables, meeting minutes and invites, agendas, letters and memos created by oppressive regime proponents to record repression-in-action have demonstrably later been used by the very victim/survivor communities they sought to repress; these contemporaneously made records are reimagined and reinterpreted in diverse legal and non-legal settings to empower affected communities and educate wider audiences, as the archives are activated along the TJ continuum.[50]

Files originally created by a repressive regime for regime purposes can mean different things to different people in different places over time. A poignant example drawn from the French Pinochet legal archive is a regime file created by DINA operatives in furtherance of the cross-border terror network codenamed Operation Condor. The record documented that an identified dissident – Claudet, one of the four French-Chilean victims subject of the French legal proceedings – "*ya no existe*" (no longer exists).[51] This file has been used in multiple cases addressing Pinochet-era crimes[52] and was accepted in the French Pinochet proceedings as persuasive evidence given it was made contemporaneous to Claudet's disappearance across Chile's border in Argentina, and the timing of its creation corresponded to the last time Claudet was reportedly seen or heard from. Recording that a target "no longer exists" was also found to be evidence of chain-of-command structures, crucial in cases asserting administrative massacre to evidence high-level individual criminal responsibility through the careful compilation of linkage evidence.[53] This file has since become synonymous with Operation Condor, given it was sent from a DINA operative in Buenos Aires, and because of its sinister nature, to clinically record a person as no longer existing.

48 McKemmish, Upward, and Reed, "Records Continuum Model," 4447.

49 Coinciding with the advent of modernity: Michelle Caswell, "Hannah Arendt's World: Bureaucracy, Documentation, and Banal Evil," *Archivaria* 70 (Fall 2010).

50 Eric Ketelaar, "Cultivating Archives: Meanings and Identities," *Archival Science* 12 (2012): 19; Verne Harris, *Ghosts of Archive: Deconstructive Intersectionality and Praxis* (Routledge, Taylor & Francis Group, 2021).

51 Declassified memoranda that was sent between Operation Condor [DINA] operatives in Argentina and Chile documented Claudet was acting as a courier when he was arrested in the Argentine capital. These records convey that following an interrogation, and removal of microfilm that Claudet reportedly had in his possession, he was confirmed to "no longer exists".

52 Interview with Himan Rights lawyer, January 16, 2023.

53 As per the French instrucción findings settled by Magistrate Sophie Clemént.

During the French investigation phase, regime records were corroborated by witness testimony taken in France, Chile, Italy, Argentina, Mexico and the US due to Le Loire's eager and inspired methods of inquiry.[54] Victims/survivors, witnesses and family members of the victims gave statements, and others travelled to France to give oral testimony that, vis-à-vis, contextualised the regime records and linked other important key pieces of archival evidence together. Witness testimony strengthened versions proffered when taken together with regime records, Truth Commission evidence and institutional records, and countered denials submitted by Pinochet cronies and compromised institution heads. By way of illustration, recommendations to prosecute were compiled for the relevant prosecutorial body at the culmination of the French instruction phase. Contained in those comprehensive recommendations were different types of archival evidence layered in a way to validate and support some versions provided and dilute or refute others. The recommendations conveyed that given various types of archival evidence, in conjunction with extensive and varied witness testimony, all supported one general proposition, that being that the Chilean State, with Pinochet at its head, had planned and implemented a system to carry out kidnappings, extrajudicial killings, enforced disappearances, systematic torture and illegal, ongoing detention under the ultimate control of Pinochet. The evidence was so diverse, pointing to the one conclusion of State-sanctioned criminality, that it was accepted to have convincingly confronted and refuted any such denials.

Declassified files like the cable mentioned earlier are of intriguing quality.[55] As transitional communities and other third-party countries come to learn about the true extent of conflict contexts and or systems of repression, documents such as these give glimpses into the intention of regime heads in a visual, highly credible way. The aesthetics and transfixing eminence of official documentation of a brutal regime, set against a cross-section of other corroborative evidence – truth commission evidence and findings, victim files compiled by the Vicariate of Solidarity, State files such as birth and marriage certificate and immigration records, together with personal items provided by families of the disappeared, such as photographs and university records – can espouse intense, emotional responses from respective audiences.

The meanings that can be drawn from these records, according to each individual audience member, are captivating and disconcerting, moving and shocking. It is precisely the responses such documentation can elucidate that forged the imperative for this corpus of material to be exhibited for wider

54 Roht-Arriaza, *The Pinochet Effect*, 118–49.

55 Jacques Derrida and Eric Prenowitz, "Archive Fever: A Freudian Impression," *Diacritics* 25 (1995): 9. According to Derrida, the archive promotes nostalgia and attracts a desire to return to the archival place and time of its origin.

audiences.[56] This material, taken together, counters deniability and profoundly illustrates how the repression operated. Coupled with audio-visual recordings of the French trial proceedings, the theatre of trial as a spectacle concerning administrative massacre is projected into a new realm of the showcase – a museum exhibition to ensure against forgetting and deniability through education and memory projects. The likeness to Proust's memory of madeleines is here unequivocally pertinent: "from a long distant past, the more persistent and more faithful recollection of things broken remain poised a long time, ready to remind us".[57]

The following section explores the activation of the French Pinochet trial legal court archive by the Museum of Memory in Santiago, Chile, with regard to their journey across geographical, temporal, cultural, political and institutional boundaries to forge and augment the collective memory of the Pinochet repression. As a corollary, facilitating factors may be elucidated by analysing the circumstances that gave rise to using archives in different spaces over time.[58] A thorough examination and discussion of the various factors at play – such as the individuals and networks involved, the locations of the archives, and the temporal gap between the creation of records during repressive periods and their later activation along the transitional justice continuum – along with the socio-political contexts in which these records are (re)interpreted, falls outside the scope of this piece. It is important in any event to highlight this area of the literature and practice that needs attention, especially because of the resurgence of popularity of expansive extraterritorial jurisdictional grounds[59] by which to pursue gross human rights violators that necessitate identification, access and use of evidence from diverse settings.[60]

4.3 Law as Memory

The French Pinochet legal archive provided "blueprints"[61] or prisms[62] from which the *Juzgar y Filmar* (Judging and Filming) exhibition may be viewed

56 Legal documents, including audio-visual recordings of trial proceedings addressing administrative massacre, can ensure deniability, denounce State-sanctioned atrocity and give power to affected communities in their quest for truth, justice and memorialisation. By revealing the banality of evil inscribed within the marks of an administrative record and showcasing the organisation of repression through cables sent through chain-of-command structures, the court records expose the insidious dictatorial regimes at the turn of modernity.

57 Proust, *Remembrance of Things Past.*

58 Anita Ferrara, "Archives and Transitional Justice in Chile: A Crucial Relationship," *Human Rights Review* 22 (2021): 253.

59 Active nationality, passive personality jurisdictional permissibilities, and 'pure' universal jurisdiction.

60 The use of different types of archives in downstream TJ processes is an integral feature of the author's PhD thesis.

61 Osiel, *Mass Atrocity.*

62 Campbell, "The Laws of Memory," 251.

and understood. The legal blueprint signals the fundamental nature of the archive, given that its role since its inception has been to record and preserve court proceedings in a visceral way. The criminal law spectrum of proceedings was captured, from the investigative instruction phase to intermittent decision and motion-making processes, through the analysis of witness testimony at trial and the adjudication of matters of law and fact during the final judgment phase. The meanings that can be elucidated from these archival remnants[63] pertain to individual criminal culpability and its place in a systematic plan of repression, as these narratives were told and "proven" through the mnemonic system of the rule of law.

International and transitional blueprints complement the legal prism;[64] while legal archives commonly hold collective memory potentiality for a country's identity and national history-making purposes, the French Pinochet legal archive is imbued with an international configuration. The global community's focus on the plight of Chileans under dictatorship peaked when Pinochet was arrested in London. International criminal justice became a system-in-action rather than an idealistic goal, which imprinted meaning onto the French legal archive. French law and procedure shaped the juridical memory infused in the archive. However, the expansive jurisdictional bases upon which the case was premised, the testimonial records gleaned from countries and people the world over, the internationalised legal outfits and investigation processes, and the involvement of political leaders from the US and Italy, Argentina and Chile, is illustrative of the archive as reinstituting universal values.[65] The transitional blueprint is cognisant of the French Pinochet trial's effect on Chile's transitional journey. Catalysing cases elsewhere and in Chile, French legal institutions and processes became mechanisms of a third-party post-conflict reckoning along the TJ continuum toward peace and justice.[66] This international and local duality is central to the *Juzgar y Filmar* exhibition.

The exhibition can be entered in one of two ways. One option is to enter via the outside of the museum's main entrance, past the museum café that flanks one of the institution's exterior walls and down a set of concrete stairs. On the descent, the viewer first sees the words "*Juzgar y Filmar*" peering out underneath an overhanging wall. A walkway is alluringly lit beside the exhibition's title, and a thick black line is identifiable on the mirroring side. Unbeknownst to the viewer at this stage of the immersive experience is the symbolic

63 Francesca Lessa, "Remnants of Truth: The Role of Archives in Human Rights Trials for Operation Condor," *Latin American Research Review* 56 (2021): 183.

64 While Campbell distinguishes these "templates", the present author links them, given that the TJ journey ought not to be confined to state boundaries, as explored by emerging scholar Kelsey Rhude in her recent doctoral research, which focusses on (in)access to TJ using a survivor/victim-centred analysis.

65 Ruti Teitel, "Human Rights in Transition: Transitional Justice Genealogy," *Harvard Human Rights Journal* 16 (2003): 69–94.

66 Campbell, "The Laws of Memory," 252–53.

nature of the black line, this heart line or fault line, and chronological timeline spans the entire exhibition, tracing the journey of judicial proceedings conducted globally to address crimes against humanity, with a special focus on the case of Alfonso Chanfreau.[67] Segments from the Nuremberg trials are airing, as well as recordings from the trial of Nazi criminal Adolf Eichman conducted in Israel after he was arrested in Argentina. These audio-visual records are situated in the centre of the space, while the Chanfreau records are presented on the exterior, encircling walls. The showcasing of extracts of these trials is representative of and central to contextualising the history of trials addressing crimes against humanity and their recording.[68]

The timeline runs in the centre of each wall of the exhibition space, intersecting with screens displaying audio-visual recordings of critical witness testimony, final judgements, commentary from lawyers involved in the legal cases and significant media coverage. The line reminds and pays respect to the enduring nature of enforced disappearances, which fatefully also stands as a testament to the enduring commitment of the families of the missing to denounce the State-sanctioned crimes committed in the Chilean context to legal accountability.[69] Recordings of the testimony given during the French trial by family members of the disappeared are emotive and moving, bringing home to the examined the ongoing pain caused by such criminality. It also axiomatically illustrates the reformation of the criminal procedure in Chile, as dictatorship-era crimes, because of the date of their commission, had to be processed under the previous inquisitorial regime that relied on documentary evidence by and large. At the turn of the century, the new criminal procedure required that greater evidentiary value be attributed to oral testimony.

Precisely because Pinochet-era crimes are adjudicated utilising the old criminal procedure, a fundamental feature of this exhibition was to fill a gap between the document-focussed judicial proceedings in Chile for summary executions, enforced disappearances, torture and illegal imprisonment committed by Pinochet's security apparatus by ventilating these procedures in a way that was far more accessible to a wider variety of audiences. That is, through the showcasing of "fragmented images, shreds of a judicial process", albeit given in France, and through the ingenious development and incorporation of a simple, double-sided two-page handout clearly explaining the old criminal procedure in Chile, the exhibition sought to educate and raise

67 Tribunal de grande instance (Paris), Order of November 2, 1998 (ordonnance disant y avoir lieu d informer) in the case of MM. Chanfreau.

68 Noting the development of the codification of the crime over time, particularly given the lacuna prevailing in the international legal armoury regarding this atrocity crime. See further Courtney Martin, "Treaty-Based Regulation and Evidence-Extradition Agreements as Critical Tools in the Fight against International Criminal Wrongdoing," *International Criminal Law Review* 22 (2021): 1168.

69 Interview with Human Rights activist, January 25, 2024.

questions about the absence of this imagery in Chile.[70] More specifically, the exhibition presented in this way, at a critical time 50 years after the coup d'état, purposefully and provocatively questioned the state of justice in Chile with regard to the value of these audio-visual archives for transparency, truth and the (ongoing) construction of collective memory.[71]

The other entrance is subsumed in the urban; audience members can access the exhibition directly from the city's main public transport service, the Metro, thereby linking locals and foreigners, commuters and tourists, in their journeys to the museum space. This seemingly has a dual purpose; from a practical viewpoint, ease of access increases visibility and, therefore, spectator numbers, while from a critical engagement perspective, this intertwining of the *everyday* with the spectacle of the exhibition represents the French Pinochet trial as "law as theatre" that disrupted the persisting impunity in dictatorial Chile. Another reading is that the meshing of the banal with the perverse and explorative subject matter of the exhibition mirrors the terror and tolerance of clandestine torture and extermination centres that were operating in plain sight in Pinochet's Chile.[72] Blending the urban with the exhibition space, the curatorial design bridges the gap between justice and citizenship. Exhibiting trial proceedings and related posters, media footage and interviews in this way invites societal reflection on the Chilean construction of democracy and, thereby, collective memory. Recalling Chile's old judicial process as reliant on documentary evidence, trial proceedings made accessible to the public in this way unveil an otherwise obstructed-from-view justice-making process.

Throughout the tenure of *Juzgar y Filmar*, educative dialogues held in the museum space are aired via multiple media platforms and on radio networks as another mechanism by which to broaden viewer capacity.[73] Discussions focussed on trials for human rights violations, with artists, lawyers, judges, researchers and other cultural agents,[74] highlight the multidisciplinary nature of the exhibition and its capacity to connect a broad intersection

70 "Exposición 'Juzgar y Filmar Los Crímenes de Lesa Humanidad'," Iniciativa Franco-Chilena de Altos Estudios, September 2, 2023, accessed November 22, 2024, https://ifcae.uchile.cl/2023/09/exposicion-juzgar-y-filmar-los-crimenes-de-lesa-humanidad/.

71 "Exposición 'Juzgar y Filmar Los Crímenes de Lesa Humanidad'."

72 Author's note: This interpretation was formed by analysing empirical data, including fieldwork interviews conducted by the author in Chile with individuals who had grown up knowing that former torture facilities operated across the road from their place of residence or where they went to school, and hearing stories about aunties, friends and cousins being disappeared or tortured by State officials. These individuals continue to grapple with the ongoing divide in Chilean society long after the fall of the dictatorship.

73 For example, within the framework of *Juzgar y Filmar*, the dialogue session "Pathways and Challenges of human rights trials" was held on July 17, 2024, at the MMDH with representatives of the *Subsecretaría de Derechos Humanos* to promote broader engagement with the exhibition.

74 Ferrara, "Bottom-Up and Thought-Provoking Sites of Memory."

of society on topics that are still contested. A special space is reserved for researchers and others interested in viewing the trial proceedings in a more intimate setting, the museum's top floor becoming a fixed viewing platform from which a more personal experience of the archive may be gleaned. As described by the creators: "These works open doors to debate and demand attention in a social scenario that is increasingly susceptible to thoughtlessness and denialism".[75]

Conclusion

"When a past is hidden somewhere outside the realm, beyond the reach of intellect, in some material object which we do not suspect, it alone can give reality and substance, it alone can bring into the light of day".[76] The "magic" of performative trials addressing administrative massacre is captured and sown into culminating court record repositories. These records ignite upon intersection with resultant TJ continuums and fortify societal efforts to deal with histories of brutal pasts. *Juzgar y Filmar* allows the exploration of memories woven into the archival compendium emanating from the French Pinochet trial. The artifactual objects expose concealed and new realities and give credence to the ongoing suffering and impact of the State-sanctioned atrocity. Parallels between the dramaturgical nature of trials as spectacle and the immersive experience offered by the exhibition invite the "unsuspecting viewer" at once to remember, to resonate, to lament while offering opportunities to learn, to broadcast, to resist.

"Seek? More than that: create".[77] The exhibition transforms into a "monumental didactic" space that emboldens discussion, generates debate and is purposefully constructed to crack open space for dialogue and memory.[78] Educative events to discuss the exhibition, its intentions and its reception with varying sectors of society are a deliberate facet of the showcase that memorialises its legacy as a living site of engagement and contestation. By coming "face to face with something which does not so far exist", memories do not recede into a forgotten realm of State-endorsed oblivion. The presentation of the audio-visual court archive in a museum institution presents confronting realities. It dually operates as an allegory for the enduring effect of State-sanctioned repression as an endless pursuit for truth, justice and accountability. With the recent passing of the 50th anniversary of the coup état, the role and significance of memory as a pillar of the ongoing transitional justice endeavour in Chile has become a reinvigorated opportunity for creativity and deliberation, typified and celebrated by the exhibition *Juzgar y Filmar*.

75 "Exposición Juzgar y Filmar Los Crímenes de Lesa Humanidad."

76 Proust, *Remembrance of Things Past.*

77 Proust, *Remembrance of Things Past.*

78 Kieran McEvoy, "Beyond Legalism: Towards a Thicker Understanding of Transitional Justice," *Journal of Law and Society* 34 (2007): 411.

Bibliography

Appadurai, Arjun, ed. *The Social Life of Things: Commodities in Cultural Perspective.* 1st ed. Cambridge University Press, 1986. https://www.cambridge.org/core/product/identifier/9780511819582/type/book. Accessed September 9, 2024.

Campbell, Kieran. "The Laws of Memory: The ICTY, the Archive, and Transitional Justice". *Social & Legal Studies* 22 (2013): 247.

Carlson, Kerstin Bree. *Model(Ing) Justice: Perfecting the Promise of International Criminal Law.* 1st ed. Cambridge University Press, 2018. Accessed November 12, 2024. https://www.cambridge.org/core/product/identifier/9781108278157/type/book.

Coen, Mark, Katherine O'Donnell, and Maeve O'Rourke, eds. *A Dublin Magdalene Laundry: Donnybrook and Church-State Power in Ireland.* Bloomsbury Academic. Accessed November 13, 2024. https://www.bloomsburycollections.com/monograph?docid=b-9781350279087.

Combs, Nancy A. *Fact-Finding without Facts: The Uncertain Evidentiary Foundations of International Criminal Convictions.* 1st ed. Cambridge University Press, 2010. Accessed October 22, 2024. https://www.cambridge.org/core/product/identifier/9780511760259/type/book.

"Corte Suprema Confirma Sentencia Contra Ex Coronel de Carabineros y Funcionario Del Ejército Por Desaparición de Alfonso Chanfreau." Accessed November 22, 2024. https://radio.uchile.cl/2024/07/23/corte-suprema-confirma-sentencia-contra-ex-coronel-de-carabineros-y-funcionario-del-ejercito-por-desaparicion-de-alfonso-chanfreau/.

Derrida, Jacques, and Eric Prenowitz. "Archive Fever: A Freudian Impression." *Diacritics* 25 (1995): 9.

"Exposición 'Juzgar y Filmar Los Crímenes de Lesa Humanidad'." Iniciativa Franco-Chilena de Altos Estudios, September 2, 2023. Accessed November 22, 2024. https://ifcae.uchile.cl/2023/09/exposicion-juzgar-y-filmar-los-crimenes-de-lesa-humanidad/.

Ferrara, Anita. *Assessing the Long-Term Impact of Truth Commissions: The Chilean Truth and Reconciliation Commission in Historical Perspective.* Routledge, Taylor & Francis Group, 2015.

Ferrara, Anita. "Archives and Transitional Justice in Chile: A Crucial Relationship." *Human Rights Review* 22 (2021): 253.

Ferrara, Anita. "Bottom-Up and Thought-Provoking Sites of Memory." In *Localising Memory in Transitional Justice, The Dynamics and Informal Practices of Memorialisation after Mass Violence and Dictatorship*, edited by Mina Rauschenbach, Julia Viebach, and Stephan Parmentier, 188–222. London: Routledge, 2022.

Harris, Verne. *Ghosts of Archive: Deconstructive Intersectionality and Praxis.* Routledge, Taylor & Francis Group, 2021.

Harry, Benjamin W.Z. *Work of Art in the Age of Mechanical Reproduction: An Influential Essay of Cultural Criticism.* 1st ed. Penguin Press, 2008.

"Historia Del Proyecto." *Expedientes de la Represión.* Accessed November 22, 2024. https://expedientesdelarepresion.cl/nuestro-proyecto/.

International Federation for Human Rights. "A Historic Trial in France on International Crimes Committed under the Chilean Dictatorship." Accessed November 22, 2024. https://www.fidh.org/en/issues/litigation/litigation-against-individuals/Pinochet-and-others-Case/A-Historic-Trial-in-France-on.

"Judging and Filming Trials for Crimes against Humanity | Part II – Museum of Memory and Human Rights." Accessed November 22, 2024. https://mmdh.cl/exposiciones/temporales/post-exposicion-5.

Ketelaar, Eric. "Tacit Narratives: The Meanings of Archives." *Archival Science* 1 (2001): 131.

Ketelaar, Eric. "Cultivating Archives: Meanings and Identities." *Archival Science* 12 (2012): 19.

Kornbluh, Peter, ed. *The Pinochet File: A Declassified Dossier on Atrocity and Accountability.* Rev. and updated ed., 40th anniversary edition. The New Press, 2013.
Lessa, Francesca. "Remnants of Truth: The Role of Archives in Human Rights Trials for Operation Condor." *Latin American Research Review* 56 (2021): 183.
Lessa Francesca. *The Condor Trials: Transnational Repression and Human Rights in South America.* Yale University Press, 2022. Accessed September 9, 2024. http://www.jstor.org/stable/10.2307/j.ctv2g591p5.
Lühe, Ulrike, and Romain Ledauphin. "From the Forerunners of Document Collection to the Trial of Klaus Barbie and beyond: The Transitional Justice Journey of the Izieu Telegram." *The International Journal of Human Rights* 25 (2021): 440.
Martin, Courtney. "Treaty-Based Regulation and Evidence-Extradition Agreements as Critical Tools in the Fight against International Criminal Wrongdoing." *International Criminal Law Review* 22 (2021): 1168.
McEvoy, Kieran. "Beyond Legalism: Towards a Thicker Understanding of Transitional Justice." *Journal of Law and Society* 34 (2007): 411.
Osiel, Mark. *Mass Atrocity, Collective Memory, and the Law.* First paperback printing. Transaction Publishers, 2000.
Proust, Marcel. *Remembrance of Things Past.* Translated by C.K. Scott-Moncrieff and Stephen Hudson. Penguin Classics, 2022.
Roht-Arriaza, Naomi. *The Pinochet Effect: Transnational Justice in the Age of Human Rights.* University of Pennsylvania Press, 2005.
Schabas, William. *Unimaginable Atrocities: Justice, Politics, and Rights at the War Crimes Tribunals.* Oxford University Press, 2012. Accessed November 22, 2024. http://www.oxfordscholarship.com/view/10.1093/acprof:oso/9780199653072.001.0001/acprof-9780199653072.
Schwartz, Joan M., and Terry Cook. "Archives, Records, and Power: The Making of Modern Memory." *Archival Science* 2 (2002): 1.
Sikkink, Kathryn. *The Justice Cascade: How Human Rights Prosecutions Are Changing World Politics.* 1st ed. Norton, 2011.
Thorne, Benjamin. *The Figure of the Witness in International Criminal Tribunals: Memory, Atrocities and Transitional Justice.* Routledge, Taylor & Francis Group, 2023.
Wilson, Richard Ashby. *Writing History in International Criminal Trials.* Cambridge University Press, 2011.

5 The Documentation Unit at the Peruvian Truth and Reconciliation Commission (TRC)

Ruth Elena Borja Santa Cruz

5.1 Historical Context (1980–2000)

Between 1980 and 2000, Peru experienced a period of violence initiated by the *Partido Comunista del Perú-Sendero Luminoso* (Communist Party of Peru-Shining Path – PCP-SL). This 20-year period was unique because Peru was not under a dictatorship. Three consecutive presidents were elected by popular vote: Fernando Belaunde Terry from 1980 to 1985, Alan García from 1985 to 1990, and Alberto Fujimori from 1990 to 1992. In 1992, Alberto Fujimori executed a self-coup, marking a breakdown of democracy. This action was supported by the people because it was a difficult time characterised by hyperinflation, violence, and corruption within the Peruvian government. Fujimori positioned himself as the nation's saviour, and the population backed him during this crisis. From 1992 onward, Alberto Fujimori governed unlawfully and implemented a series of political, economic, and social reforms included in the new constitution established in 1993. On September 12, 1992, the *Grupo Especial de la Policía* (Special Police Group – GEIN) arrested the leadership of the *Sendero Luminoso* (Shining Path – PCP-SL), which benefited the illegal government of Alberto Fujimori. However, remnants of the PCP-SL continued to threaten his administration.

At the end of the 1990s, revelations about Alberto Fujimori's government surfaced when the infamous *vladivideos* were televised.[1] These video recordings, ordered by Fujimori's advisor, Vladimiro Montesinos, were made during meetings held in the *Servicio de Inteligencia Nacional* (National Intelligence Service offices – SIN), attended by congressmen, businessmen, politicians, artists, journalists, and government officials. The videos, seen all over Peru and abroad, showed the corruption in Fujimori's government. This event was the primary reason for Alberto Fujimori's resignation via fax from Tokyo in 2000. Congressman Valentín Paniagua provisionally assumed the presidency, and

1 LUM. *Vladivideo 295A – Reunión de Alex Kouri, José Francisco Crousillat y Vladimiro Montesinos,* YouTube video, https://m.youtube.com/watch?v=DKZnoq9jF94.

DOI: 10.4324/9781003609322-7

during his short term in office, he created the Truth Commission in 2001.[2] Elections were held, and Alejandro Toledo Manrique took office. He renamed the previously created Truth Commission, Truth and Reconciliation Commission (TRC). The Commission was assigned the following tasks: 1) to establish the causes of the conflict in Peru from 1980 to 2000, 2) to clarify the human rights violations that occurred during this period, 3) to identify those responsible for these violations, 4) to propose reparations for the victims and their families, along with recommendations for reforms, and 5) to set up mechanisms for following up on its recommendations. This commission represented a new initiative for Peruvian society, drawing inspiration from the experiences of truth commissions in other countries.

5.2 The TRC's Documentation Unit

The organisational structure of the Truth and Reconciliation Commission included the *Unidad de Documentación* (Documentation Unit – UD) led by Rosario Narváez Vargas. As a historian-archivist, the author was actively involved in managing the TRC' s archives. As requests for information and the need for data collection increased, the staff of the UD expanded accordingly. The Unit provided information to various branches of the Truth and Reconciliation Commission. To that end, it requested information from various public entities, including the Judiciary, the National Prosecutor's Office, the Congress of the Republic, government ministries, and other institutions. The focus was gathering information related to judicial processes, complaints, civil registries, migratory movements, and commissions established to investigate cases of political violence from 1980 to 2000. Private entities such as universities, the printed press, television reports, ecclesiastical institutions, and human rights NGOs were also contacted to request information on the period of the *Conflicto Armado Interno* (Internal Armed Conflict – CAI).

It is important to point out that police and military institutions did not facilitate access to their archives, an issue often faced by Truth Commissions in Latin America. The secrecy surrounding their archives is notable, as they have been reluctant to disclose the level of violence they employed during the CAI. Their justification for withholding this information is similar to that of other countries: they claim that their documentation is purged every five years, meaning there is none available from the period in question. Furthermore, military and police institutions lack interest in adhering to the standards and regulations related to document destruction established by the General National Archive, which oversees the National System of Archives. Despite knowing the attitudes of the military and police institutions, the Truth and

2 The Truth Commission was created on June 4, 2001, by Supreme Decree N° 065–2001-PCM, which was ratified and complemented by Supreme Decree N° 101–2001-PCM.

Reconciliation Commission (TRC) formally requested information from the Ministries of Defense and the Interior regarding personnel stationed in conflict zones. When it became impossible for them to deny the existence of the documentation, they provided it with a confidentiality seal on every page to ensure that the information would remain confidential.[3]

5.2.1 Creation of the TRC Central Archive

The Documentation Unit created a structured functional classification table of what would later become the TRC's Central Archive: to that end the organic structure of the Truth Commission and the ISAD (G) Standards were taken into account.[4] Documentary series were created using documentation collected from other institutions, plus those generated by the different branches of the TRC. The TRC used the initial documentation for research, sensitisation, and dissemination activities. For example, public hearings, burial sites, and testimonies collected in Regional Offices were used to produce TV documentaries and publications such as "Missing Peruvians", a preliminary list of people missing due to violence (1980–2000)[5] and "*Los rostros y perfiles de la violencia*" (Faces and Profiles of the Violence).[6]

As the work of the Truth and Reconciliation Commission (TRC) progressed, the Documentation Unit team organised visits to various offices in Lima and the four Regional Headquarters. The goal was to collaborate with the secretarial staff from each office to train them in identifying and managing the various documents and files collected. Once the work at each Regional Headquarters was completed, the arranged documentation was transferred to the Documentation Unit, which was responsible for verifying and codifying all the TRC's documentation. The task was challenging because the secretarial staff at the Lima offices and Regional Headquarters had limited knowledge of archives and often followed practices that contradicted proper document management rules. Ultimately, the Documentation Unit staff had to reorganise and catalogue the documents from various headquarters and offices to ensure an adequate transfer to the *Defensoría del Pueblo* (Ombudsman's Office).

3 This occurred when the Ministry of Defense handed over the manuals used by its officers and troops during the CAI, and the Ministry of the Interior handed over the list of its police personnel from 1980–2000.

4 ISAD (G) The International Standard for General Archival Description of the International Council on Archives, ICA.

5 Comisión de la Verdad y Reconciliación, *Los peruanos que faltan, lista preliminar de personas desaparecidas por la violencia* (1980–2000) (Lima: Delivery Commission of the Truth and Reconciliation Commission, 2003).

6 Comisión de la Verdad y Reconciliación, *Informe final* (Lima: CVR, 2003), Volume I, Chapter 3: "The Faces and Profiles of Violence," Section One: General Statement of the Process; Volume IX: National Anthropological-Forensic Research Plan.

5.2.2 *The Documentary Legacy of the TRC*

The TRC operated using more than just documentation from various public and private institutions. Its most significant achievement was the development of a comprehensive database that recorded the names of victims, their relatives, locations, and instances of violence. The database included testimonies from victims, their relatives, witnesses, and, in some cases, perpetrators from across the country. This collection of accounts helped build various cases that the Truth and Reconciliation Commission (TRC) presented for prosecution and reparations and informed the public about the human rights violations that occurred during the 20 years of Internal Armed Conflict. The TRC generated the following archival material: 16,917 folders with testimonies, 13,139 printed photos, 1,109 videos, 18,696 audio cassettes, and 453 folders on 78 special cases that would end in a judicial process. There were also 1,055 folders about burial sites, which later helped in the exhumation and delivery of remains. This work is currently carried out by the General Directorate for the Search for Missing persons under the Ministry of Justice. In addition, a specialised library was created, serving as bibliographic support for researchers from the different areas of the TRC.

5.2.3 *The Transfer of the TRC Collection to the Ombudsman's Office*

The TRC operated from 2002 to 2003. Upon the conclusion of its mandate on August 29, 2003, the TRC presented its final report in the city of Huamanga. On the same day, Supreme Decree No. 078 was issued, which designated transferring commissions to facilitate the delivery of the TRC documents to the Ombudsman's Office and to the *Presidencia del Consejo de Ministros* (Presidency of the Council of Ministers – PCM). The Handover Commission, the Ombudsman's Reception Commission, and the Reception Commission for the Presidency of the Council of Ministers were established. The technical documentation, including all files, testimonies, and any materials that support investigations into human rights violations, was transferred to the Ombudsman's Office. Meanwhile, administrative documentation, such as accounting records and personnel files from the TRC, was sent to the Central Archive of the Presidency of the Council of Ministers, the government agency responsible for overseeing the TRC.

Transferring documents from the TRC to the Ombudsman and the PCM is somewhat unconventional for archivists, as we believe that the unity of the fund can not be broken. However, this approach proved helpful for a straightforward reason: after the Final Report was submitted and the *Centro de Información para la Memoria Colectiva y los Derechos Humanos* (Information Center for Collective Memory and Human Rights – CMHR) was established in the Ombudsman's Office,[7] internal control bodies that needed information about budgets, projects, salaries, and other TRC expenditures were directed

7 Created on April 19, 2004, by Ombudsman's Resolution N° 010–2003 – DP; it was first located at Jirón Miró Quesada N° 398, to date it is located at Jr. Ucayali 394, Cercado de Lima.

to the Central Archive of the Presidency of the Council of Ministers. Doing so, ensured that our time and personnel were not diverted from their primary responsibilities by dealing with administrative queries and requests. Our priority was to provide services to victims and their families, school and university students, judges, and researchers. The Ombudsman's Office established the Information Center to achieve this. This initiative received financial support from various foreign sources, which enabled us to acquire modern equipment, furniture, and the necessary conditions to preserve documents. In its early years, the Information Center employed eight specialists who assisted researchers with search and description tasks related to various documentary series in the TRC collection. With additional funding later on, the Information Center digitalised the 16,917 folders of testimony, enabling a quicker and more efficient service for the victims and relatives of the Internal Armed Conflict.

It is important to note that one of the paragraphs in the Supreme Decree that established the TRC specifies that the testimonies and documents collected by the TRC will remain confidential. The inventory of these materials was sent to the Ombudsman's Office, ensuring strict confidentiality regarding their content. However, the Law of Transparency and Access to Information[8] was enacted in August 2002, which mandated that public institutions provide information to the public. In 2004, when the Information Center was established, the Transparency Law was already in effect. This law provided the legal framework for the Information Center to disclose the TRC's information while guaranteeing individuals' security and privacy. As a result, the Information Center's operations became one of the reparations recommended by the TRC in its final report. The TRC suggested that the state should guarantee widespread dissemination of its Final Report, allowing the population to access information regarding the country's experiences during those 20 years.

5.3 Uses and Ways of Appropriation of the TRC Archives

5.3.1 School and University Students

One of the objectives of the Information Center was to reach secondary school and university students. To this end, the Information Center coordinated with school and university directors so that, through guided visits, students could learn about what happened in the country between 1980 and 2000. The objective was to help students who had not experienced that period and were unfamiliar with the internal conflict gain awareness. This would encourage them to initiate conversations with their parents to uncover family stories that had previously gone untold. Workshops were conducted with students from schools and universities, where emblematic cases presented by the Truth and Reconciliation Commission (TRC) were discussed. These included the

8 Congress of the Republic of Peru, *Law 27806 Law on Transparency and Access to Public Information*, August 2, 2002.

Chuschi, Tarata, Lucanamarca, and Accomarca cases, which exemplified the TRC's efforts to reconstruct what happened in those years. Many students started to recognise the importance of learning about their history and understanding why their parents had not shared their family stories. They also visited photographic exhibits from the conflict period, where an explanation accompanied each photograph.

5.3.2 *Relatives of Victims and Perpetrators*

Another significant group of interest was the relatives of victims, many of whom were Quechua speakers seeking information about their testimonies given before the TRC or searching for details regarding their disappeared or murdered sons, husbands, and fathers. The Information Center carefully provided explanations and follow-up with relatives so they could gather as much information as possible. The Information Center successfully reunited families that had been separated during the Internal Armed Conflict, including children taken by the PCP-SL to various locations, including their barracks or to Lima as servants. There were instances where siblings were reunited when one sibling visited the Information Center to search for his brother, believing he was dead. A search of the database revealed that the brother was alive. The Ombudsman facilitated their reunion and helped reconstruct their story. There is also the story of two brothers who, as children, were kidnapped during a PCP-SL raid and subsequently separated. Now that they were grown, they believed their siblings were dead, but thanks to a search in the database, they were able to reunite. Additionally, there is a notable case involving relatives of individuals who took up arms. These family members visited the Information Center seeking information about the detention or disappearance of their sons, husbands, or brothers who had been involved in "leftist" activities. These situations needed to be addressed in a highly personalised manner. It was essential to handle them with great care to avoid causing additional distress to the victims while still providing them with information about the detention or disappearance of their family members.

5.3.3 *NGOs and State Entities*

Human rights organizations, including APRODEH, CEAS, Paz y Esperanza, Comisedh IDL, and CEAPAZ, frequently accessed the Information Center to search for relevant information related to specific cases they were defending.[9] Other users are state entities, as the Truth and Reconciliation Commission required the state to assume responsibility toward the victims upon delivering

9 *Asociación Pro-Derechos Humanos* (APRODEH); *Comisión Episcopal de Acción Social* (CEAS); *Comisión de Derechos Humanos* (COMISEDH IDL); *Centro de Estudio y Acción para la Paz* (CEAPAZ).

its final report and recommendations. The *Comisión Multisectorial de Alto Nivel (High-Level* Multisectoral Commission – CMAN)[10] was established to oversee the government's actions and policies related to peace, collective repair, and national reconciliation. CMAN also coordinates and supervises the *Plan Integral de Reparaciones* (Comprehensive Plan of Reparations – PIR), which implements collective, individual, and symbolic reparations. The Information Center provided the Multisectoral Commission with a database of testimonies on which they could develop their individual, collective, and symbolic reparation projects.

The *Consejo de Reparaciones* (Reparations Council)[11] was established to provide individual reparations to family members who lost their parents or siblings during the Internal Armed Conflict. The Reparations Council requests specific case details from the Information Center to grant the victims' families reparations. These reparations can take various forms, including monetary compensation, educational benefits such as scholarships for the children of the victims, and symbolic reparations, which may involve improving infrastructure in affected towns or creating memorials or museums. Recently, the Reparations Council has worked with the relatives of the Accomarca Case to return the remains of family members who were killed by the Peruvian Army many years ago.[12] The Information Center has been supplying courts with information about the cases they are investigating. The Judicial Power is the institution that requests the most information from the Information Center. Even during the pandemic, staff members have been asked to provide information on files and testimonies to support prosecutions.

Finally, the *Lugar de la Memoria, la Tolerancia, y la Inclusión Social* (Place of Memory, Tolerance, and Social Inclusion – LUM) was created in 2015, not as a traditional museum but as a larger space managed by the Ministry of Culture.[13] This centre offers cultural activities aimed at learning, researching, and commemorating human rights issues, particularly focusing on the period of the Internal Armed Conflict. The Information Center has supplied the LUM with public hearings videos and essential information to support its research and dissemination efforts. The organisation promotes research and cultural and recreational activities. It works with the relatives of the victims and also with the relatives of the police and military who belong to associations that demand justice for relatives who died during the armed conflict. Military and police personnel have important stories to share, and the Place of Memory, Tolerance, and Social Inclusion provides them with a platform. Currently, the centre is facing budget constraints that necessitate seeking external

10 CMAN was created by Supreme Decree No. 011–2004-PCM.

11 The Reparations Council is the Ministry of Justice and Human Rights collegiate body.

12 On August 14, 1985, in Accomarca, 69 villagers were victims of violence perpetrated by members of the Peruvian Army.

13 The LUM was inaugurated on December 17, 2015, under the presidency of Ollanta Humala Tasso and Minister of Culture of Peru Diana Álvarez-Calderón Gallo.

funding to support its activities. There has been little progress on the issue of reparations because the state has neglected the victims and their families of the Internal Armed Conflict by reducing the budget and prioritising other activities. This is a concerning regression that directly impacts the victims.

The centre hosts recently discovered archives such as the *Confederación Campesina del Perú* (Peruvian Peasant Confederation).[14] This archive contains a wealth of information about peasant organisations from the time of the Internal Armed Conflict. It documents the incursions of armed forces and police, as well as the actions of the Peruvian Communist Party, known as the Shining Path, in villages and hamlets, including the various violations they committed. The archive has been digitalised and is accessible online through UCLA's website.[15] From a political perspective, the archive of the United Mariateguista Party (Partido Unificado Mariateguista – PUM) was discovered. This leftist organisation in Peru operated intermittently between 1984 and 2005 and played a significant role in the political landscape during the armed conflict. Its key representative was parliamentarian Javier Diez Canseco, who served in the Congress of the Republic. He was a strong advocate for human rights and a vocal critic of corruption in Peru. The Place of Memory, Tolerance, and Social Inclusion staff, with financial support from the Gerda Henkel Foundation, a German institution dedicated to preserving historical and cultural heritage, worked to rescue and organise this archive. The PUM archive contains valuable information about the party's organisation and operations, as well as accounts of how its members suffered as victims during the armed conflict due to the arbitrary treatment they faced for their political activities.

In conclusion, continuing to recover the archives of state entities and civil society strengthens our collective memory and contributes to creating a more inclusive society that respects the rights of all individuals. We must remember that forgotten archives, which are at risk of being lost, are waiting to be discovered.

Bibliography

Comisión de la Verdad y Reconciliación. *Informe final.* Lima: CVR, 2003. Volume I, Chapter 3: "The Faces and Profiles of Violence," Section One: General Statement of the Process; Volume IX: National Anthropological-Forensic Research Plan.

Comisión de la Verdad y Reconciliación. *Los peruanos que faltan, lista preliminar de personas desaparecidas por la violencia (1980–2000).* Lima: Delivery Commission of the Truth and Reconciliation Commission, 2003.

14 LUM, *+MEMORIA(S) 2018,* no. 2 (2018): 49–67.

15 MEAP, "The Peruvian Peasant Confederation Archive," accessed December 29, 2024, https://meap.library.ucla.edu/projects/the-peruvian-peasant-confederation-archive.

Congress of the Republic of Peru. *Law No. 27806, Law on Transparency and Access to Public Information*, August 2, 2002.
LUM. *+MEMORIA(S) 2018*, no. 2 (2018): 49–67.
LUM. Vladivideo 295A – Reunión de Alex Kouri, José Francisco Crousillat y Vladimiro Montesinos. YouTube video. https://m.youtube.com/watch?v=DKZnoq9jF94.
MEAP. "The Peruvian Peasant Confederation Archive." Accessed December 29, 2024. https://meap.library.ucla.edu/projects/the-peruvian-peasant-confederation-archive.

Part II

6 The Role of Transitional Justice Archives in Supporting Justice, Reconciliation, and Memory in Colombia

Flor Alba Romero Medina

Introduction

There is a close relationship between archives, human rights violations, and collective memory.[1] Colombia has experienced an armed conflict for over fifty years, resulting in a vast amount of documentation and evidence. This encompasses in-depth investigations, case studies, social movement reports, NGOs' reports, and victims' testimonies. These sources offer crucial insights into the pursuit of truth and justice. The framework for understanding archives documenting human rights violations is based on human rights and collective memory.[2] In this context, archives play a vital role in acknowledging the truth, restoring victims' rights, and promoting restorative justice. The significance of archives documenting human rights violations is also linked to their representation of a nation's collective social memory. These records are created by various contributors, including local communities, victims, academics, and the judicial system. Concerning the tools that the state employs in post-conflict processes, the United Nations emphasises that:

> Archives play a crucial role in upholding individuals' rights. They provide access to the truth about the circumstances surrounding rights violations and information regarding the fate of victims in cases of death or disappearance. Additionally, archives significantly contribute to preserving an accurate historical record and support every person's right to understand their past.[3]

1 Marta Lucía Giraldo-Lopera, "Archivos, Derechos Humanos y Memoria Colectiva: Una Revisión de la Literatura Académica Internacional," *Revista Interamericana de Bibliotecología* 40, no. 2 (2017): 125–44, https://doi.org/10.17533/udea.rib.v40n2a02.

2 Some of the most relevant scholars working on collective memory are Maurice Halbwachs, Elizabeth Jelin, and Andreas Huyssen.

3 United Nations, *Updated Set of Principles for the Protection and Promotion of Human Rights through Action to Combat Impunity*, Human Rights Council, February 8, 2005, Doc. E/CN.4/2005/102/Add.1. Principles 13–17.

DOI: 10.4324/9781003609322-9

Archives play a crucial role in documenting human rights violations. They contribute to the collective memory and help identify those responsible for the violations within the transitional justice framework. This highlights the importance of preserving, organising, and safeguarding these archives. Louis Joinet, in the document "Principles for the Protection and Promotion of Human Rights to Combat Impunity," approved in 1997 by the United Nations Commission on Human Rights,[4] emphasised that the individual right to know the truth requires the preservation of archives. These archives must be protected against theft, destruction, manipulation, or falsification. Furthermore, legislation should be implemented to ensure compliance with these protections, and violations should be subject to penalties. The "Principles for the Protection and Promotion of Human Rights to Combat Impunity" also reflects the importance of implementing effective administrative measures to manage the inventory of archives. It is essential to store these archives properly, particularly those housed in state institutions, and to ensure they are kept in specialised storage facilities. Moreover, the state must appoint qualified personnel to oversee the archives' administration and ensure its long-term preservation. Additionally, measures should be in place to allow investigators and judicial personnel to access the archives without restriction while respecting confidentiality to avoid interfering with ongoing legal procedures. In the context of the Joinet Principles, "archives" refers to:

> Collections of documents related to human rights violations and humanitarian law. These documents may come from various sources, including (a) national government agencies that have been significantly involved in human rights violations; (b) local agencies, such as police stations, that have participated in these violations; (c) state agencies responsible for protecting human rights, such as the prosecutor's office and the judiciary; and (d) materials gathered by truth commissions and other investigative bodies.[5]

Principle 1 establishes that "all individuals have the inalienable right to know the truth about events that occurred and the circumstances and motives behind them, particularly those involving massive and systematic human rights abuses that led to heinous crimes."[6] Principle 2 raises the importance of the "duty to remember," as people's understanding of their history of repression is part of their heritage and must be preserved through appropriate measures

4 The "Principles for the Protection and Promotion of Human Rights to Combat Impunity" were approved in 1997 by the United Nations Commission on Human Rights, see also Colectivo de Abogados José Alvear Restrepo, "Conjunto de Principios para la Protección y Promoción de los Derechos Humanos mediante la Lucha contra la Impunidad," accessed December 28, 2024, https://www.colectivodeabogados.org/conjunto-de-principios-para-la-proteccion-y-promocion-de-los-derechos-humanos-mediante-la-lucha-contra-la-impunidad/.

5 United Nations, *Updated Set of Principles*, Doc. E/CN.4/2005/102/Add.1.

6 United Nations, *Updated Set of Principles*, Doc. E/CN.4/2005/102/Add.1.

in line with the state's responsibility to remember.[7] The duty to remember aims to protect the archives of human rights violations, ensuring that they are not forgotten and remain part of collective memory. This serves to counteract revisionist and negationist narratives:

> Regardless of the actions they may bring before the courts, the victims, as well as their families and relatives, have the imprescriptible right to ***know the truth*** about the circumstances in which the violations were committed and, in case of death or disappearance, about the fate of the victim.[8]

The Joinet Principles establish guarantees for implementing the right to know, which includes the necessity of access to an effective judicial remedy. An independent judiciary should ensure this access, which may be supported by additional mechanisms such as truth commissions. The Joinet Principles were updated in 2005 by the independent expert Diane Orentlicher. A key highlight of the update is the general obligation of states to adopt effective measures to combat impunity, emphasising that they must ensure accountability. The guidelines for establishing and operating truth commissions and preserving and accessing archives related to human rights violations were broadened. Furthermore, concerning the principle of the right to know, it is emphasised that states must implement necessary measures to ensure its effective realisation. The Updated Principles highlight that individuals have the right to know the truth about past events, and society has the right to know and the responsibility to remember. To protect the right to know, the state must ensure the preservation of and access to archives related to human rights violations and international humanitarian law.[9]

6.1 The Precedent of the Justice and Peace Law Archives

Colombia experienced a prolonged and destructive armed conflict that significantly affected over 8 million victims. These individuals retain the rights to truth, justice, reparation, and guarantees against future violence. Transitional justice is implemented after such conflicts, emphasising the victims' right to know the truth, expectation of non-repetition and restorative mechanisms, rather than focusing solely on punishment or sentencing. In Colombia, the implementation of restorative justice began in 2005 with the approval of the Justice and Peace Law.[10] This approach to transitional justice was applied in the context of the Peace Agreements with the Self-Defense Forces.[11] This par-

7 United Nations, *Updated Set of Principles*, Doc. E/CN.4/2005/102/Add.1.

8 United Nations, *Updated Set of Principles*, Doc. E/CN.4/2005/102/Add.1. Emphasis added.

9 United Nations, *Updated Set of Principles*, Doc. E/CN.4/2005/102/Add.1.

10 Congress of the Republic of Colombia, Law 975, July 25, 2005.

11 *Autodefensas Unidas de Colombia* (AUC) are paramilitary forces that were active belligerents in the Colombian armed conflict from 1997 to 2006.

amilitary organisation had a significant presence and control over large areas of the country. It is important to note that this type of justice was not utilised in previous peace processes with guerrilla organisations.[12] The Justice and Peace Law provided the framework for how the Colombian State addressed the members of Colombia's United Self-Defense Forces, specifically the demobilised paramilitaries. This law provided former paramilitaries with reduced prison sentences in exchange for their full confessions and contributions to reparations for victims and national peace.

However, according to the Criminal Chamber of the Supreme Court of Justice, the application of this law has not been evaluated favourably.[13] The victims have expressed frustration with the slow progress, lack of guarantees, and inconsistent results in implementing this law. Law 1592 of 2012, which aimed to reform Law 975 and streamline proceedings, has proven ineffective. Some perpetrators have begun serving their sentences, while others have been deported or regained their freedom.[14] Nevertheless, it is important to note that the Justice and Peace Law played a crucial role in helping the country understand the phenomenon of paramilitarism and its criminal methods of social and territorial control. These methods involved narcotraffickers, different social sectors, and public institutions. A major achievement of the Justice and Peace Law was uncovering the truth about the identification and restitution process of some bodies of the disappeared. However, Gustavo Gallón from the Colombian Commission of Jurists states, "The known truth pales in comparison to the magnitude of the atrocities that should be brought to light."[15]

A critical assessment of the Justice and Peace Law application reveals several flaws. Firstly, access to the hearings was restricted, and the information disclosed was deemed confidential, significantly undermining the victims' right to know the truth. Additionally, another important source of information – paramilitary leaders – was obstructed due to their extradition. Furthermore, the limited participation of victims in the process, along with the murder or disappearance of numerous individuals during this time, highlights serious shortcomings in the implementation of the law. Despite all its limitations, it is essential to acknowledge that the judicial archives left behind by the Justice and Peace process contain hundreds of life stories from victims and their organisations. However, in relation to these archives, issues of confidentiality and the narratives formed during the judicial process did not shift the public discourse that legitimises state violence. Therefore, while it is crucial

12 Observatorio de Conflicto y Paz, *Verdad, Perdón y Reconciliación: Retos de la Construcción de Paz en Colombia* (Bogotá: Universidad Nacional de Colombia, July 2015), 2.

13 Andrea del Pilar Cubides, "Achievements and Challenges of Justice and Peace, 10 Years Later," 2015, https://www.ambitojuridico.com/noticias/informe/educacion-y-cultura/logros-y-retos-de-justicia-y-paz-10-anos-despues.

14 del Pilar Cubides, "Achievements and Challenges of Justice and Peace, 10 Years Later."

15 del Pilar Cubides, "Achievements and Challenges of Justice and Peace, 10 Years Later."

to respect the privacy of the victims and those participating in the process, Colombian society must understand the structural violence in the country.[16]

One of the most common criticisms of the Justice and Peace Law is the limited number of convictions it has achieved over the years. Several factors contributed to this challenge, including the high volume of cases, the unavailability of involved parties to attend hearings, limited staffing and budget, and the small number of Justice and Peace magistrates in the high courts of Bogotá, Medellín, Bucaramanga, and Barranquilla. One criticism is that the information is fragmented, separating the prosecution of paramilitaries, former members of the Revolutionary Armed Forces of Colombia (FARC), and state officials. This fragmentation hinders the ability to uncover the connections between these processes and their actors, which raises the risk of failing to fulfil the victims' right to justice. Another challenge in managing these judicial files is determining how many individuals have received full compensation. This issue arises from methodological limitations and a lack of coordination among the public entities responsible for providing reparations. Finally, information obtained from the paramilitaries may allow the Prosecutor General's Office to investigate and prosecute those complicit in paramilitarism, including state agents and private individuals.[17]

6.2 Historical Memory in Colombia

The role of archives in supporting human rights should be recognised as an essential state policy. This policy must harmonise with existing legislation without undermining prior coordinated efforts. It should be guided by a public policy outlining the necessary measures and actions to effectively fulfil this mandate.[18] Understanding past events and recounting atrocities are essential for developing a historical memory. Memory plays a crucial role in formulating social strategies to prevent such events from occurring again, enabling victims to actively participate in the process of building peace. A significant development in this effort was the establishment of the *Centro Nacional de Memoria Historica* (National Center for Historical Memory – CNMH) under Law 1448 of 2011,[19] also known as "the Victims and Land Restitution Law." This centre includes the Observatory of Memory and Conflict, the area of pedagogy of historical memory, the Museum of the Memory of Colombia,

16 CIT Pax Colombia, "Justice and Peace Law (Law 975 of 2005)," International Observatory - DDR, accessed December 28, 2024, http://www.toledopax.org/es/content/citpax-colombia.

17 Grupo de Memoria Histórica (GMH), *¡Basta ya! Colombia: Memorias de guerra y dignidad* (Bogotá: Imprenta Nacional, 2013), 24.

18 CNMH, *Política Pública de Archivos de Derechos Humanos, Memoria Histórica y Conflicto Armado* (Bogotá: Centro Nacional de Memoria Histórica, 2017), https://centrodememoriahistorica.gov.co/politica-publica-de-archivos-de-derechos-humanos-memoria-historica-y-conflicto-armado/.

19 CNMH, "Contexto," Centro Nacional de Memoria Histórica, accessed December 28, 2024, https://centrodememoriahistorica.gov.co/contexto.

and the Archive on Human Rights, which houses a collection of judgments, truth agreements, and initiatives for the construction of memory. The research and publications developed are a fundamental contribution to the right to the truth of the victims and of Colombian society, helping to avoid the future recurrence of the atrocities experienced.

The purpose of this centre is to receive, recover, preserve, compile, and analyse all documentary materials, including oral testimonies and other forms of evidence, related to human rights violations and breaches of international humanitarian law that occurred during the Colombian internal armed conflict. Additionally, the centre conducts educational activities to strengthen social relations and enhance understanding of the truth for the victims, serving as a means of reparation and promoting cultural transformation within society. The ultimate goals are to prevent the recurrence of such violations and to foster peacebuilding efforts. The National Center for Historical Memory has conducted extensive research on human rights violations and the contexts in which they occurred. This work is closely connected to the subsequent *Sistema de Verdad, Justicia, Reparación y No Repetición* (System of Truth, Justice, Reparation, and Non-Recurrence – SVJRNR)[20] established in 2016 and has shared with the state and society the expertise acquired after years of working in this area.

6.3 The System of Truth, Justice, Reparation and Non-Recurrence

In 2016, the Colombian government signed a Peace Agreement with the FARC-EP guerrilla group after five years of negotiations, establishing the framework for a transitional justice process and creating the System of Truth, Justice, Reparation and Non-Recurrence (SIVJRNR). This system includes three key components: the *Unidad de Búsqueda de Personas Dadas por Desaparecidas* (Unit for the Search of Missing Persons – UBPD), the *Comisión de la Verdad* (Truth Commission – CEV), and the *Jurisdicción Especial para la Paz* (Special Jurisdiction for Peace – JEP). While these three bodies operate independently, they work together in a coordinated manner. The establishment of this system reflects the state's commitment to fulfilling its international obligations to investigate, prosecute, and punish serious violations of human rights and international humanitarian law. It also aims to provide a pathway for Colombian society to overcome the armed conflict that has persisted in the country for over 50 years.

Every mechanism developed its public policy for document management in compliance with Colombian laws and regulations. Since its establishment, the SIVJRNR has made significant progress through collaborative efforts and learning processes. These advancements are essential for peacebuilding and

20 Also known as *Sistema Integral para la Paz* (Integrated System for Peace – SIP).

providing comprehensive reparations to the victims of the armed conflict in Colombia. The Unit for the Search of Missing Persons and the Truth Commission collect extrajudicial information and verify and cross-check their reports. These constitute vital information for the JEP and its mission of applying restorative justice. Providing contexts, facts about structural violence, and patterns of political violence gives the JEP valuable information for compiling its judicial archives.

6.3.1 The System's Archives

The JEP mission is to investigate and prosecute individuals or groups accused of serious human rights violations or breaches of International Humanitarian Law when they do not fully acknowledge their actions or take responsibility for them. Therefore, it is crucial to adopt a transparent methodology for collecting information, determining the criteria to be used, and utilising the extensive documentary resources related to victimising events in the context of armed conflict. The JEP archives serve as essential resources that uphold the rights to truth, justice, and reparation and assist affected communities in ensuring that such violations do not happen again. At the same time, every process related to transitional justice investigations and prosecutions, including judicial truth-seeking efforts, reparation initiatives, and institutional reforms to prevent the recurrence of repression or conflict, relies extensively on archives.[21]

The JEP administers the archives, guarantees the preservation and safety of information, and complies with the General Law on Archives. The JEP's actions and efforts produce judicial files that serve as the foundation for the judicial memory, which constitute information for building the country's historical memory. These documents hold legal, historical, political, and cultural significance for society. All of that highlights the importance of organising, protecting, and ensuring the accessibility of the JEP archives. These archives serve as a fundamental source of truth and are a vital resource for academic research, supporting the interpretation and understanding of events in Colombia. Moreover, the JEP has produced the "Manual for the Participation of Victims before the Special Jurisdiction for Peace"[22] in line with its mandate and in compliance with Interpretative Ruling 01, which was issued on April 3, 2019, by the Appeal Section of the JEP.[23] This outlines best practices for victim participation, emphasises the importance of maintaining a continuous

21 JEP, *AOG Agreement No. 046 of 2020 (November 11) adopting the JEP's Institutional Document Management Policy*, 8.

22 JEP, *Manual para la participación de las víctimas ante la Jurisdicción Especial para la Paz* (Bogotá, 2019).

23 JEP Appeal Section, *Interpretative Judgment TP-SA-SENIT-01*, April 3, 2019.

dialogue with human rights organisations and victims, and incorporates methodological guidelines for presenting their reports.

The integral participation of the victims, collectively or individually, means that all the legal actions submitted to the JEP, whether in the form of observations, petitions, or reports, are incorporated in the files of the JEP as a testimony of their victimisation experience within the context of the internal armed conflict. The JEP asserts that written reports from victims are essential for starting all judicial proceedings and supporting the collaborative construction of the truth. These reports help identify the facts and actions for which the alleged perpetrators should be tried and held accountable. Additionally, they contribute to defining reparative and restorative measures within the proper sanctions outlined by this transitional justice system. These documents clarify individual or group claims, current needs, and expectations regarding each procedure before the JEP.[24] To develop educational materials and communication tools for victims and key stakeholders, the JEP provides remote access to the recorded archives of the completed hearings. This access is available to victims and their representatives, and translation services are offered when necessary.

The Truth Commission, drawing on lessons learned from other truth commissions, established comprehensive records of its investigations, supplemented by materials provided by non-governmental organisations.[25] This collection includes nearly 14,000 interviews with both victims and perpetrators of the events in question, along with academic studies and other reports. The information has been digitised for easy access anywhere worldwide, ensuring long-term availability. Additionally, it contains hundreds of declassified documents from the Colombian and U.S. Army. Furthermore, the Commission transferred these archives to the National Archive, asserting that the information regarding human rights violations held by the authorities is public and should be accessible to anyone who requests it. The digital archives have adequate protection and benefit from international cooperation.[26]

The Unit for the Search of Missing Persons is dedicated to supporting the families of over 120,000 individuals reported missing. It collaborates closely with victims, communities, and various organizations, bolstered by international cooperation and academic partnerships. One of its primary functions is to collect, organise, and analyse information relevant to the search for the missing. The Unit has developed a National Plan and Regional Search Plans,

24 JEP, *Manual para la participación de las víctimas*, 125.

25 Daniel Ospina Celis, "Archivos de las Comisiones de la Verdad: la Clave para un Legado Duradero en Sociedades que Salen de un Conflicto," Dejusticia, September 23, 2023, https://www.dejusticia.org/archivos-de-las-comisiones-de-la-verdad-la-clave-para-un-legado-duradero-en-sociedades-que-salen-de-un-conflicto/.

26 These digital files are preserved through The Legacy Project, with the support of the Kroc Institute at the University of Notre Dame; a digital copy of these files, which safeguard sensitive data, is available to the Swiss government.

which involve verifying information from official sources, civil society, and confidential interviews. These efforts have allowed for the identification of many missing persons in the context of armed conflict. Additionally, the Unit has designed a registry to track graves, illegal cemeteries, and burial sites where unidentified bodies have been discovered. The Search for Missing Persons Unit staff has functional immunities regarding the confidential information it receives, systematises, or produces. It cannot be used in judicial proceedings to determine the responsibility of the perpetrators, nor can it be used as probative evidence. Those who are part of the Unit for the Search of Missing Persons (UBPD) are exonerated from reporting and cannot testify in judicial proceedings for facts they came to know in their search activities.[27]

Despite the increasing role and awareness of the importance of the archives, the information on human rights violations and breaches of international humanitarian law in Colombia faces significant challenges, given the difficulties in collecting and systematising information related to more than 50 years of conflict from reports previously collected by public institutions and non-governmental organisations. Some institutions show little interest in disclosing the truth, and many documents are disappearing; others are at risk due to the deterioration of the paper and the conditions in which they are found. The SVJRNR has discovered that many state institutions and NGOs either overlook the importance of preserving archives and information or lack the knowledge to do so effectively. The project "Mapping of Archives of the Attorney General's Office in Colombia in light of the work of Transitional Justice Mechanisms"[28] represented a significant step forward. The Prosecutor General's Office was instructed about the essential role of files and documents for implementing transitional justice through the JEP and the work of the Truth Commission.

Conclusions

Colombia has chosen a hybrid restorative-retributive system to deal with its past. Restorative justice addresses the harm caused by the crime rather than isolating the person who committed it. This approach focuses on making amends rather than on imposing punishment. The individuals responsible for the crime acknowledge their guilt and the necessity to repair the harm caused. This involves engaging in dialogue with the victim or their family, expressing remorse, and apologising or seeking forgiveness. In a country like Colombia, which has a history of prolonged armed conflict, achieving transitional

27 "*¿Qué es la Unidad para la Búsqueda de Personas Dadas por Desaparecidas en el Contexto y en Razón del Conflicto Armado?*," UBPD, https://ubpdbusquedadesaparecidos.co/wp-content/uploads/2021/03/ABC_UBPD.pdf.

28 "*Los archivos en los procesos de justicia transicional,*" *CNMH,* accessed December 28, 2024, https://centrodememoriahistorica.gov.co/los-archivos-en-los-procesos-de-justicia-transicional/.

justice – specifically regarding truth-seeking and victim reparations – is a complex challenge. The TJ mechanisms often face huge obstacles and risks in uncovering the truth, compensating victims, holding perpetrators accountable, and reforming institutions.

Implementing transitional justice in Colombia has fostered institutional learning, recognition, and profound analysis of the armed conflict. It highlighted the necessity for transitional public policies that effectively classify and utilise the archives documenting human rights violations. The sheer volume of these archives, along with reports from non-governmental organisations and academic studies, calls for creative approaches to their preservation and dissemination. This is essential for developing transitional justice mechanisms that defend and promote victims' rights, ultimately ensuring a sustainable and lasting peace. Transitional justice archives and victims' stories are crucial for uncovering the truth, restoring victims' dignity, and sharing a collective memory. This is vital to prevent the recurrence of the horrific events experienced during the prolonged armed conflict.

Bibliography

CNMH. "Los archivos en los procesos de justicia transicional." 2017. Accessed December 28, 2024. https://centrodememoriahistorica.gov.co/los-archivos-en-los-procesos-de-justicia-transicional/.

CNMH. *Política Pública de Archivos de Derechos Humanos, Memoria Histórica y Conflicto Armado*. Bogotá: Centro Nacional de Memoria Histórica, 2017. https://centrodememoriahistorica.gov.co/politica-publica-de-archivos-de-derechos-humanos-memoria-historica-y-conflicto-armado/.

Colectivo de Abogados José Alvear Restrepo. "Conjunto de Principios para la Protección y Promoción de los Derechos Humanos mediante la Lucha contra la Impunidad." Accessed December 28, 2024. https://www.colectivodeabogados.org/conjunto-de-principios-para-la-proteccion-y-promocion-de-los-derechos-humanos-mediante-la-lucha-contra-la-impunidad/.

Congress of the Republic of Colombia. *Law 975*, July 25, 2005.

Cubides, Andrea del Pilar. "Achievements and Challenges of Justice and Peace, 10 Years Later." 2015. https://www.ambitojuridico.com/noticias/informe/educacion-y-cultura/logros-y-retos-de-justicia-y-paz-10-anos-despues.

Daniel Ospina Celis. "Archivos de las Comisiones de la Verdad: la Clave para un Legado Duradero en Sociedades que Salen de un Conflicto."

DeJusticia, September 23, 2023. https://www.dejusticia.org/archivos-de-las-comisiones-de-la-verdad-la-clave-para-un-legado-duradero-en-sociedades-que-salen-de-un-conflicto/

Gallón, Gustavo. "Achievements and Challenges of Justice and Peace, 10 Years Later." Colombian Commission of Jurists, 2015. https://www.ambitojuridico.com/noticias/informe/educacion-y-cultura/logros-y-retos-de-justicia-y-paz-10-anos-despues.

Giraldo-Lopera, Marta Lucía. "Archivos, Derechos Humanos y Memoria Colectiva: Una Revisión de la Literatura Académica Internacional." *Revista Interamericana de Bibliotecología* 40, no. 2 (2017): 125–44. https://doi.org/10.17533/udea.rib.v40n2a02.

Grupo de Memoria Histórica (GMH). *¡Basta ya! Colombia: Memorias de guerra y dignidad*. Bogotá: Imprenta Nacional, 2013.

International Observatory – DDR Justice and Peace Law and CIT Pax Colombia. "Justice and Peace Law (Law 975 of 2005)." http://www.toledopax.org/es/content/citpax-colombia.

JEP. *AOG Agreement No. 046 of 2020 (November 11)*, adopting the JEP's Institutional Document Management Policy, 8.

JEP. *Manual para la participación de las víctimas ante la Jurisdicción Especial para la Paz*. Bogotá, 2019.

JEP Appeal Section. "Interpretative Judgment TP-SA-SENIT-01." April 3, 2019. https://www.coljuristas.org/observatorio_jep/documentos/seccion_de_apelacion/Sentencia-interpretativa_TP-SA-SENIT-01_03-abril–2019.pdf.

Observatorio de Conflicto y Paz. *Verdad, Perdón y Reconciliación: Retos de la Construcción de Paz en Colombia*. Bogotá: Universidad Nacional de Colombia, July 2015, 2.

United Nations. *Updated Set of Principles for the Protection and Promotion of Human Rights through Action to Combat Impunity*, Human Rights Council, February 8, 2005, Doc. E/CN.4/2005/102/Add.1.

7 The Documentary Collection of the Truth Commission of Colombia

An Unprecedented Experience in Transitional Justice Archives

Maria Prada Ramírez and Andrés Medina Valencia

Introduction

This chapter collaboratively reconstructs a specific experience of the Commission for the Clarification of the Truth, Coexistence, and Non-Repetition of Colombia (hereinafter the Commission) in regard to its archive. First, it describes contextual issues, both endogenous and exogenous, that impacted, and sometimes conditioned, the decisions and type of work that the Commission prioritised as it developed its mandate. Second, the chapter describes how the Commission's archive was built, following national and international guidelines and regulations on human rights, memory, and truth. The third section describes the Commission's legacy two years after the end of its mandate. Finally, in the fourth and last section, we offer some lessons learned from the challenges faced, reflections, and relevant recommendations for future truth and transitional justice mechanisms in Colombia and elsewhere.

7.1 Context and Background for the Work of the Truth Commission

Truth commissions are established as mechanisms for transitional justice. Their purpose is to clarify the events that occurred during periods of widespread human rights violations or dictatorships. They aim to answer questions about what happened, why it happened, how it occurred, where it took place, and who was responsible. The goal is to help close these painful periods by providing an investigative and explanatory contribution to society, hoping that such events will not happen again and that there will be no impunity. In the case of Colombia, the Commission aimed not only to clarify the truth but also to acknowledge responsibilities, strengthen coexistence in the territories, and develop proposals to prevent the recurrence of violence. The platform was created to encourage deep listening, inclusive dialogue, and active participation from all parts of society. Due to the unique characteristics and socio-political context of the internal armed conflict in Colombia, the Commission faced significant challenges in completing its mission to the highest standards.

DOI: 10.4324/9781003609322-10

These diverse challenges included external, internal, and even global issues, such as the COVID-19 pandemic.

The Commission was established as a result of the Peace Agreement in Colombia, which was signed between the Colombian Government and the Revolutionary Armed Forces of Colombia, People's Army (FARC-EP). Point 5 of this agreement is designed to protect the rights of victims. To achieve this, both parties agreed to establish an Integral System for Truth, Justice, Reparation, and Non-Repetition, later referred to as the Integral System for Peace.[1] This Agreement was intended for endorsement through an open plebiscite but ultimately did not succeed. The "NO" campaign effectively spread various fake news and misinformation regarding the Agreement's content. This tactic contributed to a majority "NO" vote in a society that has experienced extensive suffering, violence, and pain. Even more surprising was that more than 60% of the eligible voting population abstained. After jointly reviewing the 59 proposed modifications suggested by the leaders of the NO campaign, both delegations developed a new version of the agreement.[2] The Congress of the Republic ultimately endorsed this revised agreement, which was later approved by the Constitutional Court and became an official state agreement in the Constitution.[3]

The political event captured the attention of public opinion nationwide for several weeks and even made international headlines. By the end of 2016, the Peace Agreement had begun to be implemented despite the lack of domestic legitimacy.[4] It is important to note that since that time, there has been political support from the international community. This is evident in the unanimous backing of the United Nations Security Council and the presence of the Verification Mission in Colombia, which both surround and strengthen the comprehensive implementation of the Agreement.[5] The Commission's mandate was developed between 2018 and 2022, exactly during a presidential term in Colombia. This timing presented an additional political challenge for the entity. The president-elect at that time, Iván Duque, belonged to the political party that campaigned against the plebiscite. Consequently, neither the official

1 This system includes two other entities: the Special Jurisdiction for Peace (JEP) and the Unit for the Search of Missing Persons (UBPD).

2 Oficina del Alto Comisionado para la Paz, "Sistematización Opciones y Propuestas Voceros del No y lo Acordado en el Nuevo Acuerdo," November 22, 2016, https://www.juanitaenelcongreso.com/_files/ugd/883ff8_e1d0053279944cc69dfba41cc7f8c9e7.pdf.

3 Oficina del Alto Comisionado para la Paz, "Cambios, precisiones y ajustes para un nuevo Acuerdo Final para la terminación del conflicto y la construcción de una paz estable y duradera," November 12, 2016, https://www.juanitaenelcongreso.com/_files/ugd/883ff8_3fb603bd95974fd7b531c874f28f61ae.pdf.

4 "Radiografía del Plebiscito y el Posplebiscito," Ideas para la Paz (FIP), 2016, https://multimedia.ideaspaz.org/especiales/posplebiscito/index.html.

5 United Nations Security Council, *Press Release on Colombia*. UN Verification Mission in Colombia, April 15, 2024, accessed December 29, 2024, http://colombia.unmissions.org/comunicado-de-prensa-del-consejo-de-seguridad-de-las-naciones-unidas-sobre-colombia-3.

discourse of the president nor that of his party aimed to legitimise the Peace Agreement or the Integral System for Peace. In contrast, the public messages were marked by scepticism and distrust, referencing to the loss of the plebiscite. Effectively, this aimed to continually restrict the budget of the System for Peace's entities, thereby impairing their proper functioning. During its mandate, the Commission encountered significant obstacles related to the discourse and public narrative from political authorities.

In addition to the sensitive relationship with the national government and the challenges to its legitimacy following the plebiscite, a third factor affected the process: the deep-seated distrust of civil society toward all state entities. Although independent from the various branches of government, the fact that the Commission was classified as a public entity led many victims and civil society organisations to view it as part of the same state that had been responsible for human rights violations during the war or that had effectively neglected their suffering. A state with which they had frequently shared their testimonies, often leading to their re-victimization, that ultimately failed to provide reparations. In addition to the distrust of public institutions, some victims and perpetrators were sceptical or afraid to come forward, given the ongoing confrontation among various armed actors throughout the country.

At the end of its first year, the Commission had completed its planning phase, established a defined structure, hired teams, developed clear work methodologies, and created a robust territorial and extraterritorial deployment. However, it faced the challenge of the COVID-19 pandemic, which forced the Commission to reimagine and completely adjust its operations. This adjustment was necessary to ensure it could continue its work without interruption during a pandemic that impacted humanity. The deaths of Commissioners Alfredo Molano Bravo in 2019 and Ángela María Salazar in 2020 had a profound impact on the Commission team, posing significant challenges to their collective capabilities. Both individuals had established strong legitimacy with the rural population and the victims, and their absence created a pressing need to convene and select two new members to join the process. This included reaching agreements and building collective knowledge that had finally begun after numerous attempts at collaboration. With time and focus on their tasks, the two new commissioners were able to integrate into the collective process quickly.

Despite facing internal and external challenges, the Commission remained attentive to the lessons and experiences of other commissions worldwide. From the outset, it reflected on the impact of its legacy, how its report would be disseminated, the use and accessibility of its archives, and the significance of the collective, ethical, and political process for society. The Commission recognised that, in addition to producing the best possible report, the pursuit of truth and preventing future violations should continue beyond its mandate. To achieve this, the methods employed needed to be effective for social engagement and ongoing involvement. The teams internally referred to this as both the "event or positive shock", which pertains to the process, and the

"Legacy", which refers to the report, the methods, and the individuals involved in its dissemination. An example of this can be found in Recommendation for Non-Repetition 67, documented in the Volume of Findings and Recommendations, which states the following:[6]

> The different social actors, particularly those who work in pedagogy, education, and cultural management; the public and private media; the National Government, Congress of the Republic and public institutions in general; and among them, those who supported and closely accompanied the Commission's processes, are urged to get to know the legacy of the Truth Commission, disseminate it, and give it continuity at territorial, national, and international levels according to their duties, objectives, and specific missions, and rely on it to implement the recommendations made in this Report.

To this end, it is recommended*:*

- To understand and explore the physical and digital locations where the legacy of the Truth Commission is preserved, along with the actors and sectors involved in its development, in order to gain an in-depth understanding of its contents.
- To share information about the sources, characteristics, and contents of the Commission's legacy so that it reaches a wider audience, including more people, organisations, and institutions.
- To ensure continuity, include actions related to the Truth Commission's legacy. This should encompass reflections, narratives, methodologies, processes, and products aimed at truth clarification, coexistence, recognition, and preventing recurrence.

7.2 The Ethical and Political Commitment to Listen

In addition to the previously mentioned challenges, the Commission faced an unprecedented task: clarifying the causes of the armed conflict in the country that has persisted since the establishment of the National Front in 1958. This date marks the starting point of its investigation. Over the years, the Colombian conflict has exhibited a diverse range of violence, necessitating a thorough understanding of the events, the actors involved, their interests, the specific contexts of different phases, and the dynamics that characterise them. To achieve this, the Commission developed an inductive research method. This method involves open listening and observation, then contrasting and comparing findings with secondary sources, ultimately leading to

6 To know the legacy of the Truth Commission, disseminate it and give it continuity: https://www.comisiondelaverdad.co/hallazgos-y-recomendaciones.

analysis and conclusions. The research is guided by a central question: Why, despite numerous agreements and peace processes, does the armed conflict in Colombia not come to a complete end and instead continue to be recycled?[7]

Given its three-year timeframe, this task was a significant challenge. This is especially true considering that the armed conflict in Colombia has been extensively documented by numerous sources, including official records from entities such as the Unit for Integral Attention to Victims, the Ombudsman's Office, and the Prosecutor's Office. Additionally, it is important to acknowledge the valuable collection and analysis conducted by social and human rights organizations, academic institutions, the media, international cooperation agencies, communities, and their leaders, all of whom have worked diligently and independently to document the facts of the conflict. As a significant precedent, it is important to highlight the contribution of the National Center for Historical Memory (CNMH). This organisation has played a significant role in compiling and analysing historical memory since its establishment with the Victims Law (Law 1448 of 2011). By 2020, it had produced 140 reports addressing issues related to the armed conflict.[8]

The Commission did not start from scratch; its main challenge was to organise and efficiently manage the vast amount of existing information. With rigour and independence, it needed to gather the accumulated precedents and contribute to the research and analysis processes necessary for identifying the factors that perpetuate violence, as outlined in its mandate. Central to this challenge was the Mission Information System (SIM), a platform designed to ensure the effective circulation of information and knowledge relevant to fulfilling its mission. This system was implemented throughout the entire information cycle, from the initial data collection to its subsequent use and reuse. It includes key stages such as classification, preservation, processing, analysis, and information visualisation.

The SIM was designed as a technological framework to ensure that victims and citizens have the right to know. From a constructivist perspective, clarity can only be achieved through a participatory movement encouraging an informed, reflective, active, and responsible citizenry. This citizenry advocates for its collective rights and can establish a transformative consensus based on dignity.[9] The goal is not to find a single truth that removes differences but

7 Methodology called "Listening, Recognizing and Understanding to Transform" Comisión para el Esclarecimiento de la Verdad, la Convivencia y la No Repetición, "Ruta metodológica del esclarecimiento de la verdad: Informe final de la Comisión de la Verdad," https://www.comisiondelaverdad.co/como-lo-hicimos/ruta-metodologica-del-esclarecimiento-de-la-verdad.

8 Subgerencia Cultural del Banco de la República, "Las publicaciones del Centro Nacional de Memoria Histórica en la Biblioteca Virtual del Banco de la República," *La Red Cultural del Banco de la República*, https://www.banrepcultural.org/noticias/las-publicaciones-del-centro-nacional-de-memoria-historica-en-la-biblioteca-virtual-del.

9 Swisspeace, "Un marco conceptual para abordar el pasado." *Essentials* 16, https://www.swisspeace.ch/assets/publications/downloads/Essentials/bcaf54fb17/Un-marco-conceptual-para-Abordar-el-Pasado-Essential-16-swisspeace.pdf.

to accept those differences and explore alternatives that prioritise collective welfare from a place of diversity. Therefore, the Commission recognised that simply having large amounts of information was insufficient. It was essential to gather insights about common goals that could help transform the structural conditions contributing to ongoing inequality, violence, and failures in the justice system.[10] The truths proposed by the Commission aimed to explore the complex interplay of actors, interests, objectives, and practices that contributed to the ongoing conflict. These factors varied based on historical periods and specific locations, which allowed for a more nuanced understanding rather than simplistic or binary interpretations. Information should not be treated as proprietary; it must instead act as a vital resource for fostering participatory clarification and social dialogue.

Due to its institutional role and the diverse, high-volume, and rapidly changing nature of information, the SIM faced the challenge of integrating data management models from information science with the guidelines for human rights archives in Colombia, particularly those established by the CNMH. This task was based on previous work on human rights archives developed by Trudy Huskamp Peterson[11] and Antonio González Quintana[12] as well as the experiences of organisations such as Swisspeace[13] and Memoria Abierta,[14] and the reports of the International Council on Archives[15] and the United Nations Commission on Human Rights (Joinet, Orentlicher).[16]

The Joinet-Orentlicher principles were established by the United Nations Commission on Human Rights as a framework to combat impunity. They include essential legal and archival elements to ensure the rights of victims of serious human rights violations. Among the rights outlined in these documents, the recommendations concerning the "right to know" were key considerations in the design of the SIM. To grasp the significance of this right, it is important to recognise that its scope extends beyond an individual's claim to access the truth. It encompasses the collective ability to know and remember

10 United Nations, *Report of the Special Rapporteur on the Promotion of Truth, Justice, Reparation and Guarantees of Non-Repetition*, Section C: General Considerations, 2015, https://documents.un.org/doc/undoc/gen/g15/202/07/pdf/g1520207.pdf.

11 Trudy H. Peterson, *Final Minutes: A Guide to Preserving the Records of Truth Commissions* (Washington, DC: Woodrow Wilson Center Press, 2005).

12 Antonio González Quintana, "Archives and Human Rights," *ANABAD Bulletin* 49, no. 3–4 (1999): 371–89.

13 Swisspeace, "Un marco conceptual para abordar el pasado."

14 Red de Sitios de Memoria Latinoamericanos y Caribeños (RESLAC), *Experiences of Civil Society Participation in Truth Commissions in Latin America* (RESLAC, 2020), https://sitiosdememoria.org/wp-content/uploads/2020/06/Comisiones-Reslac_DIGITAL.pdf.

15 Comisión Colombiana de Juristas, *Principios sobre la impunidad y las reparaciones* (Comisón Colombiana de Juristas, 2007), https://www.coljuristas.org/documentos/libros_e_informes/principios_sobre_impunidad_y_reparaciones.pdf

16 United Nations, *Updated Set of Principles for the Protection and Promotion of Human Rights through Action to Combat Impunity*, Human Rights Council, February 8, 2005, Doc. E/CN.4/2005/102/Add.1.

the past, which serves two main purposes: (i) to preserve and share historical memory and (ii) to conduct research that helps clarify and prevent the recurrence of cycles of violence. The responsibility of the state regarding the "duty to remember" is emphasised as a means to protect information from the risk of being lost. This duty also aims to prevent interpretations that promote revisionism or denialism, which could jeopardise the comprehensive reparation of victims and affected communities.

Additionally, recommendations for preserving human rights archives were put in place to prevent the destruction of documentary records, the disintegration of collections, and the misuse of information, all of which would violate states' obligations to uphold rights. In this context, it is important to highlight the recommendations established by the Office of the High Commissioner for Human Rights of the United Nations regarding how the final disposition of documentary archives directly impacts the design, implementation, and delivery phases of related processes. These guidelines are supported by the principle of "right to memory integrity," which must be upheld, as no design of transitional justice mechanisms should compromise the integrity of the documentary collections that preserve social memory. It is important to emphasise the guarantees of habeas data and data processing concerning the records compiled by the Commission. Both victims and the accused should have the right to access documents that mention their names individually. However, their identities must be protected during public consultations in accordance with the legal guidelines established.[17] This mandate regarding personal data protection is complemented by the spirit of maximum publicity of the Final Report and its annexes, enabling the public to be fully informed of the Truth Commission's conclusions and recommendations. Based on these considerations (and other elements beyond the scope of this document), the guidelines for the design and implementation of the SIM were defined:

Ethical-political: (i) *autonomy*, the repository of information must be guarded and implemented within the Commission, independent of external resources or services; (ii) *plurality*, the archive will guarantee the safeguarding of information obtained from any available source and in all necessary formats, promoting the equitable participation of all social sectors; (iii) *neutrality*, the mechanisms provided for the preservation, consultation, processing, and contrasting of information are equitable, transparent, and technically based.

Socio-technical: (i) *transparency*, the procedures, standards, methodologies, and data structure of the SIM will be verifiable and auditable for validation, comparison, and updating; (ii) *openness*, the analytical tools, methodologies, and procedures implemented in the SIM will be open, documented,

17 Congress of the Republic of Colombia, *Law 1266,* December 31, 2008; Congress of the Republic of Colombia, Law 1581, October 17, 2012.

and available for public consultation; (iii) *accessibility*, the information system includes the technological and pedagogical mechanisms required to guarantee the effective consultation and recovery of the information by any population; (iv) *responsibility*, the necessary mechanisms will be incorporated for the proper custody of the information, its processing and analysis, as well as the protection of personal and sensitive data offering a service that guarantees the integrity of people and contributes to the building of peace.

Methodological: (i) *objectivity*, rigorous and verifiable technical tools and procedures will be used for the standardisation, analysis, verification, and contrasting both of the sources and research results; (ii) *reflexivity*, the procedures for the cataloguing, collecting, and analysing of information will take into account and make explicit the contexts of collection, production, and use of all information favouring a critical, documented, and participatory understanding of the sources; (iii) *collaboration*, promoting dialogue and the integration of knowledge, skills, and learning in the platform, to consolidate a collective knowledge supported by the use of tools for self-management, co-creation, and distributed learning.

Impact: (i) *participation*, a technological and pedagogical strategy will be created to enhance the usability of available information by strengthening communities of practice and fostering co-creation efforts that promote its adoption and social use; (ii) *care*, the design of the solutions will put its users and participants at the centre, seeking to prevent both physical and emotionally adverse impacts and ensuring to offer inputs that contribute to reparation, learning, and personal and collective healing; (iii) *sustainability*, the information, tools, codes, and documentation of the SIM will be developed with the goal of sustainability, thinking of its future use and proliferation; (iv) *appropriation*, the embodiment of the right to know lies in the strengthened skills of its users to access, analyse, and understand the knowledge incorporated into the SIM, as well as the capacity to co-create, adjust, and reuse its tools, methodologies, and procedures.

The implementation of these guidelines aimed to ensure the protection of citizens' right to know and the Commission's duty to remember. This serves as a transitional mechanism for uncovering the truth. However, it is important to note that the Colombian case has specific characteristics that set it apart from the processes described in previous literature. The Commission adopted modern technological developments and designed the SIM following current standards for information management, big data, and data science. This innovative approach of creating a completely digital Commission made it possible to overcome the previously identified technical challenges and face contingencies such as the COVID-19 pandemic during a large part of its development. In addition, the commitment to address the complexity, dynamism, and variety of information requires a collection of plural voices, which calls for a transdisciplinary approach incorporating mixed methodologies for capturing, processing, and analysing information in multiple formats.

The SIM was developed as a technological platform designed to facilitate the flow of information in a feedback loop, enabling users to consult, interact, and collaboratively build knowledge. After an initial assessment of requirements, it was determined that no existing tool on the market could fully address the entity's information needs or align with its mission objectives. In response, a proposal was made to integrate a suite of tools around a central repository. This approach would provide a robust solution that ensures the interoperability of information, secure preservation, and relevant functionalities tailored to the needs of working teams.

The Commission decided to create a customised software solution based on the principles of autonomy, transparency, and neutrality. This solution was developed within its own infrastructure using free and open-source tools. This approach provided greater control over information, ensured independence from external services, and allowed for ongoing adaptation to meet the evolving needs of its mission. Importantly, this was achieved without compromising the security of the information or the integrity of its donors and users. The following brief describes the phases of the information cycle and details the technological, methodological, and strategic solutions implemented to meet the Commission's technical and functional requirements:

Collection: The objective of this phase is to capture, catalogue, classify, and pre-process the information for its subsequent integration and preservation in the central repository. Considering the large volume of information available and respecting the guidelines of plurality and participation, the SIM considered three primary information flows: mission information, external sources, and knowledge production within the entity.

First, by executing the mandate of deep listening, during the three years of its mission, the Commission collected the voices of 28,603 people from diverse sources, such as individual and collective interviews, public meetings, and life histories.[18] Each scenario was carried out following established methodological guidelines, enabling information capture, organisation, processing, and analysis. In total, different organisations and individuals voluntarily submitted 1,221 reports and 438 cases. The submissions were gathered, catalogued, and organised as documentation for an investigation.[19] Likewise, the Commission collected a large amount of content from external sources, resulting in 214 documentary collections from 68 entities and 561 data sets from 148 public and private institutions.[20] In addition, a bibliographic corpus of 12,112 titles related to the Colombian internal armed conflict was created in multiple

18 Comisión para el Esclarecimiento de la Verdad, la Convivencia y la No Repetición, "Datos de la escucha y fuentes externas de la Comisión," https://www.comisiondelaverdad.co/datos-de-la-escucha-y-fuentes-externas-de-la-comision.

19 Comisión para el Esclarecimiento de la Verdad, la Convivencia y la No Repetición, "Informes y casos," https://www.comisiondelaverdad.co/informes-y-casos

20 Comisión para el Esclarecimiento de la Verdad, la Convivencia y la No Repetición, "Bases de datos," https://www.comisiondelaverdad.co/bases-de-datos.

formats.[21] The internal knowledge management exercise allowed the permanent flow of narratives, reports, and research documents among the various technical areas of the Commission and registered SIM technical developments, such as source code, maps, analyses, and visualisations, that were made available for internal consultation and subsequent public dissemination.

Information processing: To improve the accessibility and usefulness of the gathered information, specific procedures were established for processing it in relation to the previously mentioned input flows. The interviews collected, which formed the basis of the research, were prioritised for transcription and coding. The Commission employed a team of over 100 professional analysts to facilitate this process. This team was supported by psychosocial specialists with expertise in documentary analysis, who coordinated the tasks and provided self-care and emotional support to their colleagues. Additionally, training sessions were organised to enhance understanding of research concepts; update the coding framework; and analyse findings, cases, and significant trends, allowing for feedback from the research team.

In collaboration with the research groups, a thesaurus containing 12,341 entries was developed, along with a Wiki that provides definitions for 377 analytical categories, classified into 11 thematic domains.[22] This standardisation of the language was key not only for the documentary analysis of the interviews but also for documentary cataloguing, information management, and massive data analysis. External information was safeguarded with a hash code to verify its authenticity. Then, when necessary, standardisation and optimisation procedures were carried out, such as OCR for physical documents, data quality for structured information, or digitisation for material support. The SIM believed that any object with symbolic value or information relevant to the mission should be documented. Accordingly, material objects and audiovisual records resulting from mission operations were kept. These tasks were supported by developing more than 30 procedures configuring information flows and standardised formats and procedures created to capture, process, analyse, preserve, and use the documentary corpus.

Integration: Regardless of their origin and format, all of the Commission's mission-related documents were stored in a central repository that provided advanced tools for searching, retrieving, and consulting documents. Various solutions were implemented at the core of this ecosystem of tools to ensure robust and efficient access to information backed by a hyper-convergent technological infrastructure. Data integration was implemented in a non-relational database supported by an Elasticsearch engine that indexed 2,453,980 resources

21 Comisión para el Esclarecimiento de la Verdad, la Convivencia y la No Repetición, "Bibliografía abierta del informe final," https://www.comisiondelaverdad.co/bibliografia-abierta-del-informe-final.

22 Comisión para el Esclarecimiento de la Verdad, la Convivencia y la No Repetición, "Recursos (Lenguaje Natural)," https://www.comisiondelaverdad.co/recursos-lenguaje-natural.

in multiple formats. Additionally, by incorporating a data repository, information flows were optimised, and efficiency increased in the processing and analysing of massive data aggregates. It should be emphasised that by integrating these technologies, a system capable of optimally materialising the principles of plurality, neutrality, transparency, and accessibility from a technological solution implemented in-house and tailored to the Commission's mission needs was developed.

Analytical: As part of the information management cycle, the information analysis phase was of fundamental interest for extracting knowledge, contrasting versions, and verifying hypotheses. Similarly to the previous phases, the SIM was oriented toward forming a qualified team equipped with the necessary technological tools to meet the research needs. For this purpose, specialised teams were formed to address different types of analysis. The Geographic Information System team developed the Geoportal, producing cartographies, viewers, and geo-statistical analysis; the Data Visualisation Team created interactive dashboards and infographics with tools using open libraries to simplify the exploration of data sets; the Data Analytics Team, using rigorously documented protocols, led the data modelling to support the research; and the Language Processing Team[23] identified patterns of unstructured data sets, relying on elaborating a lexicon on the Colombian armed conflict.

Due to the complexity and volume of the information, the Data Analytics Team collaborated with the research teams to develop information analysis projects. Each process adhered to a protocol that included thorough documentation and feedback from peer seminars, ensuring both technical validity and theoretical relevance. The analyses carried out with R and Python, were documented on GitHub following the Human Rights Data Analysis Group (HRDAG) quantum workflow methodology,[24] which gave transparency, verifiability, and the ability to reuse the code for future studies.

One noteworthy project is the "Data Integration and Statistical Estimation" initiative, which was implemented in collaboration with the Human Rights Data Analysis Group (HRDAG), led by Patrick Ball. This project integrated a total of 112 statistical sources to assess victimisation across five types of violence in the Colombian conflict: homicides, kidnappings, disappearances, illegal recruitment, and displacement. Through advanced analytical algorithms, the data were unified and underreporting rates were calculated, requiring specialised equipment and computational resources restricted to the Commission and the JEP (Special Jurisdiction for Peace). The results served both entities in their research work, and the methodology developed continues to serve the

23 Comisión para el Esclarecimiento de la Verdad, la Convivencia y la No Repetición, "Analítica de datos (información y recursos) | Informe Final de la Comisión de la Verdad," https://www.comisiondelaverdad.co/analitica-de-datos-informacion-y-recursos.

24 Human Rights Data Analysis Group (HRDAG), "The Task is a Quantum of Workflow," June 14, 2016, http://hrdag.org/2016/06/14/the-task-is-a-quantum-of-workflow/.

JEP and has also been incorporated into the National Statistics Department (DANE).[25]

Knowledge management: SIM's knowledge management strategy was based on three fundamental pillars: self-management of information, collaborative construction of knowledge, appropriation, and social use. Different scenarios were created to incorporate these commitments integrally and dynamically to achieve these commitments. From the design and development phase, the tools were planned with user-friendly interfaces and functionalities that responded to the needs of the researchers. The Commission's mission team underwent continuous training to enhance its capabilities and fulfil support and usability requirements. As a result of this training and with the involvement of the SIM development team, new functionalities were created, and existing ones were adjusted. A notable example of this happened during the COVID-19 pandemic. As the number of infections surged globally, the focus shifted toward adapting tools for secure use on the Internet, as many were previously restricted to intranet access. Due to the effective efforts of the development team, a secure solution for internet use was implemented just in time for the lockdowns. Collaborative knowledge development presented a design challenge that resulted in integrating features and functions promoting distributed work and learning. Notable examples include the Wiki, which features a collaborative dictionary of terms, and the Module for Collaborative Cataloging, which aims to incorporate content and facilitate teamwork among the mission team openly.

In alignment with its role as a living archive for the Commission's legacy, priority was given to organising the SIM, resulting in technical documentation for external use and the validation and reuse of its tools.[26] Other mission areas were also modified to create collections that included replicable and expandable methodologies, promoting participatory knowledge management by citizens and communities. This practice was strengthened by consolidating communities of practice aimed at giving sustainability to the processes of clarification and restoration, assisting researchers and creating pedagogical spaces to amplify the Commission's impact on peacebuilding. An example of this activation was seen in the Community of Pedagogical Practices for Truth, Memory and Non-repetition, "Let the Truth be Told", with the participation of teachers from Bogota and Valle del Cauca.[27]

25 HRDAG – Human Rights Data Analysis Group, "HRDAG – Human Rights Data Analysis Group," http://hrdag.org/colombia-faq/.

26 As a result of this exercise, a technical description of all SIM tools was made in GitBook format. These resources are available in the methodological sections of the transmedia; see for example: Comisión para el Esclarecimiento de la Verdad, la Convivencia y la No Repetición, "Gitbook | Archivo de Esclarecimiento [GitBook]," https://docsarchivoesclarecimiento.comisiondelaverdad.co.

27 Comisión para el Esclarecimiento de la Verdad, la Convivencia y la No Repetición, "Pedagogía: Informe Final de la Comisión de la Verdad," https://www.comisiondelaverdad.co/pedagogia.

Archive for the Clarification of the Truth:[28] this platform was designed with an innovative approach to information management, integrating principles, methods, and tools from information sciences, museology, and human rights archiving. The objective, in line with the principles of the SIM, was to encourage public participation, access, and social use of the information accumulated by the Commission. This involved making the information available to the public, providing resources for contextual and critical analysis, and illustrating methodological and interpretative approaches to aid in understanding past events. Additionally, it aimed to inspire reflections and actions that promote citizen learning and transformation. This material was created to support social activations "outside the system", allowing these initiatives to serve as a living archive. This approach encourages the transfer of knowledge to the most important source of information: people and communities. Therefore, the communities of practice sought to establish themselves in people's daily lives, with their own experiences, trajectories, meanings, and knowledge, in order to promote the re-signification of their past, the reflective understanding of violence, and its subsequent participatory transformation.[29]

7.3 The Legacy of the Colombian Truth Commission

The Commission's commitment extended beyond producing the report and encouraging social dialogue throughout its three-year mandate. It also created a legacy strategy aimed at embedding the results of its efforts within a medium – and long-term social and political framework. This strategy seeks to contribute to meaningful impacts on coexistence and prevent future conflicts.

The Truth Commission defines its legacy as

> a collection of reflections, narratives, actions, products, and educational processes – both tangible and intangible – that result from its mission. This legacy allows society, the State, the Integral System for Peace, the international community, and various networks to engage with the Final Report fully. Most importantly, it encourages key social actors to commit to implementing its recommendations.

This definition is grounded in an ethical and political interpretation of the Commission's mandate and its dedication to fostering a long-term transitional

28 Comisión para el Esclarecimiento de la Verdad, la Convivencia y la No Repetición, "Archivo El Esclarecimiento de la Verdad (Truth Clarification Archive)," https://archivo.comisiondelaverdad.co.

29 Comisión para el Esclarecimiento de la Verdad, la Convivencia y la No Repetición, "Guía de proceso de guion expandido," https://www.comisiondelaverdad.co/guia-de-proceso-de-guion-expandido.

process.[30] In practical terms, this was realised through three main pillars: (i) the content provided by the Commission, (ii) the methods used to disseminate this content, and (iii) the individuals and opportunities to encourage public debate and establish an ongoing national conversation to prevent re-occurrences.

7.3.1 The Website: www.comisiondelaverdad.co

The Truth Commission presented a transmedia report accessible in various formats for consultation and understanding. The "There Is Future if There Is Truth" report comprises ten written volumes.[31] There is a public digital platform that provides permanent access to society, enabling a more immersive exploration of the stories, experiences, testimonies, cases, and files collected and lived during the armed conflict in Colombia.[32]

The report contains approximately 1TB of public information collected and produced by the Commission, organised into 22 components. Its design allows for exploration throughout Colombia and beyond, including the experiences of those in exile. The aim is to shed light on places and situations that may be unfamiliar or mystified, providing a clearer narrative of the experiences of individuals who have lived through the armed conflict. The material is sourced from various primary and secondary documents, videos, audio files, timelines, testimonies, links, databases, and multiple formats from diverse actors and sectors of society. Moreover, the webiste contains essential resources to reach various audiences. This includes manuals tailored for journalists, over 50 artistic pieces intended for screening and stimulating discussions, and specific tools designed for teachers and the educational community to use in the classroom. Additionally, there are summary guides for each report volume, accompanied by an animated series that highlights the key contents in audiovisual format.

One of the 22 components of the digital platform is the Truth Clarification Archive mentioned earlier.[33] This specific component displays the contents that belonged to the SIM and corresponds to information available for public use – after some adjustments were made to its interfaces and tools for open access. A new user experience design (UX) was developed for its publication, and a content aggregator was developed that allowed the elaboration of

30 Comisión para el Esclarecimiento de la Verdad, la Convivencia y la No Repetición, "La narrativa del legado," https://www.comisiondelaverdad.co/la-narrativa-del-legado.

31 Comisión para el Esclarecimiento de la Verdad, la Convivencia y la No Repetición, *Hay futuro si hay verdad: Informe Final de la Comisión de la Verdad* (Bogotà, 2022), https://www.comisiondelaverdad.co/hay-futuro-si-hay-verdad.

32 Comisión para el Esclarecimiento de la Verdad, la Convivencia y la No Repetición, "Apertura: Informe Final de la Comisión de la Verdad," https://www.comisiondelaverdad.co/.

33 Comisión para el Esclarecimiento de la Verdad, la Convivencia y la No Repetición, "Archivo El Esclarecimiento de la Verdad."

27 curatorial narratives with the participation of the mission teams. Likewise, to deliver this digital platform, 2,240 mission interviews were published and anonymised through artificial intelligence with manual verification, ensuring open access without compromising privacy.[34] It should also be noted that the materials published on this platform are under Creative Commons licenses (CC BY-NC-SA 4.0), integrating accessibility standards (WCAG 2.0) in a significant portion of resources.[35]

The University of Notre Dame, under the leadership of the Kroc Institute and the Lucy Family Institute for Data and Societies, recognises the significance of this material and its historical and political scope in terms of memory and cultural heritage. With the support of the Humanity United Foundation, it is committed to hosting the transmedia platform and keeping it running in perpetuity.[36] As part of this commitment, in May 2024, it enabled the download of the offline version of the transmedia platform, allowing navigation and access to 65% of its contents without needing a permanent internet connection. This favours access to the contents in the national territory, especially in remote and dispersed rural areas most affected by the internal armed conflict.[37]

7.3.2 The Exhibition: "There Is Future if There Is Truth"

Another element of the transmedia report is the travelling exhibition "*Hay Futuro Si Hay Verdad*" ("There Is Future if There Is Truth"). This experience focuses on the Report's Findings and Recommendations, encouraging us to shift our perspective from a Wounded Colombia to a Possible Colombia. It begins with a Call for a Great Peace to later place the audience within the context of the Truth Commission, framed by the Peace Agreement and as part of the Integral System for Peace. A following section called "Wounded Colombia" shares heartbreaking data alongside the faces and testimonies that illustrate the impacts of the armed conflict on individuals. The victims recount violations of human rights and breaches of international humanitarian law. In a later section, the exhibition provides a historical perspective to help us understand the factors contributing to the ongoing armed conflict, which can be examined chronologically or thematically. It then proceeds to "Deep Colombia", which explores the manifestations, impacts, and resistances

34 Comisión para el Esclarecimiento de la Verdad, la Convivencia y la No repetición, 2022.

35 Comisión para el Esclarecimiento de la Verdad, la Convivencia y la No Repetición, "Términos y condiciones para el acceso y uso de los contenidos de la plataforma digital del Informe Final," https://www.comisiondelaverdad.co/terminos-y-condiciones-para-el-acceso-y-uso-de-los-contenidos-de-la-plataforma-digital-del-informe.

36 Comisión para el Esclarecimiento de la Verdad, la Convivencia y la No Repetición, "Plataforma Digital Transmedia," https://www.comisiondelaverdad.co/plataforma-digital-transmedia.

37 Comisión para el Esclarecimiento de la Verdad, la Convivencia y la No Repetición, "Versión Offline," https://www.comisiondelaverdad.co/version-offline.

related to the armed conflict in each region, accompanied by maps and sounds from 11 sub-regions of the country. Finally, it presents an area called "Possible Colombia", which invites an ongoing conversation about the country, by closing with words, reflections, and feelings regarding the recommendations for non-repetition and envisioning the Colombia of the future – a future to which we are deeply committed.

7.3.3 The Truth Commission Documentary Fund

The depth and persistence of the armed conflict and the processes deployed by the Commission to arrive at the report "There is a Future if There is Truth" is reflected in the approximately 130 TB of files with mission, strategic, support, and evaluation information. It is a digital archive with different formats, including textual, sound, videos, photographs, and databases. It contains all the primary and secondary information that supports the report (mission file): the material that guided the vision, mission, infrastructure, and communications of the Commission (strategic file); as well as all the sources that account for the administrative, legal, and financial management of the Commission (support and evaluation file).

Under these circumstances, once the Truth Commission wrapped up in May 2023, the Documentary Fund remained under the ownership of the JEP as an institution of the Integral System for Peace that can guarantee its autonomy and under the administration of the General Archive of the Nation AGN – an entity with the mandate to protect and manage the Nation's archives – recognised as a human rights archive and cultural interest asset by the AGN. It should be noted that the Documentary Fund was recently received by UNESCO's Memory of the World Program (MoWLAC).[38] In addition, because of an international alliance with the Embassy of Switzerland and Swisspeace, a safe-haven copy of the Documentary Fund rests in the Swiss Confederation.[39]

In conclusion, the three key components – the Documentary Fund, the Digital Transmedia Platform, and the Exhibition – have ensured that the report does not remain hidden. They have allowed the documentary legacy to continue beyond the end of the mandate, presenting it as a dynamic process. These transmedia initiatives facilitate the delivery and management of historical memory, enable its analysis, and support restorative actions for future generations.

38 Comisión para el Esclarecimiento de la Verdad, la Convivencia y la No Repetición, "Versión Offline."

39 UNESCO, "Documentary Fund of the Commission for the Clarification of Truth, Coexistence and Non-Repetition (CEV)," Memory of the World – Latin America and the Caribbean, https://www.unesco.org/en/memory-world/lac/documentary-fund-commission-clarification-truth-coexistence-and-non-repetition-cev.

The achievements outlined in territorial reach and diversity of voices, especially considering the limited timeframe and the impact of COVID-19, would not have been possible without the collaborative efforts of over 3,000 national and international partners.[40] The Commission was established due to a social movement for peace and human rights that has been active in the country since the 1950s. From the outset, it aimed to collaborate closely with various social and political actors. The contributions of over 150 universities and think tanks from Colombia and around the world, more than 1,000 civil society organisations, political support from countries across all continents, and the unanimous backing of the United Nations Security Council were all essential for achieving this ambitious process of social dialogue.

This commitment to collaboration helped bridge gaps of mistrust and improved the processes of listening and participation in a more efficient and trustworthy way. As its mandate came to a close, the Commission enhanced this collaborative effort through an initiative it referred to as Networking among Allies, which aimed to ensure sustainability both in terms of time and space.[41] This commitment continued for two years after the report's publication, promoting the Commission's legacy and the utilisation of the report and its archives. This process remains a legacy in various sectors and regions in Colombia and beyond. It involves collaboration with the Committee for Follow-up and Monitoring of the Implementation of the Recommendations for Non-Repetition, as developed by the Commission.

7.4 Final Thoughts on Future Engagements With Archives and Transitional Justice Mechanisms

After a careful process of learning, continuous observation, and reflective analysis – some elements influenced by the recommendations of Pablo de Greiff, the former United Nations Special Rapporteur on truth, justice, and non-repetition – we have identified several key lessons, reflections, and recommendations for this type of work.[42]

Collaborate through alliances and acknowledge the importance of civil society's role: The Commission benefitted from the support of various organizations and initiatives that focused on archives, memory, and museums to promote the truth and defend human rights. The advancements achieved by the CNMH and the AGN in managing human rights archives provided valuable resources for the development of the Commission's documentary collection. Likewise, the process and its subsequent sustainability were nourished by the

40 Comisión para el Esclarecimiento de la Verdad, la Convivencia y la No Repetición, "Con Quién Lo Hicimos: Informe Final de la Comisión de la Verdad," https://www.comisiondelaverdad.co/con-quien-lo-hicimos-0.

41 Comisión para el Esclarecimiento de la Verdad, la Convivencia y la No Repetición, "Trabajo en Red con Aliados," https://www.comisiondelaverdad.co/trabajo-en-red-con-aliados.

42 United Nations, *Report of the Special Rapporteur.*

experience of partner organizations such as Swisspeace, *Verdad Abierta* (Open Truth), the International Coalition of Sites of Conscience, the Colombian Network of Sites of Memory, DeJusticia (Of Justice), the University of Notre Dame, and Humanity United. Their backgrounds, knowledge, and political will were crucial for the development and implementation of the provisions and practices that contributed to the implementation of the citizenry's right to know and to the creation of the Commission's Legacy.

Interventions in both cultural and individual sphere: In line with its mission, the Commission has committed to conducting an archiving exercise that incorporates various practices for advocacy and social participation, including education, the arts, psychosocial approaches, and technology. Future archiving efforts could be enhanced by integrating these areas into the flow of information. The Transmedia and the Archive of Clarification were initiatives aimed at addressing this issue. These strategies, significant from the standpoint of human rights archives, differ from conventional archival practices. This presented an additional challenge for the Commission, as it needed to balance document management requirements with a collection strategy incorporating elements from information sciences and modern museology. It is indeed an open debate, and the Commission's experience highlights the necessity of adopting an interdisciplinary approach to understand and manage documentary aggregates that comprise such diverse resources.

Storage and custody of the archive: Aware of its mandate's context and aiming for neutrality, the Commission chose to develop an Information System specifically designed for its mission requirements, hosted on its own infrastructure. While this alternative promotes a message of independence and transparency, it also suggests that considerable effort will be required for its implementation and management. Identifying the depositary entity from the beginning can help streamline and enhance the processes related to the delivery, availability, and accessibility of information during the closing of the transitional mechanism.

The relationship between digital archiving and knowledge management: Due to the extensive information needed for the research exercise, we decided to implement a digital documentary collection from the outset. This approach enabled us to incorporate data management, analysis, and circulation procedures, enhancing the collection's usability and adaptability. However, it should be noted that the incorporation of technological tools and advanced algorithms only serves as catalysts for the knowledge management carried out by the analysis and research teams. The report is primarily the outcome of a process involving dialogue, analysis, and mobilization. It reflects the voices and intentions of a society affected by armed conflict, which actively and proactively sought to contribute to peace.

The limits of technology: Despite the successful results of the commitment to a digital archive based on information sciences, its limits and possibilities must also be considered. Undoubtedly, human capital is the most valuable resource of the Commission that was based on the work of a highly qualified team. An example of this is the case of transcription tasks; although an advanced model of automated transcription with AI (Artificial Intelligence) was implemented, its performance was precarious due to the specificities in jargon and diction, the emotional nature of the stories, and the environmental conditions. To address this challenge, a team of analysts was assembled to transcribe and tag the interviews. They played a crucial role in the interviewing process and knowledge management. It is evident that relying solely on automated processing would not have provided the same depth and breadth of research.

The care of the team: Faced with these technological challenges, and in general with this type of work of documenting, analyzing, and clarifying long periods of human rights violations and breaches of international humanitarian law, based on deep listening, it is essential to provide for the psychosocial care of the research teams – especially those involved in the transcription and interviewing processes. Although the Truth Commission implemented a permanent process during the development of the mandate,[43] over time, after the project's end, physical, emotional, and psychological impacts were evident in some people, and for this reason, there should be a possible accompaniment route that extends for a period after the mandate's end.

Methodological and knowledge management provisions: In response to its "duty to remember" mandate, the clarification process must be based on explicit ethical, technical, and legal principles. Consequently, its operation must be transparent, and its practices rigorously documented. The legitimacy of the process rests on the pertinence and technical consistency of its methodologies and procedures, which must be open, rigorous, and verifiable. From the Commission's guidelines on the clarification process, clear methodological protocols were defined, and likewise, the SIM procedures were created and documented with transparency for their suitability, verification, and replication. This implied the availability of human, technical, and financial resources to comply with these standards during the mandate, including the promotion of appropriation actions that encourage its use and allow its evolution in other related scenarios.

The balance between disclosure and protection: Any mechanism that defends the guarantee of the right to know is obliged to maximize accessibility to its documentary corpus. However, it also requires an unwavering mandate for the security and integrity of the actors involved in their accounts. Consequently, the relevant provisions and procedures must be designed to ensure broad and transparent access to the information without violating the right to privacy or the integrity of the actors involved. This balance requires,

43 Comisión para el Esclarecimiento de la Verdad, la Convivencia y la No Repetición, "Acompañar el camino de la escucha: Experiencia y aprendizajes de la Estrategia de Cuidado," *Archivo del Esclarecimiento de la Verdad*, https://archivo.comisiondelaverdad.co/acompanar-el-camino-de-la-escucha:-experiencia-y-aprendizajes-de-la-estrategia-de-cuidado.

for example, the elaboration of consent forms with the authorization, or not, of the use and disclosure of the information provided by its contributors. Likewise, at the end of the mandate, a review process of all the documentary aggregates is required to determine their level of publicity and access from the legal entity.

Information classification: As part of the information governance policy, the necessary classification levels should be established from the beginning of the collection process for setting parameters around the access and use of documents during and at the end of the mandate. It is also essential to define user profiles consistent with these classification levels and to implement monitoring and surveillance tools that allow the traceability of information flows. The documentary collection must also provide for the differential rights of victims, family members, specific populations, and other social or administrative instances for the assignment of specific access permissions. The Commission carried out a classification exercise at the beginning of its activities, which was later verified and adjusted for the delivery of its documentary collection. With greater knowledge of the regulatory provisions in force at the beginning of the mandate, this activity would have been more efficient.

Information governance: To meet the aforementioned challenge, clear guidelines must be established to direct the processes of collection, management, preservation, and use of information, as well as guarantee the right to information, promote accountability and auditability, and concurrently contribute to participatory and open historical reconstruction exercises. For example, a challenge for the Commission was to establish and guarantee information security measures equivalent to or superior to those provided in the source repositories and, likewise, to ensure compliance with the chain of custody for documents with private, reserved, or judicial interest information. It also defined the information access profiles for its users and shielded the information with the necessary IT, physical, legal, and pedagogical barriers to prevent incidents that could violate the integrity of the people involved (workers, victims, collaborators, defendants, etc.).

Preservation and sustainability: Due to its nature as a mechanism aimed at clarification and reconciliation, based on the guarantee of the right to know and the integrity of memory, the Commission faced the challenge of securing its legacy of information and knowledge and establishing a social heritage. To achieve this, a strategy was implemented through the SIM and transmedia to maximize public access to documents and maintain the documentary fund for long-term preservation and access. As mentioned earlier, its declaration as cultural heritage, its inclusion in the Memory of the World, and its long-term support have been achieved in alliance with the JEP and the General Archive of the Nation, as well as with international allies such as the University of Notre Dame, the Humanity United Foundation, and Swisspeace. Likewise, its legacy continues to be disseminated in different scenarios, and its methodological and information resources are kept open for public access and social use. A Follow-up Committee has also been established as an entity that monitors compliance with the Commission's recommendations. Two sections of these, aimed at safeguarding its documentary integrity, are worth mentioning: (i) protect, preserve, and guarantee access to the archives on human rights, historical memory, and armed conflict;[44] and (ii) learn about the legacy of the Truth Commission, disseminate it, and give it the continuity mentioned at the beginning of this report.[45]

In conclusion, according to the experience of the Commission and, in particular, of its documentary collection, the following are of note: (i) a human rights archive is currently intended to safeguard large volumes of information, varied and in permanent flux; (ii) more than an information system, it is a physical, social, and technological space for knowledge management; (iii) this scenario involves human and non-human actors around research, co-creation, and learning, to have an impact on social transformation, through the mobilisation of wills, agreements, and initiatives; (iv) technology is not politically neutral, and its implementation involves an ethical-political proposal that cannot be veiled; (v) the strategies for managing knowledge reveal the social contract that is at stake, and the design of the archive must be consistent with them; (vi) in this, the Commission sought to provide resources and promote spaces for the strengthening of citizen capabilities so that the exercise for the clarification of the truth would also be the path towards reconciliation and the restoration of a society wounded by violence. These elements were and continue to be challenges for an effective guarantee of the right to know, promoting the strengthening of an informed, reflective, and transformative citizenry.

Bibliography

ComisiónColombiana de Juristas. *Principios sobre la impunidad y las reparaciones.* Comisión Colombiana de Juristas, 2007. https://www.coljuristas.org/documentos/libros_e_informes/principios_sobre_impunidad_y_reparaciones.pdf.

Comisión para el Esclarecimiento de la Verdad, la Convivencia y la No Repetición. "Acompañar el camino de la escucha: Experiencia y aprendizajes de la Estrategia de Cuidado." https://archivo.comisiondelaverdad.co/acompanar-el-camino-de-la-escucha:-experiencia-y-aprendizajes-de-la-estrategia-de-cuidado.

Comisión para el Esclarecimiento de la Verdad, la Convivencia y la No Repetición. "Analítica de datos (información y recursos) | Informe Final de la Comisión de la Verdad." https://www.comisiondelaverdad.co/analitica-de-datos-informacion-y-recursos.

44 "To the Special Jurisdiction for Peace, to order or extend, as the case may be, the precautionary measures necessary to protect, preserve and guarantee access to the archives identified by the Commission as information, documents and archives on human rights, historical memory and armed conflict, in particular those corresponding to (i) the Brigade of Military Institutes; (ii) the Intelligence and Counterintelligence Battalion Gr. Ricardo Charry Solano, of the XX Brigade of the National Army; (iii) Network No. 7 of the National Navy; and (iv) the Administrative Department of Security (DAS)." Seremos, "Recommendation #44," *Seremos*, https://www.seremos.co/recomendaciones-para-la-convivencia/.

45 Seremos, "Recommendation #67," *Seremos*, https://www.seremos.co/recomendaciones-para-la-convivencia/.

Comisión para el Esclarecimiento de la Verdad, la Convivencia y la No Repetición. "Apertura: Informe Final de la Comisión de la Verdad." https://www.comisiondelaverdad.co/.

Comisión para el Esclarecimiento de la Verdad, la Convivencia y la No Repetición. "Archivo El Esclarecimiento de la Verdad (Truth Clarification Archive)." https://archivo.comisiondelaverdad.co/.

Comisión para el Esclarecimiento de la Verdad, la Convivencia y la No Repetición. "Bases de datos." https://www.comisiondelaverdad.co/bases-de-datos.

Comisión para el Esclarecimiento de la Verdad, la Convivencia y la No Repetición. "Bibliografía abierta del informe final." https://www.comisiondelaverdad.co/bibliografia-abierta-del-informe-final.

Comisión para el Esclarecimiento de la Verdad, la Convivencia y la No Repetición. "Con Quién Lo Hicimos: Informe Final de la Comisión de la Verdad." https://www.comisiondelaverdad.co/con-quien-lo-hicimos-0.

Comisión para el Esclarecimiento de la Verdad, la Convivencia y la No Repetición. "Datos de la escucha y fuentes externas de la Comisión." https://www.comisiondelaverdad.co/datos-de-la-escucha-y-fuentes-externas-de-la-comision.

Comisión para el Esclarecimiento de la Verdad, la Convivencia y la No Repetición. "Gitbook | Archivo de Esclarecimiento [GitBook]." https://docsarchivoesclarecimiento.comisiondelaverdad.co.

Comisión para el Esclarecimiento de la Verdad, la Convivencia y la No Repetición. "Guía de proceso de guion expandido." https://www.comisiondelaverdad.co/guia-de-proceso-de-guion-expandido.

Comisión para el Esclarecimiento de la Verdad, la Convivencia y la No Repetición. *Hay futuro si hay verdad: Informe Final de la Comisión de la Verdad*. Bogotá, 2022. https://www.comisiondelaverdad.co/hay-futuro-si-hay-verdad.

Comisión para el Esclarecimiento de la Verdad, la Convivencia y la No Repetición. "Informes y casos." https://www.comisiondelaverdad.co/informes-y-casos.

Comisión para el Esclarecimiento de la Verdad, la Convivencia y la No Repetición. "La narrativa del legado." https://www.comisiondelaverdad.co/la-narrativa-del-legado.

Comisión para el Esclarecimiento de la Verdad, la Convivencia y la No Repetición. "Pedagogía: Informe Final de la Comisión de la Verdad." https://www.comisiondelaverdad.co/pedagogia.

Comisión para el Esclarecimiento de la Verdad, la Convivencia y la No Repetición. "Plataforma Digital Transmedia." https://www.comisiondelaverdad.co/plataforma-digital-transmedia.

Comisión para el Esclarecimiento de la Verdad, la Convivencia y la No Repetición. "Recursos (Lenguaje Natural)." https://www.comisiondelaverdad.co/recursos-lenguaje-natural.

Comisión para el Esclarecimiento de la Verdad, la Convivencia y la No Repetición. "Ruta metodológica del esclarecimiento de la verdad: Informe final de la Comisión de la Verdad." https://www.comisiondelaverdad.co/como-lo-hicimos/ruta-metodologica-del-esclarecimiento-de-la-verdad.

Comisión para el Esclarecimiento de la Verdad, la Convivencia y la No Repetición. "Términos y condiciones para el acceso y uso de los contenidos de la plataforma digital del Informe Final." https://www.comisiondelaverdad.co/terminos-y-condiciones-para-el-acceso-y-uso-de-los-contenidos-de-la-plataforma-digital-del-informe.

Comisión para el Esclarecimiento de la Verdad, la Convivencia y la No Repetición. "Trabajo en Red con Aliados." https://www.comisiondelaverdad.co/trabajo-en-red-con-aliados.

Comisión para el Esclarecimiento de la Verdad, la Convivencia y la No Repetición. "Versión Offline." https://www.comisiondelaverdad.co/version-offline.

Congress of the Republic of Colombia. *Law 1266*, December 31, 2008.

Congress of the Republic of Colombia. *Law 1581*, October 17, 2012.

González Quintana, Antonio. "Archives and Human Rights." *ANABAD Bulletin* 49, no. 3–4 (1999): 371–89.
Human Rights Data Analysis Group (HRDAG). "The Task is a Quantum of Workflow." June 14, 2016. http://hrdag.org/2016/06/14/the-task-is-a-quantum-of-workflow/.
Human Rights Data Analysis Group (HRDAG). "HRDAG – Human Rights Data Analysis Group." http://hrdag.org/colombia-faq/.
Oficina del Alto Comisionado para la Paz. "Cambios, precisiones y ajustes para un nuevo Acuerdo Final para la terminación del conflicto y la construcción de una paz estable y duradera." November 12, 2016. https://www.juanitaenelcongreso.com/_files/ugd/883ff8_3fb603bd95974fd7b531c874f28f61ae.pdf.
Oficina del Alto Comisionado para la Paz. "Sistematización Opciones y Propuestas Voceros del No y lo Acordado en el Nuevo Acuerdo." November 22, 2016. https://www.juanitaenelcongreso.com/_files/ugd/883ff8_e1d0053279944cc69dfba41cc7f8c9e7.pdf.
Peterson, Trudy H. *Final Minutes: A Guide to Preserving the Records of Truth Commissions.* Washington, DC: Woodrow Wilson Center Press, 2005.
"Radiografía del Plebiscito y el Posplebiscito." Ideas para la Paz (FIP). 2016. https://multimedia.ideaspaz.org/especiales/posplebiscito/index.html.
Red de Sitios de Memoria Latinoamericanos y Caribeños (RESLAC). "Experiences of Civil Society Participation in Truth Commissions in Latin America." RESLAC, 2020. https://sitiosdememoria.org/wp-content/uploads/2020/06/Comisiones-Reslac_DIGITAL.pdf.
SubgerenciaCultural del Banco de la República. "Las publicaciones del Centro Nacional de Memoria Histórica en la Biblioteca Virtual del Banco de la República." La Red Cultural del Banco de la República. https://www.banrepcultural.org/noticias/las-publicaciones-del-centro-nacional-de-memoria-historica-en-la-biblioteca-virtual-del.
Swisspeace. "Un marco conceptual para abordar el pasado." Essentials 16. https://www.swisspeace.ch/assets/publications/downloads/Essentials/bcaf54fb17/Un-marco-conceptual-para-Abordar-el-Pasado-Essential-16-swisspeace.pdf.
United Nations. *Updated Set of Principles for the Protection and Promotion of Human Rights through Action to Combat Impunity.* Human Rights Council, February 8, 2005. Doc. E/CN.4/2005/102/Add.1.
United Nations. "Report of the Special Rapporteur on the Promotion of Truth, Justice, Reparation and Guarantees of Non-Repetition, Section C: General Considerations." 2015. https://documents.un.org/doc/undoc/gen/g15/202/07/pdf/g1520207.pdf.
UNESCO. "Documentary Fund of the Commission for the Clarification of Truth, Coexistence and Non-Repetition (CEV)." Memory of the World – Latin America and the Caribbean. https://www.unesco.org/en/memory-world/lac/documentary-fund-commission-clarification-truth-coexistence-and-non-repetition-cev.
United Nations Security Council. "Press Release on Colombia." UN Verification Mission in Colombia, April 15, 2024. http://colombia.unmissions.org/comunicado-de-prensa-del-consejo-de-seguridad-de-las-naciones-unidas-sobre-colombia-3.

8 The Precautionary Measures of the JEP and the DAS Archives

Fostering Public Dialogue on the Role of Secret Archives in the Colombian Armed Conflict

Oscar Parra-Vera, Natalia Andrea Herrera Gálvez, and Aurora Yezzenia Ávila-Quintero

Introduction

Since its establishment, the *Jurisdicciòn Especial Para la Paz* (Special Jurisdiction for Peace – JEP)[1] has implemented preventive precautionary measures to preserve, protect, and provide access to the archives of military and intelligence agencies. These archives have the potential to clarify information regarding serious human rights violations, breaches of International Humanitarian Law (IHL), and events related to armed conflict. This effort aims to ensure the rights to truth, justice, reparation, and guarantees of non-recurrence.

Therefore, this chapter describes the precautionary measures adopted by the *Sala de Reconocimiento de Verdad, de Responsabilidad y de Determinación de los Hechos y Conductas* (Chamber of Acknowledgment of Truth, Responsibility, and the Determination of Facts and Conduct – SRVR) or Chamber of Acknowledgment of the JEP concerning the intelligence, counterintelligence, and reserved expenses files of the now-defunct *Departamento Administrativo de Seguridad* (Security's Administrative Department – DAS) of Colombia. This chapter first outlines the context of the DAS and the reasons for its dissolution, particularly focusing on the involvement of former agency members in serious human rights violations. Next, it discusses the fate of the documentary collection and the regulations that govern access to it. Lastly, it examines and assesses the precautionary measures the SRVR implemented concerning the defunct DAS's intelligence, counterintelligence, and financial archives.

1 The JEP is the judicial component of the Comprehensive System of Truth, Justice, Reparation and Guarantees of Non-Repetition (SIVJRNR), created from the Final Peace Agreement signed between the Colombian Government and the guerrilla group of the Revolutionary Armed Forces of Colombia – People's Army (FARC-EP). It has the function of administering transitional justice and hearing crimes committed in the framework of the armed conflict committed before December 1, 2016, to satisfy the rights of victims to truth, justice, and reparation, to build a stable and lasting peace in Colombia.

DOI: 10.4324/9781003609322-11

The chapter also discusses the debates and public conversations surrounding the adoption of precautionary measures regarding the DAS archives. These deliberations involved various entities, including the Colombian State, the United Nations, civil society organisations, academic experts, victims, judicial representatives, and other stakeholders; these archives have been defined as an Asset of Cultural Interest (BCI) and Memory of the World by the United Nations Educational, Scientific and Cultural Organization (UNESCO). In conclusion, the chapter examines the significance of archives in ensuring human rights and implementing the constitutional principles of a social state that adheres to the rule of law.

8.1 The Security's Administrative Department (DAS) and Human Rights Violations

The DAS was a Colombian State agency created by Decree 1717 of 1960 during President Alberto Lleras Camargo's administration. It replaced the operations of its predecessor, the Administrative Department of the Colombian Intelligence Service. The DAS performed several key functions, including acting as a judicial police. It assisted the judicial branch, the Ministry of Justice, and the Public Prosecutor's Office in crime investigations. It cooperated in maintaining public order and monitored immigration and foreign residents within the national territory.[2]

In 1989, Decree 512 was issued by then-President Virgilio Barco, modifying the structure of the DAS. The agency was assigned new responsibilities, which included generating the internal and external intelligence information needed by the State to prevent and address acts that could disrupt security and undermine constitutional and legal order. Additionally, the agency was responsible for protecting the president, his family, and former presidents. It also provided security services to individuals who, due to their position, role, functions, or special circumstances, may be at risk of attacks against themselves or their property. Furthermore, the agency was required to maintain criminal and identification records, issue judicial and police certificates, and serve as the *Oficina Central Nacional* (National Central Office – OCN) of the International Criminal Police Organization (OIPCINTERPOL).[3]

Subsequently, during the administration of then-President Álvaro Uribe Vélez, Decree 643 of 2004 again modified the structure of the DAS, incorporating among its general functions those of carrying out counterintelligence actions aimed at protecting the interests of the State against hostile activities

2 Presidency of the Republic of Colombia, *Decree 1717*, issued by Alberto Lleras Camargo, Bogotá, July 18, 1960.

3 Presidency of the Republic of Colombia, *Decree 512*, issued by Virgilio Barco Vargas, March 13, 1989.

of internal or external origin.[4] This State agency responsible for, among other things, improving intelligence and counterintelligence in Colombia, operated until 2011, when then-President Juan Manuel Santos sanctioned Decree 4057, which abolished the DAS, and its functions were re-distributed among other State agencies. The suppression of the DAS was due to several reasons, among them the involvement of some of its officials and employees in serious human rights violations, and their links with paramilitary groups, as well as the improper use of intelligence for the persecution of political opponents and critics of the government, facts that have been proven both nationally and internationally.

To cite some domestic cases, the *Sala de Casación Penal de la Corte Suprema de Justicia* (Criminal Cassation Chamber of the Supreme Court of Justice – CSJ) twice convicted Jorge Aurelio Noguera Cotes, former director of the DAS[5] between 2002 and 2005, during the term of then-President Álvaro Uribe Vélez. First, in 2011, Noguera was sentenced to 25 years in prison for the crime of destruction, suppression, and concealment of public documents, misuse of confidential information, aggravated conspiracy, and the murder of university professor Alfredo Correa De Andreis. It was proven that Noguera supplied paramilitary groups, specifically the Northern Block, with lists of trade unionists, students, and leftist leaders. This included the name of professor and sociologist Correa De Andreis, which ultimately led to his murder.[6]

In 2017, the CSJ sentenced Noguera to seven years in prison for actions that became widely known in the local media as the "*chuzadas*," or wiretapping, carried out by the DAS. As the agency's director, it was determined that he had established the *Grupo Especial de Inteligencia* (Special Intelligence Group or G3). This group conducted interceptions, surveillance, and monitoring of private communications without obtaining warrants from a judicial authority. Their targets included human rights defenders from non-governmental organisations, journalists, and individuals viewed as opponents of the national government.[7]

Recently, the Superior Court of the Judicial District of Bogotá sentenced former DAS agent Ronal Harbey Rivera Rodríguez to 150 months in prison for the crime of aggravated torture against journalist and human rights defender Claudia Julieta Duque, finding that between 2001 and 2004, this former agent tortured, harassed, made intimidating calls, and conducted prolonged

4 Presidency of the Republic of Colombia, *Decree 643*, issued by Álvaro Uribe Vélez, March 2, 2004.

5 Fernando Ariza, "Noguera, el hombre que tuvo que dejar el DAS y consulado por delitos," *El Tiempo*, October 20, 2020, https://www.eltiempo.com/justicia/delitos/perfil-de-jorge-noguera-cotes-exdirector-del-das-que-recupera-su-libertad-544354.

6 Criminal Cassation Chamber of the Supreme Court of Justice of Colombia, *Single Instance Judgment* 32000, Judge Alfredo Gómez Quintero, September 14, 2011.

7 Criminal Cassation Chamber of the Supreme Court of Justice of Colombia, *Judgment SP13920–2017*, Judge Luis Guillermo Salazar Otero, September 6, 2017.

surveillance against the victim in retaliation for an investigation she conducted into the murder of journalist and comedian Jaime Garzón,[8] confirming the nature of crimes against humanity for the continuous torture to which Duque was subjected to by several State agents of the now-defunct DAS.[9] Additionally, in the framework of the criminal proceedings against the former director of the DAS, José Miguel Narváez Martínez, for his alleged responsibility in the events of which Duque was a victim, the Tenth Criminal Court of the Specialized Circuit of Bogotá, in a February 5, 2024, Decree, declared the crime of torture as a crime against humanity because it could be proven:

> That the acts of torture committed . . . were the product of a preconceived plan or policy of the Security's Administrative Department (DAS) that targeted, among others, NGOs that defended human rights, accusing them of being associated with subversive groups dedicated to discrediting the government of the day.[10]

In the framework of the transitional justice process carried out by the JEP, it has also been possible to prove the participation of former members of the DAS in cases of serious human rights violations. In Case 03 of the Chamber of Acknowledgment of the JEP, titled "Killings and Forced Disappearances Presented as Casualties in Combat by State Agents," the Order Sub-D-Subcase Casanare-055 was issued on July 14, 2022. This Order determined that the acts qualified as murders and forced disappearances, which occurred in the department of Casanare between 2005 and 2008, and were attributable to certain members of the XVI Brigade of the National Army. These acts were committed by State agents, not members of the Public Force (AENIFPU) or civilian third parties. This judicial ruling by the Chamber of Acknowledgment of the JEP concluded that a complex criminal organisation was established within the XVI Brigade. This organisation exploited the structure, functions, and resources of the Brigade's units and dependencies, as well as the national defence sector policies and the Army's institutional policies. They aimed to misrepresent murders and forced disappearances of defenceless individuals as combat casualties. Among the individuals involved in the illegal structure identified by the SRVR is Mr. Orlando Rivas Tovar, who served as the director

8 Fernando Vergara, "Foundation for Press Freedom," November 27, 2023, https://flip.org.co/pronunciamientos/condenan-a-exagente-del-das-por-tortura-agravada-contra-la-periodista-claudia-julieta-duque.

9 Superior Court of Bogotá, *Second Instance Judgment in the Case of Claudia Julieta Duque Orrego*, Defendant Ronal Harbey Rivera Rodríguez, Radication 110013107010202200090 02, November 20, 2023.

10 *Decree ruling on the appeal of the judgment on the crime of aggravated torture in the case of Claudia Duque*, defendant José Miguel Narváez Martínez, 2024, 16.

of the Casanare Sectional DAS at the time of the incidents. He has been recognised as the person most responsible for these actions.[11]

According to the Chamber of Acknowledgment, between April 2005 and November 2007, during the time Rivas Tovar served as director of the Casanare Sectional DAS, he had active and decisive participation in the criminal activities widely described in the judicial order, contributing in an essential way to the criminal plan that led to the murder and disappearance of persons marked as being guerrilla fighters, guerrilla supporters, or belonging to criminal groups, who were illegitimately presented as killed in combat.[12]

At the international level, it is worth noting that within the framework of the Case *Rodríguez Vera et al. (missing persons from the Palace of Justice) v. Colombia*, the Inter-American Court of Human Rights (IACtHR) identified several acts demonstrating the Colombian State's failure to comply with its obligation to prevent human rights violations during the seizure and retaking of the Palace of Justice in 1985.[13] Among these were, in August 1985, the sending of radiograms to State entities, including the DAS, that warned of the possibility of a terrorist act against the installations of the Palace of Justice and the adoption of a state of exceptional protection for the Palace of Justice from October 17 until early November 1985, consisting of police personnel, escorts from the institution, guards from the Colbasec LTD. company, and members of the DAS.[14]

Additionally, on November 21, 2018, the Inter-American Court issued a judgment in the Case of *Omeara Carrascal et al. v. Colombia*, establishing the relationship maintained in 1994 between paramilitary groups from the Department of Cesar with the National Anti-Kidnapping and Extortion Unit, formed by the National Army and the DAS, that manifested itself in actions

11 Chamber of Acknowledgment of Truth, Responsibility, and the Determination of Facts and Conduct of the Special Jurisdiction for Peace, *Order SRVR-SUB-D-055*, July 14, 2022.

12 Chamber of Acknowledgment of Truth, Responsibility, and the Determination of Facts and Conduct of the Special Jurisdiction for Peace, *Order SRVR-SUB-D-055*, July 14, 2022.

13 The facts of the case are framed within the events known as the seizure and retaking of the Palace of Justice, which occurred in Bogota on November 6 and 7, 1985. On those dates, the guerrilla group M-19 violently took over the Palace of Justice, where the Supreme Court of Justice and the Colombian Council of State were located, taking hundreds of people hostage, including magistrates, assistant magistrates, lawyers, administrative and service employees, as well as visitors to both judicial corporations. After this armed action by the guerrilla group, known as the "seizure of the Palace of Justice," the response of the State security forces is known as the "retaking of the Palace of Justice." Internal courts and the Truth Commission on the Palace of Justice events have considered this military operation disproportionate and excessive. As a consequence of these events, hundreds of people were killed and wounded, and several forced disappearances and tortures occurred, for which the Colombian State was condemned. Official Summary Issued by the *Inter-American Court, Rodríguez Vera and Others (Palace of Justice Disappeared) v. Colombia*, Inter-American Court of Human Rights, 2.

14 *Rodríguez Vera and Others (Palace of Justice Disappeared) v. Colombia*, Inter-American Court of Human Rights, November 14, 2014.

and omissions that ended with the death of the three members of the Omeara and Álvarez families.[15] Given the context of the DAS and its role in serious human rights violations, the next section will outline how the intelligence agency's archives were utilised after its dissolution and the regulations governing access to these documents.

8.1.1 The Fate of the DAS Archives Following the Agency's Dissolution: Location and Accessibility

Article 3 of Decree-Law 4057 of 2011 outlined the entities that would take over the functions of the DAS following its dissolution. The responsibilities of judicial police were transferred to the Attorney General's Office (FGN). The tasks related to immigration control for nationals and foreigners were assigned to the Special Administrative Unit of *Migración Colombia* (Colombia Migration). The Ministry of National Defense, through *MinDefensa*, its Judicial Police, was designated to manage criminal and identification records and issue judicial certificates. Lastly, the responsibility for providing protection and security was transferred to the National Protection Unit (UNP).[16] In relation to the fate of the DAS files containing intelligence information, it is necessary to point out that Article 24 of Decree-Law 4057 of 2011 determined that the custody and conservation of such files would continue to be the responsibility of the DAS under suppression, that their access and consultation would be subject to legal reserve, and that information would only be provided to administrative and judicial authorities and those entities that required or requested the information within the framework of their functions and competencies for reasons of national security and defence. For its part, Article 23 of said decree provided that the files related to the functions of the DAS that were transferred to other entities would be received by such entities in the state in which they are found.[17]

In 2014, once the DAS suppression process concluded, Decree 1303 was issued, which regulated Decree 4057 of 2011. Thus, Article 1 of Decree 1303 of 2014 established that the preservation and safekeeping of the DAS's intelligence, counterintelligence, and reserved expenses archives would be "in charge of the *Archivo General de la Nación* (General Archive of the Nation – AGN) from the completion of the process of suppression of the entity, on behalf of the *Direccion Nacional de Inteligencia* (Directorate of

15 *Omeara Carrascal and Others v. Colombia*, Inter-American Court of Human Rights, November 21, 2018.

16 Presidency of the Republic of Colombia, *Decree 4057*, issued by Juan Manuel Santos Calderón, October 31, 2011.

17 Presidency of the Republic of Colombia, *Decree 4057*, issued by Juan Manuel Santos Calderón, October 31, 2011.

National Intelligence – DNI)."[18] The DNI assumed the country's intelligence and counterintelligence responsibilities. Furthermore, the decree specified that

> the DNI would be the competent authority responsible for authorising access, consultation, and provision of these files, which would be subject to a legal reserve. Information would only be provided to the judicial authorities that request it within a judicial process or the controlling entities that require or request it.[19]

Additionally, the rule provided that the DNI would be in charge of developing and adopting the necessary security protocols for access and consultation activities. The General Archive of the Nation was responsible for most archives' custody, protection, and administration, granting it the authority to issue labour certifications and process requests or applications related to these archives.

However, the archives of the DAS after its suppression were left in the custody of various entities. The AGN, affiliated with the Ministry of Culture, received most of the archives from the now-defunct DAS. This includes all documents related to intelligence, counterintelligence, confidential expenses, and the agency's general archives. Following the abolition of the DAS, the functions previously handled by this agency were transferred to several entities, including the *Fiscalía General de la Nación* (Attorney General's Office), *Migración Colombia*, the Ministry of Defense, and the *Unidad Nacional de Protección* (National Protection Unit). These organisations were provided with the relevant files associated with their responsibilities after the dismantling of DAS. In 2018, the Special Jurisdiction for Peace issued preventive precautionary measures due to the potential of the extinct DAS files and archives to illuminate serious human rights violations involving former intelligence agency members.

8.2 Precautionary Measures Adopted on the Intelligence, Counterintelligence, and Reserved Expenses Archives of the Extinct DAS

This section discusses the JEP's role in managing the intelligence and counterintelligence files of the defunct DAS over the past five years and details how the JEP's Chamber of Acknowledgement ordered precautionary measures. Transitional precautionary measures, as part of the JEP, serve as a procedural mechanism to prevent or stop situations that threaten or violate the rights to truth, justice, reparation, and non-repetition for victims of non-international

18 Presidency of the Republic of Colombia, *Decree 4057*, issued by Juan Manuel Santos Calderón, October 31, 2011.

19 Presidency of the Republic of Colombia, *Decree 1303*, issued by Juan Manuel Santos Calderón, July 11, 2014, 2, Art. 1.

armed conflicts (NIAC);[20] they can also apply to natural or legal persons other than the procedural subjects under the competency of the Jurisdiction. In the context of this procedural mechanism, the Constitutional Court of Colombia stated in Judgment C-007 of 2018 that adopting precautionary measures helps protect and promote victims' rights. It emphasised that applying special regulations is particularly relevant during the transition from conflict to peace.[21] Under the same logic, the Procedural Law of the JEP establishes that one of the guiding principles of this jurisdiction is the effectiveness of restorative justice, which implies "the clarification of the truth in favour of the victims and society,"[22] which, according to the jurisprudence that has been developed by the Tribunal for Peace of the JEP, implies "the re-establishment of human rights, and restorative and reparative measures in relation to individual and collective victims."[23] As a result, the transitional judicial authorities take the lead in protecting victims' rights, but within the limits of their powers. They should strive to coordinate and integrate both judicial and non-judicial mechanisms in line with national laws, such as Law 1448 of 2011, which has:

> Expressly enshrined the need to ensure the external coherence of the "different efforts of the State to guarantee the rights to truth, justice, and reparation for the victims." . . . So, in transitional justice scenarios, where it is essential to reconstitute the social fabric and recover confidence in the institutions, the opposing actions of the mechanisms established to ensure the transition can have harmful effects on the fulfillment of the objectives pursued, especially when such contradiction entails the risk of re-victimization.[24]

Precautionary measures may be adopted to protect and preserve information held in public or private archives.[25] Precautionary measures are classified as preventive, conservative, anticipatory, or suspensive, enabling the Chambers and Sections, among others, to issue orders to protect and preserve information.[26] In this regard, the SRVR has stated that precautionary measures aimed at such protection and preservation must be preventive to the extent that they seek to avoid restrictions on the realisation of the right to truth, justice, and information of victims and Colombian society.[27] Thus, the

20 Appeal Section of the Tribunal for Peace of the Special Jurisdiction for Peace, *Order TP-SA 714*, January 27, 2021, 25.
21 Constitutional Court, Judgment C-007/18, 2018.
22 Congress of the Republic of Colombia, Law 1922, July 18, 2018.
23 *Order TP-SA 714*, 2021, 26.
24 *Order TP-SA 714*, 2021, 42.
25 Congress of the Republic of Colombia, *Law 1922*, July 18, 2018.
26 Congress of the Republic of Colombia, *Law 1922*, July 18, 2018.
27 Chamber of Acknowledgment of Truth, Responsibility, and the Determination of Facts and Conduct of the Special jurisdiction for Peace, Order 215, October 2, 2019, 7.

precautionary measures decreed on the archives of the extinct DAS are preventive measures.[28]

These measures were taken by Order 001 of March 12, 2018, by the Executive Secretary of the JEP to preserve such information against possible risks of destruction, theft, or alteration.[29] Subsequently, when the JEP began to operate, these measures were placed under the direction and monitoring of Judge Oscar Parra-Vera, who issued Order 73 on October 26, 2018.

In this court order, the Chamber of Acknowledgment made a normative and jurisprudential reconstruction regarding the right to truth based on the considerations developed by the Constitutional Court, the Set of Principles for the Protection and Promotion of Human Rights for the Fight against Impunity of the United Nations Commission on Human Rights (Joinet Principles), and Additional Protocol I of the 1949 Geneva Convention, relating to the Protection of Victims of International Armed Conflicts of 1977. Based on this background, the SRVR highlighted obligations of the State related to guaranteeing the right to truth as (i) the obligation to search for persons reported missing, (ii) clarifying the conditions under which human rights violations occurred, (iii) the duty to remember; and (iv) the adoption of measures to implement the right of victims to know the truth, highlighting principle 5 of the Joinet Principles which expressly stipulates the obligation of states to ensure the preservation of archives on violations of human rights and humanitarian law and the opportunity of consulting them.[30]

In addition, the SRVR brought up the jurisprudential advances of the IACtHR court regarding the right to truth to hold up the dual dimension of this right, its importance as an autonomous right, the possibility that its violation may affect other rights recognised in the American Convention, and the obligations it entails for the States. In particular, the Chamber discussed the progress made in the case of *Gudiel Álvarez et al. v. Guatemala (Diario Militar)* – regarding the problems of access to information to the Historical Archive of the Police associated with serious human rights violations – and the case of *Gomes Lund et al. v. Brazil*, on access to archives related to the dictatorship in that country.

The Chamber of Acknowledgment also reported the comparative experience of the importance of intelligence and counterintelligence archives in

28 "The precautionary measures that were decreed by the Executive Secretariat of the SJP in Order 001 of 2018 are not conservative, but preventive, as they do not seek simply to maintain a certain status quo, but to prevent it from occurring in harm, given the possible existence of a risk that has been documented" Chamber of Acknowledgment of Truth, Responsibility, and the Determination of Facts and Conduct of the Special Jurisdiction for Peace, *Order No. 73*, October 26, 2018, 18.

29 Executive Secretariat of the Special Jurisdiction for Peace, *Order No. 001*, March 12, 2018.

30 Chamber of Acknowledgment of Truth, Responsibility, and the Determination of Facts and Conduct of the Special Jurisdiction for Peace, *Order No. 73*, October 26, 2018, 25.

transitional contexts and the historically implemented policies to ensure their preservation and access. In particular, the SRVR incorporated the categorisation of secret surveillance archives for political reasons according to their different access levels, based on the study carried out in 16 countries by archivists Katherine Wisser and Joel Blanco. Based on the proposals made by the archivists, four categories emerge, namely: (i) open access with clear policies, (ii) open access with practical restrictions, (iii) no access because they are closed, and (iv) no access due to destruction or ignorance of their whereabouts.[31] The Chamber reviewed various archives from cross-national cases that fit each category.

On the other hand, Order 73 of 2018 addresses Colombian regulations concerning access to public information, highlighting the tensions with national security and defence. It explicitly states that archives cannot be classified as confidential when they contain information related to human rights violations or crimes against humanity. The Special Jurisdiction for Peace also assessed Statutory Law 1621 of 2013, which issues regulations to strengthen the legal framework of agencies that carry out intelligence and counterintelligence operations. The law stipulates that, in case of dissolution, this activity, must not affect the preservation of files that contain information about serious human rights violations.[32] The JEP ordered measures for the preservation of the archives and highlighted the need to access the security protocols applied by the DNI and the AGN to verify that the consultation processes were carried out with adequate controls and to prevent the purging of intelligence files that put at risk relevant information to determine human rights violations.[33]

In terms of the need to protect the archives, the Chamber of Acknowledgment made references to the public policy on "archives of human rights, historical memory, and armed conflict," as well as the "Protocol for Documentary Management of Archives" referring to severe and gross violations of human rights and breaches of international humanitarian law that occurred during the internal armed conflict. The *Centro Nacional de Memoria Histórica* (National Centre for Historical Memory – CNMH)[34] issued the aforementioned documents for historical memory. This policy

31 Ana María Ramírez Mouraille, Maria Paula Ángel Arango, Mauricio Albarracín Caballero, Rodrigo Uprimny Yepes, and Viviana Newman Pont, *Acceso a los archivos de inteligencia y contrainteligencia en el marco del posacuerdo* (Bogotá: Dejusticia, 2017).

32 Chamber of Acknowledgment of Truth, *Order No. 73*, October 26, 2018.

33 Chamber of Acknowledgment of Truth, *Order No. 73*, October 26, 2018.

34 The National Center for Historical Memory, established under Law 1448 of 2011, titled "*Por la cual se dictan medidas de atención, asistencia y reparación integral a las víctimas del conflicto armado interno y se dictan otras disposiciones*" ("By which measures of attention, assistance, and comprehensive reparation for the victims of the internal armed conflict are established and other provisions are issued"), published in the Official Gazette No. 48,096 on June 10, 2011, is the institution responsible for compiling, preserving, and disseminating the historical memory of human rights violations and breaches of international humanitarian law within the context of Colombia's armed conflict. Its mission is to contribute to truth, justice, comprehensive reparation, and guarantees of non-repetition for victims, while promoting reconciliation and an inclusive society.

paper establishes the principle of protection and safeguarding of archives, a necessary factor to mitigate the risks of destruction, alteration, falsification, subtraction, or modification that may happen due to actions of armed groups, environmental impacts, vulnerability of the institutions in charge of their custody, or improper handling, among others.[35] In addition, the public policy and the protocol contemplate special measures for the protection of, and access to, human rights archives, emphasising the temporary suspension of any process of elimination of documents, particularly in archives such as those of the extinct DAS, relevant to guaranteeing the rights to truth, justice, and reparation of the victims.[36]

The preceding framework allowed the SRVR to emphasise the duty to adopt measures to identify and assess the possible risks the archives face. This, coupled with other elements, allows the assessment of possible destruction or alteration of the archives of the extinct DAS, such as (i) the ruling of the CSJ that declares Jorge Aurelio Noguera, former director of the DAS, criminally liable for the crimes of destruction, suppression, and concealment of public documents that show his link with the Northern Block (paramilitaries); (ii) judgment of the CSJ of October 28, 2016, by which four officials of the Strategic Intelligence Group of the extinct DAS were convicted for crimes related to illegal interceptions; and (iii) complaints by human rights organisations warning of the alleged loss, concealment, and destruction of information from the computer files of the extinct DAS, among other irregularities.[37]

The Chamber of Acknowledgment emphasised that the complaints filed occurred between 2011 and 2017 when protection, preservation, purging, and access mechanisms were to operate under the responsibility of the AGN and the DNI. The JEP assessed the current risk status and concluded that one of the most significant risks is the lack of clarity regarding the management processes related to the documentary collection of the defunct DAS. As a result, a critical risk is the uncertainty surrounding which materials are available, what has already been organised, and in what format. What materials used years or even decades ago could be reprocessed for readability and preservation with today's technology? Currently, the Chamber lacks the information needed to identify which materials are at risk of deteriorating, particularly those printed with inks that may fade. It is unclear how these documents will be preserved in the future. It is important to understand the formats in which documents are recorded, the timing of their issuance, and how they are managed. Additionally, there is no clear information on which materials are confidential and which are not.[38]

35 CNMH, *Política pública de archivos de derechos humanos, memoria histórica y conflicto armado* (Bogotá: Centro Nacional de Memoria Histórica, 2017).

36 Chamber of Acknowledgment of Truth, *Order No. 73*, October 26, 2018.

37 Chamber of Acknowledgment of Truth, *Order No. 73*, October 26, 2018.

38 Chamber of Acknowledgment of Truth, *Order No. 73*, October 26, 2018, 56.

8.2.1 Technical Roundtables and Public Debates About the DAS Files

Order 73 of 2018, issued by the JEP, ordered the creation of a technical roundtable with the participation of the *Procuraduria General de la Nacion* (Attorney General's Office), the *Fiscalía General* (Prosecutor General's Office), the Office of the United Nations High Commissioner for Human Rights in Colombia (OHCHR), the *Ministerio de Justicia y Derecho* (Ministry of Justice and Law), the Ministry of Defense, the AGN, the National Center for Historical Memory, the DNI, victims, and civil society organisations representing victims of agents of the former DAS. The goal of the technical roundtable was to collaboratively identify measures to preserve the integrity of the archives of the former DAS. Additionally, the group aimed to ensure that implementing security protocols for access and consultation does not create unnecessary restrictions beyond those legally established.[39] The first technical roundtable was held on January 30, 2019.[40] The institutions discussed the current state of the archives and the challenges of creating an inventory. Human rights organisations highlighted the various obstacles and restrictions that hinder access to the archives. Meanwhile, civil society organisations pointed out that the archives of the defunct DAS were not designated as "human rights or international humanitarian law archives." They stated that while the specific contents of the archives are unknown, it has been judicially established that multiple officials of the former DAS, including several of its directors, committed human rights violations.[41]

After the first technical roundtable, the AGN and the *Consorcio Fondo Colombia en Paz* (Colombia in Peace Fund Consortium) signed a contract to provide comprehensive services for the inventory of documents of the now-defunct DAS. Under this contract, the JEP received a proposal from the AGN for a methodology for conducting the inventories.[42] Based on this proposal and using Order OPV 182 dated April 25, 2023, the SRVR authorised the AGN, as the governing body of Colombia's archival policy, to conduct a comprehensive diagnosis, classification, organisation, and technical inventory of all the archives. This authorisation aims to make progress in identifying which DAS files correspond to human rights archives. Implementing a records

39 Chamber of Acknowledgment of Truth, *Order No. 73*, October 26, 2018, 56.

40 The hearing of the first session of the technical roundtable can be viewed at: https://www.youtube.com/watch?v=bfVL44ODhok (part 1) https://www.youtube.com/watch?v=vgZwp36dAPE.

41 Mesa por la Justicia Transicional de la Coordinación Colombia Europa Estados Unidos (CCEEU), *Intervención de organizaciones defensoras de DD.HH. y de víctimas parte de la Mesa por la Justicia Transicional de la Coordinación Colombia Europa Estados Unidos (CCEEU) en la Mesa Técnica para la protección de archivos del DAS* (Bogotá: CCEEU, 2019), https://www.jep.gov.co/Biblioteca/Das/das3.pdf.

42 Archivo General de la Nación, *Propuesta de intervención sobre los medios y soportes de almacenamiento de datos, en el que se identifiquen los escenarios y actividades que podrían llevarse a cabo y estimación de costo, tiempo, tecnología y personal para cada una de estas actividades* (Bogotá: AGN, 2021).

management procedure for archives concerning severe and gross human rights violations and breaches of international humanitarian law is essential during internal armed conflict.

Regarding the latter, it is important to note that, in making this decision, the Chamber of Acknowledgment considered multiple regulations and concepts, emphasising the provisions of the Inter-American Commission on Human Rights (IACHR) related to access to information documenting human rights violations, which considers the States have the duty to manage the archives:

> As an essential effort for the re-establishment and recognition of the historical truth, . . . therefore, the States must ensure the preservation, classification, and systematization of documents that may contain information related to serious human rights violations or of any nature that may assist in their investigation.[43]

The SRVR decided to hold a second technical roundtable session to discuss the observations regarding the proposed methodology for organising the documents of the now-defunct DAS. This session was held on June 6, 2023, with the participation of the AGN Directorate, the Minister of Defense, the Director of the DNI, the Ministry of Justice, the Unit for the Search for Missing Persons, civil society organisations, a former director of the DAS, victims of the forced disappearances in the Palace of Justice, the Investigation and Prosecution Unit of the JEP, the Office of the United Nations High Commissioner for Human Rights, and the National Center for Historical Memory.[44] The different interventions highlighted the importance of precautionary measures in fostering public dialogue and accountability concerning the future of the archives. On September 25, 2023, the SRVR released the written observations submitted by participants from the second session of the technical roundtable to the Colombian public, setting a deadline for receiving comments.[45]

*8.2.2 **Gradual Access to DAS Archives***

The Chamber of Acknowledgement has evaluated various requests to access the archives of Colombia's defunct Department of Administrative Security (DAS). In 2023, responsibility for this access was transferred from the DNI to the JEP to enhance the safeguarding of sensitive information. Over five years, 38 orders were issued to address 53 requests for archival access, primarily

43 Inter-American Commission on Human Rights, "Principios sobre políticas públicas de memoria en las Américas," in *Documentos básicos en materia de derechos humanos en el Sistema Interamericano* (OAS, 2020), 343–44.

44 The nine-hour hearing of the second session of the technical roundtable can be viewed at https://www.youtube.com/watch?v=QIMCmseIEnA.

45 Special Jurisdiction for Peace, 2023.

by judicial authorities and occasionally by victims and their representatives. Under Decree 1303 of 2014, DAS files are accessible only to judicial authorities involved in official investigations. However, in cases of significant international interest – such as the Palace of Justice disappearances – the Chamber of Acknowledgement has granted exceptional access to victims, citing the files as "human rights files" not subject to confidentiality.

To facilitate victim participation, the JEP mandated that victims in certain high-profile cases, like those before the Inter-American Court, be granted access to relevant DAS records. Recent decisions have reinforced this stance, authorising access in forced disappearance cases. The JEP's approach aligns with a pro-victim principle, prioritising victims' rights to dignity and information access in human rights cases. The following is an account of the debates that have arisen in recent years in the context of public deliberations on the archives in question.

8.3 Challenges and the Future of the DAS Archives

As a follow-up to the precautionary measures, the JEP Rapporteur Office has been involved in the efforts undertaken by the National System for the Purging of Colombian Intelligence and Counterintelligence Archive Data.[46] This involvement relates to managing these archives and other activities to ensure the right to the truth. However, one of the main challenges in this area is the lack of classification and inventory of the documentary collection from the now-defunct DAS. Having clear information about the number of archives containing human rights records is essential for ensuring access and consultation for both victims and Colombian society as a whole. This is especially important given that,

> Court rulings and the public debate arising from interceptions and illegal surveillance conducted between 2002 and 2010 highlight the potential of these files to clarify issues regarding the treatment of various actors. These include opposition political forces, human rights organizations, social leaders, community leaders, and academics, all within the context of the security policies implemented by different governments.[47]

One of the challenges in classifying and inventorying the archives is the sheer volume of documents involved, which complicates the process in terms of

46 System created as "an integrated and coordinated mechanism between the intelligence community, government institutions, control agencies and judicial authorities" and, in turn, "a set of instances, orientations, activities, resources, definitions, programs and institutions that enable the implementation of the general principles and provisions on updating, correction and withdrawal of intelligence and counterintelligence data and files." Presidency of the Republic of Colombia, *Decree 2149*, issued by Juan Manuel Santos Calderón, December 20, 2017.

47 Centro Nacional de Memoria Histórica, *Política pública de archivos de derechos humanos, memoria histórica y conflicto armado*, 76.

time, space, and resources. To address this issue, the AGN has estimated that the cost of conducting the inventory and evaluation will be approximately USD 2.5 million. This estimate reflects the need for techniques that go beyond a simple inventory; it requires classification, organisation, and description of the archives. This work is essential to uphold the rights of victims of serious human rights violations and international humanitarian law. Moreover, inter-institutional coordination, including international cooperation, is crucial for securing the financial resources necessary to carry out the inventory and mitigate the risks facing the archives.

8.3.1 Tension Between the Principle of Legal Reserve and the Right of Access to Information

Statutory Law 1621 states that files created by intelligence and counterintelligence agencies are protected by legal confidentiality for a maximum of 30 years from the date the information is collected.[48] By judgment C-540 of July 12, 2012, the Constitutional Court of Colombia declared this reserve constitutional by considering that "to the extent that such limits are legitimate for the purpose they pursue, the reserve is temporary, and the term is reasonable and proportional to the legal assets sought to be protected."[49] Additionally, access to and consultation of the DAS files is subject to legal reserve, which states that "information will only be provided to the judicial authorities that request it within a judicial process or the control entities that require or request it."[50]

This legal reserve must be examined within the context of the Constitution. Law 1712 of 2014 sets forth a principle of maximum disclosure, which states that all information held by regulated entities is considered public unless restricted by specific constitutional or legal provisions.[51] While limited exceptions exist to protect fundamental rights and public interests (such as national security and public health), these must meet the principle of proportionality.[52]

Exceptions to access include potential harm to individuals' rights and require a written description of the specific damage. Information related to national security must be justified, demonstrating a present, probable, and significant risk.[53] Article 28 of the law requires a "harm test" to determine if the potential harm from disclosure exceeds the public's interest in access. Crucially, Article 21 states that exceptions based on national security do not apply in cases of

48 Congress of the Republic of Colombia, *Statutory Law 1621*, April 17, 2013, Art. 33.

49 Constitutional Court of Colombia, *Judgment T-540,* Judge Jorge Iván Palacio Palacio, July 12, 2012.

50 Presidency of the Republic of Colombia, Decree 1303, issued by Juan Manuel Santos Calderón, July 11, 2014, Art. 1.

51 Congress of the Republic of Colombia, *Law 1712,* March 6, 2014, Art. 2.

52 Constitutional Court of Colombia, *Judgment T-451*, Judge Humberto Antonio Sierra Porto, May 26, 2011.

53 Constitutional Court of Colombia, Judgment C-274, Judge María Victoria Calle Correa, May 9, 2013.

human rights violations or crimes against humanity. Partial disclosure is also required when only parts of the information are exempt, ensuring transparency. There is a tension between the legal reserve of the now-defunct DAS archives and the right to access public information, which demands maximum disclosure. As outlined in existing regulations and the jurisprudence established by the Constitutional Court, this tension must be resolved by applying a "harm test." Therefore, access to the archives of the defunct DAS can only be denied if it can be demonstrated that there is a present, probable, and specific risk of causing harm to the protected interest. Additionally, the potential damage must be significant.

The Directorate of National Intelligence must guide its decisions by considering the insights provided by the Constitutional Court regarding the balance between legal reserve and the right to access reserved public information. This requires assessing each case to determine whether denying access to information is reasonable and proportionate, particularly in light of the interests protected by the right to public information.[54] Furthermore, the analysis conducted by the Directorate of National Intelligence should adhere to the principle of maximum disclosure and the prohibition against applying exceptions for accessing confidential information related to human rights violations or crimes against humanity.

8.3.2 The Now-Defunct DAS as Human Rights Archives

Law 1448 of 2011 assigned the CNMH the responsibility of collecting, preserving, and safeguarding archives related to violations of International Humanitarian Law (IHL) and serious breaches of international human rights norms during the Colombian armed conflict. In light of this mandate, the CNMH and the AGN have collaborated to implement the Protocol for Document Management of Human Rights and IHL Archives. However, to effectively work with the archives of the now-defunct DAS, it is essential to determine the nature of these archives. The CNMH, along with the Transitional Justice Committee of the Coordination Colombia, Europe, and the United States (CCEEU),[55] representatives from the Technical Committee of Archives, and victims from the Palace of Justice, have all emphasised the importance of identifying, locating, protecting, and providing access to the

54 Constitutional Court of Colombia, Judgment C-274, Judge María Victoria Calle Correa, May 9, 2013.

55 Formed by Colectivo de Abogados José Alvear Restrepo; Fundación Comité de Solidaridad con Presos Políticos; Movimiento Nacional de Víctimas de Crímenes de Estado; Corporación Jurídica Yira Castro; Humanidad Vigente Corporación Jurídica; Observatorio de la Coordinación Colombia Europa Estados Unidos; Equipo Colombiano Interdisciplinario de Trabajo Forense y Asistencia Psicosocial – Equitas; Colectivo Orlando Fals Borda; Corporación Jurídica Libertad; Asociación para la Promoción Social Alternativa MINGA; and, Comisión Colombiana de Juristas.

DAS Archives. This is essential for making reparations to the victims and fulfilling the State's duty to memory. The CNMH also claims that the DAS took violent actions contributing to the internal armed conflict.[56] The Office of the United Nations High Commissioner for Human Rights in Colombia believes that preserving the archive of the dismantled DAS is crucial for achieving the objectives of the SIVJRNR. Therefore, efforts to maintain this archive should be geared towards preventing collective memory loss. This approach aligns with the Set of Principles and the Global Principles on National Security and the Right to Information, commonly known as the Tshwane Principles.[57]

8.3.3 On Accessibility to the Archives of the Now-Defunct DAS and Its Preservation

The CCEEU has stated that there should be no restrictions on accessing the archives of the defunct DAS, especially since these archives relate to human rights violations. This position aligns with the principles the Colombian Constitutional Court established in judgments C-274 of 2013, C-017 of 2018, and C-018 of 2018, which are grounded in the Law on Transparency and Access to Information.[58] Similarly, the Minister of Defense pointed out that access to archives should not be denied for national security reasons, citing the international experiences of Argentina and Guatemala. These countries have taken measures regarding access to archives of human rights violations. In the Guatemalan case, historical archives played a role in the investigation of serious crimes and the search for missing persons.[59]

The Ministry of Justice and Law has emphasised the importance of classifying and publishing the archives, stating that any access limitations must be proportional and necessary following the test of proportionality (suitability, necessity, and proportionality). Expert Juan Carlos Upegui, who represented the Ministry at the technical roundtable, noted that Colombia continues to face challenges concerning this issue. It has been observed that even the Constitutional Court has issued rulings in specific cases where the principle of proportionality did not play a decisive role in determining the publication of personal information held by the State. This indicates that there may be reasons for its limited

56 Centro Nacional de Memoria Histórica, "Informe presentado por el Centro Nacional de Memoria Histórica (CNMH) en el marco de las acciones de la mesa técnica, realizada el día 30-01-2019," Bogotá, 2019, https://www.jep.gov.co/Biblioteca/Das/das5.pdf.

57 Office of the United Nations High Commissioner for Human Rights, "Concepto técnico respecto del Auto del 10 de enero de 2019 sobre 'Convocatoria mesa técnica para verificarlas condiciones de preservación y acceso a los archivos de inteligencia, contrainteligencia y gastos reservados del DAS'," Bogotá, 2019.

58 Centro Nacional de la Memoria Histórica, "Informe presentado por el Centro Nacional de la Memoria Histórica."

59 Special Jurisdiction for Peace, 2023.

effectiveness.[60] In light of these observations, Judge Oscar Parra-Vera decided to grant progressive access to the information in the intelligence, counterintelligence, and reserved expenses files of the now-defunct DAS. This decision will respect the current protocols and consider this documentary fund's ongoing evaluation and classification.[61]

The AGN has acknowledged the importance of incorporating the archives of the defunct DAS into its classification and inventory efforts. Although these records are not currently in its possession, they are part of the broader documentary collection. The Chamber of Acknowledgment is currently assessing this issue. The objective is to centralise all documents in the AGN, ensuring effective data preservation and accurately determining the preservation model for both physical and technological stability.[62] A clear example of the importance of this approach is that documentation related to resumes and administrative matters typically isn't linked to specific intelligence operations. However, this information can be relevant for cross-referencing indications or other forms of evidence related to crimes under the jurisdiction of the JEP.

In this regard, the Unit for the Search for Missing Persons (UBPD) has also expressed its concern, emphasising the need for the classification and inventory process to include the administrative archives of the DAS and not only the intelligence, counterintelligence, and reserved expenses archives, since there is no certainty about their content and nature, and this does not mean that information related to human rights violations cannot be found.[63] It is important to note that the inventory and classification work conducted by the AGN encompasses not only the intelligence, counterintelligence, and confidential expense archives of the defunct DAS but also its entire documentary collection. This collection includes documents that date back to before the establishment of the DAS in Colombia (1960). The Attorney General's Office has put forward a series of recommendations to implement actions before evaluating and inventorying the archives. This process will assess the preservation status of the documents. A maintenance procedure for the documentary conservation units should be established. This would enable intervention in as many archives as possible within the documentary collection of the now-defunct DAS.[64]

60 Juan Carlos Upegui Mejía, *Transparencia estatal y datos personales: El problema de la publicidad de la información personal en el poder del Estado* (Bogotá: Externado University of Colombia, 2020), 157, https://bdigital.uexternado.edu.co/handle/001/2819.

61 Special Jurisdiction for Peace, 2023.

62 Archivo General de la Nación, *Informe de los Archivos de Inteligencia, Contrainteligencia y Gastos Reservados del extinto Departamento Administrativo de Seguridad* (Bogotá: AGN, 2018).

63 Unidad para la Búsqueda de Personas Dadas por Desaparecidas, "Respuesta a los autos OPV-181 y OPV-231 de 2023," Bogotá, June 8, 2023.

64 Procuraduría General de la Nación, "Intervención de la PGN en la mesa técnica de las MC DAS del 30 de enero de 2019," Bogotá, 2019.

8.3.4 *The Defunct DAS Archives: An Asset of Cultural Interest and Memory of the World by UNESCO*

In response to a request from human rights organisations, the Documents Evaluation Committee of the General Archive of the Nation (AGN) issued Resolution No. 545 on July 11, 2023. This resolution declared the DAS archives an "Asset of Cultural Interest of Archival Documentary Collection in the national public sphere." This declaration aligns with the Decision adopted by the Special Jurisdiction for Peace specified in Order OPV 182 of 2023. As a result, the DAS documentary collection, which consists of more than 60,000 boxes and various storage units, will now be considered assets of collective interest for the nation. This collection includes intelligence, counterintelligence, reserved expense archives, and general or administrative archives. The decision aims to support human rights and fulfil the requirements of the Comprehensive System of Truth, Justice, Reparation, and Non-Repetition.[65]

The decision adopted by the AGN highlights how the precautionary measures implemented by the Chamber of Acknowledgment of the JEP have created a space for public dialogue about the significance of intelligence, counterintelligence, and the reserved expenses archives related to the armed conflict. These precautionary measures have not only activated the authority of the JEP but also involved other entities, such as the General Archive of the Nation, in protecting victims' rights to the truth. The discussions stemming from the JEP's precautionary measures regarding the DAS archives have led to reflections on the need to safeguard these archives and ensure citizens can access their information. This remains a priority despite the identified challenges related to resources and time. It is also noteworthy that the archives of the Truth Commission and the now-defunct DAS have been included in the regional registry of UNESCO's Memory of the World Program (MoWLAC). This recognition aims to preserve historical documents and clarify the truth about Colombia's past. According to UNESCO, the DAS documentary collection

> "represents a source of documentation that reveals the truth about the war in Colombia, highlighting its role as an intelligence agency and identifying actions that attribute responsibility for human rights violations and breaches of international humanitarian law."[66]

65 Archivo General de la Nación, *Resolución No. 545* (Bogotá: Archivo General de la Nación, 2023).

66 "Archivos de la Comisión de la Verdad y del extinto DAS entran a hacer parte de la lista regional de Memoria del Mundo de la UNESCO," Ministerio de las Relaciones Exteriores de Colobia, https://www.cancilleria.gov.co/newsroom/news/archivos-comision-verdad-extinto-das-entran-hacer-parte-lista-regional-memoria-mundo.

8.3.5 Order of the Inter-American Court in CAJAR v. Colombia *Within the Framework of the Precautionary Measures Issued by the JEP*

Another important aspect to consider regarding the precautionary measures issued by the Chamber is the recent ruling from the Inter-American Court of Human Rights on December 18, 2023, in the case of *Members of the Corporation Collective of Lawyers "José Alvear Restrepo" (CAJAR) v. Colombia*. This ruling is considered a landmark decision as it recognises the right to defend human rights and emphasises the importance of transparency in handling State information. In this ruling, the IACtHR condemned the Colombian State for its systematic persecution of CAJAR members and their families. This persecution was carried out through various actions, including illegal and arbitrary surveillance conducted by the Department of Administrative Security. It is important to emphasise that the DAS files played a crucial role in the analysis conducted by the IACtHR in this case. The Court determined that the Colombian State collected and stored a significant amount of information about CAJAR members through "arbitrary intelligence activities that harmed the victims." These activities continued during the enforcement of Law 1621 of 2013. As a result, the Court concluded that "the victims experienced various acts of violence, harassment, and intimidation, some of which involved direct participation by state agents."[67]

The IACtHR ruled that the victims have not had access to all the documents and data stored in the Colombian government's intelligence files. This lack of access has hindered their ability to fully understand the extent of the arbitrary intelligence activities conducted by the authorities against them. The Inter-American Court of Human Rights stated that this situation not only violated the victims' right to access information but also their right to informational self-determination.[68] It is also important to highlight that one of the comprehensive reparation measures ordered by the IACtHR, which the Colombian State must implement, is the timely reviewing of the files from the defunct DAS, as well as the files of the National Police, the Army's Artillery School, and the Military Intelligence Center of the Army. This measure aims to ensure that individuals who request access can effectively retrieve the information and data stored in these files. It is essential to uphold their right to "eventual rectification, cancellation, or deletion of the data contained in the files."[69]

67 Inter-American Court of Human Rights, *Official Summary of the Judgment in the Case of Members of the Corporation Collective of Lawyers "José Alvear Restrepo" (CAJAR) v. Colombia*, October 18, 2023.

68 Inter-American Court of Human Rights, *Official Summary of the Judgment in the Case of Members of the Corporation Collective of Lawyers.*

69 Inter-American Court of Human Rights, *Official Summary of the Judgment in the Case of Members of the Corporation Collective of Lawyers.*

The IACtHR's order has generated considerable debate at the domestic level. This is especially relevant in the context of the precautionary measures issued by the Chamber of Acknowledgment concerning the DAS files, which specifically mandated that these files should not be purged. A dialogue has been established between the Inter-American Commission on Human Rights, the victims, and the Special Jurisdiction for Peace. This dialogue aims to find a way to comply with the international court's decision through precautionary measures. This includes a restitution measure focused on reviewing and accessing intelligence files. This approach aligns with the Colombian State's obligation for due diligence in the investigations of crimes against human rights defenders.

Conclusions

Protecting the DAS archives is essential for investigating serious crimes that took place during the Colombian armed conflict. Due to the former DAS officials' involvement in severe human rights violations, it is crucial to emphasise the archives' potential to shed light on numerous events and reveal other unknown facts that have not yet been examined. This is essential for upholding victims' rights and Colombian society as a whole, particularly regarding truth, justice, reparation, and guarantees of non-repetition. These files may contain valuable information about serious human rights violations, such as torture, arbitrary detentions, forced disappearances, and extrajudicial executions. Furthermore, they could incorporate information about espionage and illegal surveillance targeting citizens, journalists, human rights defenders, public officials, and political leaders. The archives may also document cases of political persecution, including instances where intelligence has been used to intimidate, threaten, or undermine political opponents. It is essential to recognise how these archives can enhance transparency and accountability, vital components of a democratic society. By promoting these values, the archives can strengthen democracy and uphold human rights, build public trust in Colombian institutions, and acknowledge the State's responsibility for serious human rights violations.

In light of the ongoing debates surrounding the conflict between legal reserves and the right to access information, the chapter emphasises the importance of the entities responsible for reviewing access requests – namely the Directorate of National Intelligence and, in exceptional cases, the Special Jurisdiction for Peace – of applying the "proportionality test" established by the Constitutional Court in each case. Their evaluations should adhere to constitutional principles aimed at upholding and fulfilling the rights of victims and Colombian society, especially the rights to truth and memory. Furthermore, this discussion highlights that the precautionary measures related to the archives of the now-defunct Administrative Department of Security (DAS) signify a major advancement in the restorative transitional justice processes supported by the Special Jurisdiction for Peace (JEP). Despite the challenges mentioned in this chapter, significant progress has been achieved in protecting these archives and in ensuring gradual access to them. This is essential for conducting thorough investigations into State criminality in Colombia.

Bibliography

Appeal Section of the Tribunal for Peace of the Special Jurisdiction for Peace. *Order TP-SA 714*. January 27, 2021.

Archivo General de la Nación. *Informe de los Archivos de Inteligencia, Contrainteligencia y Gastos Reservados del extinto Departamento Administrativo de Seguridad*. Bogotá: AGN, 2018.

Archivo General de la Nación. *Propuesta de intervención sobre los medios y soportes de almacenamiento de datos, en el que se identifiquen los escenarios y actividades que podrían llevarse a cabo y estimación de costo, tiempo, tecnología y personal para cada una de estas actividades*. Bogotá: AGN, 2021.

Archivo General de la Nación. *Resolución No. 545*. Bogotá: Archivo General de la Nación, 2023.

Ariza, Fernando. "Noguera, el hombre que tuvo que dejar el DAS y consulado por delitos." *El Tiempo*, October 20, 2020. https://www.eltiempo.com/justicia/delitos/perfil-de-jorge-noguera-cotes-exdirector-del-das-que-recupera-su-libertad-544354.

Chamber of Acknowledgment of Truth, Responsibility, and the Determination of Facts and Conduct of the Special Jurisdiction for Peace. *Order No. 73*. October 26, 2018, 25.

Chamber of Acknowledgment of Truth, Responsibility, and the Determination of Facts and Conduct of the Special Jurisdiction for Peace. *Order 215*. October 2, 2019.

Chamber of Acknowledgment of Truth, Responsibility, and the Determination of Facts and Conduct of the Special Jurisdiction for Peace. *Order SRVR-SUB-D-055*. July 14, 2022.

Centro Nacional de Memoria Histórica (CNMH). *Política pública de archivos de derechos humanos, memoria histórica y conflicto armado*. Bogotá: Centro Nacional de Memoria Histórica, 2017.

Centro Nacional de Memoria Histórica. "Informe presentado por el Centro Nacional de Memoria Histórica (CNMH) en el marco de las acciones de la mesa técnica, realizada el día 30-01-2019." Bogotá, 2019. https://www.jep.gov.co/Biblioteca/Das/das5.pdf.

Congress of the Republic of Colombia. *Statutory Law 1621*. April 17, 2013.

Congress of the Republic of Colombia. *Law 1712*. March 6, 2014, Art. 2.

Congress of the Republic of Colombia. *Law 1922*. July 18, 2018.

Constitutional Court of Colombia. *Judgment T-451*. Judge Humberto Antonio Sierra Porto, May 26, 2011.

Constitutional Court of Colombia. *Judgment T–540*. Judge Jorge Iván Palacio Palacio, July 12, 2012.

Constitutional Court of Colombia. *Judgment C-274*. Judge María Victoria Calle Correa, May 9, 2013.

Constitutional Court of Colombia. *Judgment C-007/18*. 2018.

Criminal Cassation Chamber of the Supreme Court of Justice of Colombia. *Single Instance Judgment 32000*. Judge Alfredo Gómez Quintero, September 14, 2011.

Criminal Cassation Chamber of the Supreme Court of Justice of Colombia. *Judgment SP13920–2017*. Judge Luis Guillermo Salazar Otero, September 6, 2017.

Decree Ruling on the Appeal of the Judgment on the Crime of Aggravated Torture in the Case of Claudia Duque. Defendant José Miguel Narváez Martínez, 2024.

Executive Secretariat of the Special Jurisdiction for Peace. *Order No. 001*. March 12, 2018.

Inter-American Commission on Human Rights. "Principios sobre políticas públicas de memoria en las Américas." In *Documentos básicos en materia de derechos humanos en el Sistema Interamericano*. OAS, 2020.

Inter-American Court of Human Rights. *Official Summary of the Judgment in the Case of Members of the Corporation Collective of Lawyers "José Alvear Restrepo" (CAJAR) v. Colombia*. October 18, 2023.

Mesa por la Justicia Transicional de la Coordinación Colombia Europa Estados Unidos (CCEEU). *Intervención de organizaciones defensoras de DD.HH. y de víctimas parte de la Mesa por la Justicia Transicional de la Coordinación Colombia Europa Estados Unidos (CCEEU) en la Mesa Técnica para la protección de archivos del DAS*. Bogotá: CCEEU, 2019. https://www.jep.gov.co/Biblioteca/Das/das3.pdf.

Ministerio de las Relaciones Exteriores de Colombia. "Archivos de la Comisión de la Verdad y del extinto DAS entran a hacer parte de la lista regional de Memoria del Mundo de la UNESCO." Accessed January 2, 2025. https://www.cancilleria.gov.co/newsroom/news/archivos-comision-verdad-extinto-das-entran-hacer-parte-lista-regional-memoria-mundo.

Office of the United Nations High Commissioner for Human Rights. "Concepto técnico respecto del Auto del 10 de enero de 2019 sobre 'Convocatoria mesa técnica para verificarlas condiciones de preservación y acceso a los archivos de inteligencia, contrainteligencia y gastos reservados del DAS'." Bogotá, 2019.

Official Summary Issued by the Inter-American Court. *Rodríguez Vera and Others (Palace of Justice Disappeared) v. Colombia*. Inter-American Court of Human Rights.

Omeara Carrascal and Others v. Colombia. Inter-American Court of Human Rights, November 21, 2018.

Presidency of the Republic of Colombia. *Decree 1717 of 1960*. Bogotá, July 18, 1960.

Presidency of the Republic of Colombia. *Decree 512 of 1989*. Bogotá, March 13, 1989.

Presidency of the Republic of Colombia. *Decree 643 of 2004*. Bogotá, March 2, 2004.

Presidency of the Republic of Colombia. *Decree 4057 of 2011*. Bogotá, October 31, 2011.

Presidency of the Republic of Colombia. *Decree 1303 of 2014*. Bogotá, July 11, 2014.

Presidency of the Republic of Colombia. *Decree 2149 of 2017*. Bogotá, December 20, 2017.

Procuraduría General de la Nación. "Intervención de la PGN en la mesa técnica de las MC DAS del 30 de enero de 2019." Bogotá, 2019.

Ramírez Mouraille, Ana María, Maria Paula Ángel Arango, Mauricio Albarracín Caballero, Rodrigo Uprimny Yepes, and Viviana Newman Pont. *Acceso a los archivos de inteligencia y contrainteligencia en el marco del posacuerdo*. Bogotá: Dejusticia, 2017.

Rodríguez Vera and Others (Palace of Justice Disappeared) v. Colombia. Inter-American Court of Human Rights, November 14, 2014.

Superior Court of Bogotá. *Second Instance Judgment in the Case of Claudia Julieta Duque Orrego*. Defendant Ronal Harbey Rivera Rodríguez, Radication 11001310701020220009 02, November 20, 2023.

Unidad para la Búsqueda de Personas Dadas por Desaparecidas. "Respuesta a los autos OPV-181 y OPV-231 de 2023." Bogotá, June 8, 2023.

Upegui Mejía, Juan Carlos. *Transparencia estatal y datos personales: El problema de la publicidad de la información personal en el poder del Estado*. Bogotá: Externado University of Colombia, 2020.

Vergara, Fernando. "Condenan a exagente del DAS por tortura agravada contra la periodista Claudia Julieta Duque." *Fundación para la Libertad de Prensa*, November 27, 2023. https://flip.org.co/pronunciamientos/condenan-a-exagente-del-das-por-tortura-agravada-contra-la-periodista-claudia-julieta-duque.

9 Traces of Disappearance

A Groundbreaking Archive of Transitional Justice, From Investigation to Exhibition

Fernanda Barbosa Dos Santos and Folco Zaffalon

Introduction

In this chapter, we reflect on the exhibition "Traces of Disappearance," which is a novel transitional justice archive. This research project was completed through a partnership between the Colombian Truth Commission and the multidisciplinary research group Forensic Architecture of Goldsmiths, University of London.[1] "Traces of Disappearance" was designed and produced, through its methodologies and formats, to generate a broad and novel impact on Colombian and international audiences. The research carried out for the "Traces of Disappearance" project focused on three cases/episodes that reflect significant dynamics of the Colombian armed conflict.[2]

The first topic concerns the forced disappearances that occurred during the Retake of the Palace of Justice, a response by the Colombian State to the M-19 guerrilla group's seizure and retention of judicial officials on November 6, 1985. The violence continued until November 7 and resulted in approximately 100 deaths, along with an unknown number of missing persons. The second issue involves the dispossession and memory of the land in the District of Nueva Colonia, a subregion of Urabá Antioqueño.[3] This case highlights the complex web of factors that led to the forced displacement of peasants and the appropriation of land for agro-industrial banana monoculture. It includes instances of massacres, intimidation, environmental degradation, and

1 Forensic Architecture (FA) is a research agency based at Goldsmiths, University of London. FA develops spatial and media investigations into human rights and environmental violations cases. Investigations are conducted with and on behalf of communities affected by political violence, human rights and environmental groups, and the media. FA presents its work in national and international courts, in parliamentary committees, to the public, and in exhibitions at major art and cultural institutions worldwide.

2 The full *Huellas de desaparición* (Traces of Disappearance) project narrative and digital material (including videos) are available at: https://www.comisiondelaverdad.co/violaciones-de-derechos-humanos-infracciones-al-derecho-internacional-humanitario-y/huellas-de.

3 Subregion in the Colombian Department of Antioquia.

DOI: 10.4324/9781003609322-12

a network of legal, financial, and institutional mechanisms that conceals transfers of land ownership.

The third presents, through a mural at the entrance of the exhibition, the negative impacts on the territory and the indigenous Nukak people.[4] The mural focuses on a 37,000 km^2 region in the Guaviare department, an area deemed empty and vulnerable to colonisation and exploitation. Based on data collected since 1987, the mural illustrates various forms of violence and environmental destruction, including deforestation, burning, fumigation, cattle ranching, and development projects. These activities are leading to the decline of Amazonian life, particularly affecting the Nukak people. In this chapter, we reflect on our experience coordinating this project, which involved creating, developing, and publishing this new transitional justice archive.[5]

We begin by examining the limitations and innovative strategies the Truth Commission employs to access information while gathering data from various archives. We refer to "conflict archives" as those created during a political confrontation between a government and an armed opposition and preserved for public access.[6] We examine the research practices related to the presence and absence of conflict archives. Next, we will provide examples of how new archives are created using specific tools and technologies from Forensic Architecture. These tools facilitated the selection and development of the final products, including the videos, murals, and other evidence and objects displayed in the exhibition.

Additionally, we outline the strategies and challenges associated with the exhibition, particularly the dilemma of providing public access to archives and information sources related to human rights violations. This challenge is heightened by the risks faced by individuals involved in the cases and the investigations. Finally, we consider the distinction between a published and a living archive. The latter not only concerns the storage and availability of

4 The Nukak traditionally inhabit small groups in the deep forest, located between the Guaviare and Inírida rivers in southeast Colombia, away from the rivers.

5 Our role as members of the team of Commissioner Alejandro Valencia Villa, who directed the project, was to coordinate various aspects of the project in permanent dialogue with Forensic Architecture. Among other aspects of the work, we took care of obtaining the documentation and archives of the project; we managed the relationship with the communities, victims' families, human rights organisations, experts, and other project stakeholders; also, in the final stage, we took care of the dissemination and pedagogical aspects. Therefore, this article deals mainly with the aspects of the project in which we had a direct role. For more information on other aspects of the research, in particular on the case of dispossession in Urabá Antioquia, see Hannah Meszaros Martín and Oscar Pedraza, "The Memory of Earth and Land Dispossession in Urabá," *Planning Theory* (2022), https://journals.sagepub.com/doi/10.1177/14704129211072651.

6 Laia Balcells and Christopher M. Sullivan, "New Findings from Conflict Archives: An Introduction and Methodological Framework," *Journal of Peace Research* 55, no. 1 (2018): 1, https://doi.org/10.1177/0022343317750217.

information but also focuses on how this information is assimilated and appropriated by a broader audience. This chapter outlines the stages of research and dissemination of the project's results while also addressing the questions that arose during the process. We reflect on our experiences using theoretical references related to conflict archives and connect various human rights standards to the Truth Commission's approach to information. Our aim is for this chapter to contribute to discussions on transitional justice processes and archives, presenting a perspective from an innovative project that employs unique analysis methodologies, presentation formats, and diverse dissemination practices.

9.1 Access to Information: Limitations and New Pathways

This section explores the significance of public access to conflict archives and highlights the limitations imposed by the Colombian government's insufficient response to information requests. Drawing on experiences from two cases within the project, it outlines the solutions developed by the team to address the challenges encountered while searching for sources in various types of archives.

9.1.1 Open, Confidential, and Declassified Files Regarding the Dispossession of Land in Urabá Antioqueño

In March and April of 1988, the massacres in Honduras, as well as in La Negra and Punta Coquitos – rural communities in Nueva Colonia, municipality of Turbo (Urabá Antioqueño) – made headlines in the media. Both newspapers and television broadcasts reported on the violent events that led to the murder of over 40 individuals. In May 1988, the *Semana* magazine published a special article detailing the Honduras and La Negra massacres based on information from a confidential report by the Administrative Department of Security (DAS).[7] In 2019, 31 years later, researchers of this project sought documentation to clarify the dynamics behind the land dispossession in Urabá Antioqueño. Their analysis initially focused on the massacres in the village of Nueva Colonia but later expanded to examine the transformation of the territory and landscape. They also investigated the network of actors involved in this dispossession, including transnational banana companies, banks, trusts, paramilitary groups, and state institutions.

The gathered sources included testimonies from peasants, satellite and aerial images, press reports, documentaries, academic research, financial statements, certificates of land ownership history, legal judgments, land restitution processes, maps, plans, and official testimonies. The search for available archives became a fundamental practice for the research project. Interns began exploring libraries in Bogotá, including the Luís Ángel Arango Library,

7 Colombia's intelligence and counterintelligence service between 1960 and 2011.

which is managed by the Banco de la República. In addition to specialised and general press clippings, they discovered something unexpected: a confidential DAS report published by the *Semana* magazine in the 1980s that included a previously unknown annexe. This document contained photographs, drawings of the victims and alleged perpetrators, hand-drawn maps of the farms, and a layout of the buildings. Since the project's central methodology was to reconstruct the events in a three-dimensional format digitally,[8] the DAS document was a valuable starting point. In 2019, the Honduras and La Negra farms were already covered by banana plantations, concealing the sites of the massacres. The annexe allowed the comparison of the drawings made at the time with aerial images from 1989 and with the locations reported by a local farmer. This allowed for the reconstruction of the massacre sites in a digital environment.

The DAS report serves as an example of the conflict archives we worked with. In Colombia, which has experienced over 60 years of conflict involving various armed factions – including state actors, paramilitary groups, and guerrilla movements – conflict archives have been created from multiple perspectives over the decades. These archives reflect the views of the state, armed actors, victims, and civil society organisations. As they are contemporaneous with periods of violence, such archives illuminate "how different actors perceive their strategic environment in real-time and provide insights into their behaviours."[9] Access to these documents varies based on specific conditions. On one hand, there are open archives provided by libraries and other organisations. Notably, the library mentioned earlier, along with the Archive of Bogotá, the General Archive of the Nation, and the National Library, served as valuable resources for the project in the Colombian capital. The presence of well-preserved and organised conflict archives significantly enhances researchers' access. Some archives are not always accessible, particularly concerning state documents related to the Public Forces and intelligence services. Accessing these documents can uncover discrepancies in official accounts of events[10] and may reveal concealed strategies related to political violence.[11] For that reason, various truth commissions have struggled to obtain documents, especially from the military and police.[12]

8 The reconstruction of the events in the digital models was carried out through the collection of interviews and testimonies, aerial and satellite images, photographs, and videos taken in the places where the cases occurred and data of various types. This information was analyzed and became the basis for the development by Forensic Architecture of 3D animations and virtual reality environments, based on software used to create video games.

9 Balcells and Sullivan, "New Findings from Conflict Archives," 2–3.

10 Richard Cox, "Archives, War, and Memory: Building a Framework," *Library & Archival Security* 25, no. 1 (2012): 21–57, https://doi.org/10.1080/01960075.2012.657945.

11 Balcells and Sullivan, "New Findings from Conflict Archives."

12 United Nations, Office of the High Commissioner for Human Rights, *Instruments of the Rule of Law for Societies Emerging from Conflict: Archives* (Geneva: United Nations, 2015), 36, https://www.ohchr.org/sites/default/files/Documents/Publications/HR_PUB_14_4_Archives_en.pdf.

In Colombia, the Constitutional Court clarified the extent of the Truth Commission's authority to access information under Ruling C-017 of 2018. This ruling affirms the constitutionality of Decree 588 of 2017, which established the entity.

> Judicial and extrajudicial bodies involved in the official investigation of truth and the reconstruction of memory in transitional scenarios must have complete access to all public information. This access is essential for upholding the rights of victims and society to know the truth.[13]

This access prerogative for transitional justice entities, grounded in international human rights standards highlighted in various United Nations reports and resolutions (1997, 2005, 2015), was not fully granted to the Colombian Truth Commission. During a hearing before the Inter-American Commission on Human Rights (IACHR) in December 2020, Commissioner Alejandro Valencia Villa expressed concern over the government entities' failure to comply with the Truth Commission's requests for information. He urged the IACHR to request that the Colombian government cooperate.[14]

What would occur if confidential files were made public in Colombia after the legally required time to keep them reserved has passed? One answer can be found in the research: having access to and the ability to use the complete 30-year-old DAS report allowed for a better understanding of both the intelligence services' perspective on the massacres and the details of the locations recorded at the time, enhancing our comprehension of what happened. We consulted international public archives to address the lack of access to official documentation in Colombia, especially confidential or reserved documents. Documents from U.S. government agencies were declassified following requests from the non-governmental organisation National Security Archive (NSA).[15] They submitted over 15,000 declassified documents to the Truth Commission regarding the Colombian conflict, including details about the involvement of international banana companies in funding paramilitary groups in the Urabá region of Antioquia.[16]

13 Constitutional Court of Colombia, *Judgment C-017/18*, 2018.

14 The Truth Commission published a note on the petitions sent by the commissioner to the Inter-American Court of Human Rights, which is published at https://web.comisiondelaverdad.co/actualidad/noticias/cinco-peticiones-comision-verdad-a-cidh-para-facilitar-acceso-informacion.

15 Based on the Freedom of Information Act (FOIA), NSA requests the declassification of files from different U.S. government agencies. That is, to issue a public version of documents that were previously classified as confidential. More information about NSA can be found at https://nsarchive.gwu.edu/about.

16 The declassified U.S. agency documents used by the Colombian Truth Commission are available in the Commission's archive: https://www.comisiondelaverdad.co/anexo-archivos-desclasificados-national-security-archive.

9.1.2 *The "Black Boxes" and Online Archives on the Retaking of the Palace of Justice*

The second case of Traces of Disappearance investigated the evidence surrounding a significant case from the armed conflict in Colombia, which has had lasting effects on the country's democracy, the retaking of the Palace of Justice. The digital environment has opened up new possibilities for accessing information relevant to the project. In this case, open and freely accessible archives played a crucial role in reconstructing places otherwise closed to the public. For example, a video posted on YouTube featured aerial footage of Cantón Norte, an Army installation in northern Bogotá that includes infantry and cavalry schools. This video highlighted military participation in sporting events and was instrumental in reconstructing an important aspect of our research.

Understanding the physical layout of Cantón Norte, where the Army detained and tortured individuals following the seizure and retaking of the Palace of Justice on November 6 and 7, 1985, is crucial for tracing the path of those who disappeared after leaving the building. The project investigators referred to the inaccessible locations and archives for their investigation as "black boxes."[17] In the case of Cantón Norte, they could not obtain complete information about the events that took place there following the retaking of the Palace of Justice.

> Black boxes are areas where information is concealed, enabling a cycle of impunity. They can be locations of detention, torture, murder, or burial. Additionally, black boxes serve as archives where information is destroyed or inaccessible. Our work aims to define these boxes' shape, contours, and volume and connect them to other boxes within a larger system to understand their functioning.[18]

The Prosecutor's Office file 9755 of 2005, regarding the Palace of Justice case, allowed for a reconstruction of events that took place in Cantón Norte during that time. This reconstruction was based on statements from witnesses and alleged perpetrators gathered during the judicial process and various documents, including confidential ones, discovered during inspections of military installations and officers' residences. To accurately represent this space in a 3D digital format, researchers needed to pinpoint these accounts within the Cantón Norte facilities. They were able to find the necessary references through YouTube videos. Most conflict archive documents originate

17 *Judgment C-017/18* (2018).

18 "The Black Boxes of Enforced Disappearance," Truth Commission and Forensic Architecture, 2022, https://www.comisiondelaverdad.co/violacion-derechos-humanos-y-derecho-internacional-humanitario/las-cajas-negras-de-la-desaparicion.

from state efforts, but various actors produce others without an initial intention to be archived.[19]

Content is available to anyone with access when stored in a digital archive like YouTube. Mbembe notes that the archiving process involves releasing ownership of the information.[20] While open access does not equate to free use and reproduction of materials, it enables a broad audience to consult the information. It encourages various potential uses as a research source. Conflicts fuel the creation of content related to the violence experienced or witnessed and promote the use of information technologies.[21] A prime example is the variety of online videos documenting the seizure and retaking of the Palace of Justice. This instance illustrates how, in a protracted armed conflict, the motivation to produce such content is continually renewed over time.

Access to conflict archives was crucial for developing the investigation and products of "Traces of Disappearance." While the team was able to obtain confidential information from archives and state entities, the state itself also imposed limitations. To navigate these challenges, the team explored alternative methods, such as declassified documents and utilising online archives available on platforms like YouTube. The use of information technologies and the creation of archives during times of violence proved to be powerful tools for accessing relevant information. The next step in the research involved analysing and processing this information, which posed challenges related to both the lack and the excess of data.

9.2 Between Absence and Abundance

The abundance and lack of conflict archives influenced the final results and were regarded as both a limitation to the analysis and a benefit for the process. A notable example of our research focused on understanding land distribution in Urabá Antioqueño. We aimed to access information from the land registry and the official inventory of farm ownership, and we made requests through various institutional channels. In December 2019, we decided to conduct fieldwork to obtain documentation directly. We visited the mayor's office in Turbo (Antioquia) along with the project's lead researcher and requested to speak with an official from the land registry, who graciously met with us. The response arrived swiftly: the land registries from the 1980s were not available in digital form, nor were they organised in a physical archive. We had expected to find at least a few boxes of disorganised papers, which would have made

19 Achille Mbembe, "The Power of the Archive and Its Limits," in *Refiguring the Archive*, eds. Carolyn Hamilton, Verne Harris, Jane Taylor, Michele Pickover, Graeme Reid, and Razia Saleh (Cape Town: David Philip Publishers, 2002).

20 Mbembe, "The Power of the Archive and Its Limits."

21 Cox, "Archives, War, and Memory."

the task more time-consuming but still feasible. However, the documents had turned to ashes years ago; according to the official, a fire had consumed them.

The institutions' failure to respond to the project's requests further highlighted the lack of archival materials. Although the Truth Commission had the legal right to unrestricted access to state information, this was not always granted. For instance, we requested information from the National Police's Anti-Narcotics Directorate (DIRAN), the Integrated Illicit Crop Monitoring System (SIMCI), and the Ministry of Defense regarding three decades of aerial fumigation in the Guaviare department. This research aimed to investigate the impacts on the territory and the Nukak people, which was our third research topic. However, most of the requested information was not granted to the Truth Commission.[22] The lack of responses from other institutions prompted us to display the emails containing unanswered or partially answered requests in the museums hosting "Traces of Disappearance."

Along with the absence of documents, we faced the opposite issue: an overabundance. When researching the case related to the seizure and retake of the Palace of Justice in late 2020, and as isolation measures due to the COVID-19 pandemic were lifting in Colombia, we visited the Attorney General's Office and a court in Bogotá to gather information about the case. The files in the Attorney General's Office were stored in albums and towers containing CDs, DVDs, and Blu-rays. Unfortunately, we could not access the Blu-rays because the playback drive was incompatible with that media type. However, we managed to copy the other files and delivered approximately 60 gigabytes of data to the Truth Commission. During our visit to the tribunal, instead of receiving digital data, we were given numerous sheets of paper, delivered in a wheelbarrow and organised into bundles tied with ropes.

A wealth of archival sources was obtained while investigating the three cases. In the case of the Palace of Justice, we had access not only to sentences, trials, and interviews but also to over 40 hours of newsreel footage. For the Urabá case, the Land Restitution Unit provided us with hundreds of digital documents, though they were disorganised, lacking any particular order. In the study focusing on the territory and the Nukak people, the Agustín Codazzi Geographic Institute (IGAC) sent us more than 5,000 aerial and satellite images. This large number of sources facilitated a more accurate investigation, as Forensic Architecture employed extensive and detailed data mining methodologies. However, this approach also faced several management challenges. How can we avoid losing crucial information amidst a vast number of documents? What strategies can we use to process and organise the large volume of data collected over three years of work? How can we securely and

22 "The Detected Jungle," Truth Commission and Forensic Architecture, 2022, https://www.comisiondelaverdad.co/violacion-derechos-humanos-y-derecho-internacional-humanitario/la-selva-detectada.

digitally share information among members of a transnational investigation, including Forensic Architecture and the Commission?

To effectively process the data, it was crucial to assemble a transdisciplinary team comprising investigators, research assistants, and practitioners who focused on data mining under the guidance of Forensic Architecture. However, sharing information proved a significant challenge, requiring hours of effort to upload and download documents and audiovisual materials. We conducted interviews and conversations with human rights organisations and lawyers to manage the extensive court files without getting lost. Among these was Ángela María Buitrago, the prosecutor responsible for reopening the Palace of Justice case, which is documented in file 9755 of 2005. The former prosecutor secured new testimonies from victims and alleged perpetrators and gathered hours of audiovisual material using television programming systems, which helped clarify several case details.

The presence or absence of conflict archives created during periods of violence can lead to different interpretations. According to Cox, during conflicts, both the creation of memories surrounding violence and efforts to erase those memories tend to increase.[23] Additionally, the extensive production of archives is an inherent function of the state, which systematically records its processes.[24] However, this abundance of archives can pose risks for the state, potentially prompting attempts to destroy information. Conversely, lacking an archive can lend it symbolic significance and heighten interest in its contents. The Truth Commission and the Forensic Architecture investigation focused on two key issues regarding state archival documents: the lack of official documentation and the overwhelming amount of existing but unorganised documents. On one hand, the absence of information from official sources impeded progress on certain matters. On the other hand, the vast quantity of disorganised and repetitive documents contributed to a sense of silence, making it easy to become overwhelmed by data. This vastness often made it difficult to find important information.

The project investigated alternative methods to address the situation caused by official sources. The archives of human rights organisations, along with testimonies from victims' families, peasants, journalists, academics, activists, and television producers, proved essential and offered us new perspectives. Months before we obtained the Palace of Justice files, two individuals provided us with videos from their personal archives, and a human rights organisation shared relevant documents with us. Additionally, the files from relatives of the disappeared persons included details about their experiences of resistance and efforts to uphold human rights, which were not available in the official documents.

The personal notebook of lawyer Enrique Rodriguez, who passed away in 2010, offers valuable insights into his efforts as a father searching for his son, Carlos Augusto Rodriguez Vera, who went missing during the retaking of the

23 Cox, "Archives, War, and Memory."
24 Mbembe, "The Power of the Archive and Its Limits."

Palace of Justice. It also reveals 25 years' worth of requests that Rodriguez made to various authorities and public entities. The challenges a truth commission faces stem from the lack and the abundance of conflict archives. In "Traces of Disappearance," the imposed silences were recognised as significant elements of the research findings and were included in the exhibition. Along with the sources gathered from conflict archives and analysed by the team, additional materials created during the research process contributed to establishing a new archive, which will be explained in further detail next.

9.3 New Pieces of the Puzzle Surfaced

The methodologies and technologies employed by Forensic Architecture facilitated the creation of the exhibition's final elements, such as videos, murals, relationship maps, and both digital and physical 3D reconstructions. In December 2020, we gathered in-person testimonials with Nueva Colonia, Turbo farmers. Forensic Architecture developed this method, which involves having interviewees interact with a digital environment reconstructed in 3D from sources uncovered during the investigation. For the Nueva Colonia case, Forensic Architecture specialists reconstructed 100 square kilometres of the township, highlighting both dispossessed land and land at risk of disappearing. Angel Montalvo, one of the farmers interviewed, demonstrated where mangoes and other trees should be planted to reconstruct his house accurately. He also highlighted the erosion caused by the advancing sea and assisted the researchers in identifying a type of plantain that closely resembles the ones harvested in Nueva Colonia. Additionally, Gilberto Pérez, an Afro-descendant peasant who lived in the village, illustrated in the virtual environment how he fled during the Punta Coquitos massacre on April 11, 1988. The memories shared by the interviewees were closely tied to their connection to the land, as described in the project documentation.[25]

This research portrays the environment as an active participant in conflict rather than a passive element in dispute. In the context of dispossession, land is a political and social actor that affects the distribution of violence. The "land memory" concept provides insights into dispossession practices and the historical context of armed conflict.[26] The land serves as a record of experiences and events. During further fieldwork, we visited the rural village of California in the Nueva Colonia township to interview John Jairo Pérez Negrete, a peasant leader who regained his land in 2020. As we walked through his banana plantations, he reflected on the layout of the land before his dispossession and

25 Meszaros Martín and Pedraza, "The Memory of Earth and Land Dispossession in Urabá."

26 "Despojo y memoria de la tierra" (Dispossesion and Memory of the Land) research on Urabá from Traces of Dissapearance available at: https://www.comisiondelaverdad.co/violacion-derechos-humanos-y-derecho-internacional-humanitario/despojo-y-memoria-de-la-tierra

displacement. We discovered a piece of glass buried in the ground. "This was a glass, look. This tells me that the house was here," John Jairo explained in an excerpt from the interview recorded for the "Dispossession and Land Memory Project."

In Coquitos, our methods for collecting data enabled us to gain insight into what had been archived and concealed both on land and in the sea. We used a GoPro camera mounted on a pole to capture a series of photographs of every centimetre of the area. Through photogrammetry, we were able to reconstruct the landscape and track erosion changes over time. Additionally, we employed satellite and aerial imagery to visualise the loss of shoreline since the 1980s. The combination of audio and visual recordings, along with GPS points that marked paths, trees, and water outlets, formed the foundation of the material we collected in the field. This work emphasised one of the most overlooked aspects of land dispossession: the gradual degradation of territory and the environment. The collaboration between researchers, technology, farmers, and the land helped gather new information. The Truth Commission and Forensic Architecture archived these findings and compiled them into a final product. Each component included data from previously consulted archives, such as written documents, aerial and satellite images, judicial records, videos, and interviews.

The United Nations report on archives as tools for the Rule of Law in societies emerging from armed conflict states that transitional justice initiatives, such as truth commissions, require access to various documents to fulfil their mandates and create new records. These documents form a rich and invaluable source of information about the country and its people; therefore, they should be preserved and made accessible to future users.[27] As different pieces were collected and developed, strategies were devised to select and organise them into visual narratives of the research findings. This selection process gives archival status to the documents, whether sourced from other archives or created through the research.[28] This selection enables the preservation of some documents while allowing others to be forgotten or destroyed. In "Traces of Disappearance," the methodologies are crucial to the selection and assembly process.

One of these methodologies was data mining, which Forensic Architecture developed.[29] During the investigation, parts of the collected files were extracted and organised following the central questions of the inquiry, which

27 United Nations, *Instruments of the Rule of Law: Archives.*

28 Mbembe, "The Power of the Archive and Its Limits"; Cox, "Archives, War, and Memory."

29 Data mining is the practice of creating a database by extracting information from text or video documents of multiple formats. It can be done manually, algorithmically, or a combination of both. Manual data mining begins by determining a set of organising principles for the data, including how the information should be classified. These principles are determined not only by the content of the source material but also by how that information will ultimately be analysed or presented. Retrieved from https://forensic-architecture.org/methodology/data-mining-2.

will later be reflected in the final product. In the case of the Retake of the Palace of Justice, we identified the locations and vehicles linked to over 22 missing persons from the Palace of Justice, as reported by various sources. This investigation enabled us to outline their known route in both time and space, from when they left the Palace to where they were last seen alive. In some instances, we also pinpointed where their remains were eventually discovered.

In summary, "Traces of Disappearance" involved a thorough documentary search, compiling testimonials and creating new works that shed light on the dynamics of violence in the Colombian armed conflict. The gathered materials created a new archive, establishing connections in space, time, and materiality, culminating in a final construction representing a complete puzzle linking various pieces. The final outcome was made accessible to the public through museum exhibitions and the Truth Commission and Forensic Architecture websites. However, to protect the safety of the sources, additional precautions were necessary due to the openness of this information.

9.4 The Risks Involved in Opening Archives

In this section, we discuss the challenges and dilemmas we faced while publicly opening the archives and sources of information related to disseminating the results from the "Traces of Disappearance" project. We will mainly focus on the risks encountered by individuals involved in cases of human rights violations and those who participated in the investigation. With the opening of the exhibition and the publication of the "Traces of Disappearance" archives just a few weeks away, the Truth Commission thoroughly reviewed the materials proposed for publication, printing, and exhibition at the museum. Some of the files included in the exhibition consisted of military plans, diaries from the victims' relatives, certificates of tradition and freedom documenting the history of the Urabá properties, statements compiled by the Attorney General's Office, and an annexe to the previously mentioned confidential report from the DAS.

One of the most sensitive situations involved data mining in the Palace of Justice case. By including the entire case as one of the exhibition's books, the project researchers aimed to publicly showcase the methodological process and the sources of their investigation. This approach aligned with Forensic Architecture's proposal for open verification.

> Open verification requires a continuous and transparent presentation of every step involved in the work: the circumstances surrounding it, the people involved, the materials used, the locations where each piece of evidence was found, the methods of authentication, and how different pieces of evidence were combined to build a case. This approach allows the public to engage in a process similar to scientific peer review, enabling others to examine the underlying data and replicate and test the

processes. This is why much of the content in our video investigations is structured as a 'how-to'.[30]

Forensic Architecture emphasises transparency by openly sharing verification processes and results. It believes that the elements used to create its narratives should be understandable to a general audience, including non-experts in specific research areas. The organisation seeks to integrate its work into social and political contexts by providing access to data, sources, and methodologies. This approach encourages ongoing research and allows those who visit the exhibition to verify the conclusions presented. This aligns with the mandate for maximum transparency in human rights archives established by a truth commission, which connects to the principle of maximum disclosure found in international human rights law. The principles for protecting and promoting human rights, as outlined by the United Nations in 1997, emphasise the "right to know" as a collective right rooted in history. This right aims to prevent future violations from happening again. The principles stress that "a people's knowledge of the history of its oppression is part of its heritage and should therefore be preserved." Additionally, it states that the final report of a truth commission "should be made public and disseminated as widely as possible."[31]

Article 10 of the "Global Principles on National Security and the Right to Information," also known as the "Tshwane Principles," states that information related to human rights violations is particularly significant to the public.[32] This information is crucial in democratic oversight and upholding the rule of law. Therefore, there is a strong presumption – sometimes even a compelling need – that such information should be publicly and proactively disclosed.[33] In Colombia, the principle of maximum disclosure at the national level is established by the Law on Transparency and Access to Public Information.[34] Additionally, public policy concerning archives related to human rights, historical memory, and armed conflict has been developed by the National Center of

30 Eyal Weizman, "Open Verification," *e-flux Architecture*, Becoming Digital, 2019, https://www.e-flux.com/architecture/becoming-digital/248062/open-verification/.

31 United Nations, *Question of the Impunity of Perpetrators of Human Rights Violations (Civil and Political): Revised Final Report Prepared by Mr. Joinet Pursuant to Sub-Commission Decision 1996/119*, UN Doc. E/CN.4/Sub.2/1997/20/Rev.1, 6–7 (Geneva: United Nations, 1997), https://documents.un.org/doc/undoc/gen/g97/141/42/pdf/g9714142.pdf.

32 Open Society Justice Initiative, *Global Principles on National Security and the Right to Information* (New York: Open Society Justice Initiative, October 23, 2013), https://www.justiceinitiative.org/uploads/bd50b729-d427-4fbb-8da2-1943ef2a3423/global-principles-national-security-10232013.pdf.

33 Open Society Justice Initiative, *Global Principles on National Security and the Right to Information*, 25.

34 Congress of the Republic of Colombia, *Law 1712*, March 6, 2014.

Historical Memory.[35] The Constitutional Court has stated that "the right of access to public information is governed by the principle of maximum disclosure, which means that, as a general rule, information held, controlled, or managed by a regulated entity must be public."[36] Additionally, the prohibition against withholding information on human rights violations was a central tenet in the Truth Commission's norms.

The Constitutional Court, in its judgment reviewing these norms, stated that the objectives of the Truth Commission largely centre on investigating and clarifying human rights violations and breaches of international humanitarian law. Consequently, prohibiting the reproduction of documents related to these issues would significantly hinder the Commission's work. Furthermore, regarding intelligence and counterintelligence documents, if the information pertains to human rights violations, crimes against humanity, or breaches of international humanitarian law, there should be no foreseeable limitations on accessing this information in the context of the Commission's work, including its reproduction.[37]

Upon reviewing the data mining related to the Palace of Justice case, we realised that some information sources available to us in the project could pose risks if publicly disclosed in their entirety. The tension between the pursuit of truth and the safety of victims, witnesses, and human rights defenders has been evident throughout the nearly 40-year history of the fight against impunity in this case. A notable example is the case of Eduardo Umaña Mendoza, a lawyer who defended several relatives of the disappeared. He was murdered on April 18, 1998, in Bogotá. Additionally, the relatives of the disappeared, witnesses, and those who supported or investigated the case faced numerous threats over the years, and some were forced to leave the country in exile. The responsibility of the Truth Commission and everyone involved in this project was to minimise the risk of exposing individuals to potential human rights violations. This was especially important for the relatives of the disappeared, as well as for experts, human rights defenders, and other collaborators in the project. It is clear that the information obtained through data mining could pose such risks.

The tension between maximum disclosure and safeguarding the integrity and lives of victims and those involved in human rights investigations is evident in international standards. The United Nations Principles and Guidelines on the Rights of Victims (2005) outline the restrictions on disclosing data and information related to human rights violations that could expose victims to discrimination and persecution. They emphasise that "victims should be treated with humanity and respect for their dignity and human

35 Centro Nacional de Memoria Histórica, *Política pública de archivos de derechos humanos, memoria histórica y conflicto armado* (Bogotá: Centro Nacional de Memoria Histórica, 2017).
36 Constitutional Court of Colombia, *Judgment SU355/22*, 2022, para. 98.
37 *Judgment C-017/18* (2018), para. 236.4.

rights. Appropriate measures must be taken to ensure their safety, physical and psychological well-being, privacy, and that of their families."[38] Similarly, Principle 10 of the Tshwane Declaration states that "the names and other personal details of victims, their families, and witnesses may be withheld from disclosure to the general public as a necessary measure to prevent further harm to them."[39]

The Truth Commission decided to take a sample from the 244 pages of the Data Mining book and anonymise all references to victims, family members, and witnesses. Sensitive information was crossed out while the rest of the information remained accessible. After this initial sampling, the remaining pages were represented by a blank page with a notice stating, "Information not included due to the risk to individual persons." This result serves as a symbolic and aesthetic reminder to the public and society that, in Colombia, it is not yet possible to fully open the archives and sources of information regarding human rights violations. This is set against a backdrop of widespread impunity and ongoing disputes about the truth.

In conclusion, the proposals and principles aimed at maximising the disclosure of information sources by the Commission and Forensic Architecture have provided the public with significant access to the Transitional Justice Archive and its sources. This includes, for example, the intelligence manuals related to the Palace of Justice case and the economic transactions in the dispossession case in Urabá Antioqueño. However, to mitigate security risks for interviewees and victims involved in these cases, certain information sources were identified as unsuitable for public release at the time of the presentation. Once the information was published, it reached a new level of accessibility. Control of the archives shifted away from the institutions that conducted the research. The documentation became open for public interaction, allowing individuals and groups to appropriate that information.

9.5 Transitioning From a Published Archive to a Living Archive

In this final section, we discuss the shift from a published archive to a living one that can be utilised, transformed, and shared by the public and the individuals who discover and engage with it. In today's world, where information is abundant, having information available to the public does not mean that society is necessarily aware of or has absorbed it. For instance, thousands of documents in libraries and public archives are rarely consulted.

38 United Nations, *Basic Principles and Guidelines on the Right to a Remedy and Reparation for Victims of Gross Violations of International Human Rights Law and Serious Violations of International Humanitarian Law* (Geneva: United Nations, 2005), https://www.ohchr.org/en/instruments-mechanisms/instruments/basic-principles-and-guidelines-right-remedy-and-reparation

39 Open Society Justice Initiative, *Global Principles on National Security and the Right to Information*, 27.

This highlights the importance of the medium and format used to publish information, as they significantly influence how well it is known and understood. The decision to create an exhibition and audiovisual products, rather than rely on less accessible formats like books, has been a key motivation behind this project.

The exhibition launch at the Miguel Urrutia Art Museum in downtown Bogotá on International Human Rights Day, December 10, 2021, generated an immediate impact. The large murals, the extensive information available, and the detailed narratives presented in the videos and on evidence tables captivated visitors. The international recognition of Forensic Architecture and the anticipation surrounding the disclosure of one of the initial results of the Truth Commission's investigation drew a public audience. Although the press had hesitated before the exhibition's launch, they began to support its promotion in the following weeks and months. Between 2021 and 2024, at least 24 national and international publications mentioned the exhibition, as noted by Forensic Architecture's tracking.[40]

Making the information and sources of this project publicly available in a prominent setting, such as a major museum in the country, allowed casual observers to engage with it. This included individuals who may not have expertise or knowledge about armed conflict and those who might be indifferent or uninterested. Publishing in an eye-catching format is insufficient without mediation and a pedagogical process to start a dialogue between the published archive and the public.[41] This represented a new area of understanding that enabled us to exceed our expectations during the planning and execution of this project. It was a collective space where knowledge was created and emotional experiences were shared.

Simultaneously, it was also a personal and intimate space that stirred various emotions as one engaged with the material. The number of visitors has increased significantly, especially since February 2022, when schools and universities began to request guided tours. Originally scheduled to run until April, the exhibition was extended until July. After seven months, the Banco de la República Museum in Bogotá welcomed more than 50,000 visitors, making it one of the most visited exhibitions in its history. The three institutions involved designed the exhibition not only as an accessible archive for the public but also as a living archive.

40 Survey available on the project website at: https://forensic-architecture.org/investigation/enforced-disappearance-at-the-palacio-de-justicia.

41 Some of the main mediation and pedagogical initiatives carried out around the exhibition "Traces of Disappearance," both by the Pedagogical Team of the Banco de la República and the Truth Commission, are available at https://www.comisiondelaverdad.co/violaciones-de-derechos-humanos-infracciones-al-derecho-internacional-humanitario-y/huellas-de and at https://www.banrepcultural.org/exposiciones/huellas-de-desaparicion/estrategias-de-mediacion.

The International Coalition of Sites of Conscience refers to the concept of living archives in a guide for civil society organisations in creating oral human rights archives,[42] a concept similar to what Osuna refers to as living memory:

> Living memory involves transforming it into a public educational space for learning and dialogue. This approach transcends the limitations of the physical building where it is housed, allowing it to engage with citizens in their everyday environments. Breathing life into memory means putting it to use: building, sharing, disseminating, and making it visible while also teaching others. This is the essential mission of the Archive in our time.[43]

In "Traces of Disappearance," one of the most challenging aspects to convey to the public was the mural created from the research conducted on the territory and the Nukak people, which is displayed at the entrance of the exhibition. Despite the explanatory texts in front of the mural, interpreting its meaning has proven difficult. The Truth Commission, in collaboration with the Banco de la República, created this mural to promote coexistence between the Nukak communities and the farmers of the Guaviare department. This spurred the activities of the Ethnic Peoples Directorate and the Commission's Orinoquia territorial team, which were presented on April 21, 2022, at the Luis Ángel Arango Library.[44] Before the event, we visited the exhibition with representatives from both communities. When we reached the mural, the Nukak authorities highlighted several locations on the map, explaining the significance of each one. For instance, they pointed out Cerbatana Hill, a sacred site they could not access due to the ongoing armed conflict. A dialogue facilitated by a translator and interpreter allowed us to engage deeply with the mural on display.

Various activities were held during the exhibition, including ones with the relatives of those who disappeared from the Palace of Justice. One noteworthy initiative was the pedagogical space created by the educational team of the Banco de la República, known as Polifonías. In this space, objects belonging to loved ones who were victims of forced disappearance were displayed. This exhibit fostered conversations about memory, enhancing the narrative

42 International Coalition of Sites of Conscience, *Live Archives: Introductory Guide for Civil Society Organizations in the Creation of Oral Human Rights Archives and the Organization of Their Documentation*, 2020, https://gijtr.org/wp-content/uploads/2021/12/Living-Archives-Toolkit-6x9-EN-final.pdf.

43 Francisco Javier Osuna Currea, "Proceso de Cambio y Memoria Histórica: Los Archivos Como Testimonio," in *Memorias: Seminario Internacional Desafíos para la Reparación Integral a las Víctimas del Conflicto Armado Interno en Colombia*, ed. Dary Luz Nieto Sua (Bogotá: Alcaldía Mayor de Bogotá, 2012).

44 Video of the event available at https://www.banrepcultural.org/multimedia/conferencia-acuerdo-de-voluntades-entre-el-pueblo-nukak-y-el-campesinado-del-guaviare-0.

and concepts presented in the main areas of the exhibition. In this space, the pedagogical team facilitated a dialogue between peasants from the villages of Nueva Colonia (Turbo) and exhibition visitors. The drawings left in the room by the children of peasant leaders, along with the parents' account of the current situation in the territory, enriched the collective memory of the land, aligning with the research goals.

Bringing the exhibition archives to life has also meant emotionally impacting the public. The living archive aimed to foster a deep understanding and assimilation of the information presented and honour the emotions associated with pain and resistance. This approach was framed in a *sentipensante* (thinking/feeling) manner,[45] in which reason and emotions support and influence the public's interpretation. *Sentipensante*, moreover, "promotes an understanding that aligns intuition with experiential knowledge,"[46] and helps integrate the information presented with the references, contexts, and emotions of those receiving it. When people come across information about violence in audiovisual formats, it evokes emotions like surprise, fear, joy, anger, and sadness. These emotions enable the audience to connect with certain content more deeply than others, prompting discussions about how this information affects them physically and mentally.

This tension between the intimate and the collective had different manifestations on the exhibition, "Traces of Disappearance"; some were prompted by the project and others were the result of the initiatives of the people and groups that visited it. Thanks to the alliance with the Cinemateca de Bogotá, the videos of the Palace of Justice and Urabá cases were presented as a film in a movie theatre. Showing the archives on the big screen created a uniquely intimate experience, allowing viewers to focus, understand, and absorb the information more deeply. In the video rooms of the Miguel Ángel Urrutia Museum, visitors often struggled to assimilate the information thoroughly due to the noise and distractions from the crowd in the exhibition space. However, these more open rooms fostered an empathetic experience, promoting an emotional connection between visitors. This interaction enabled personal and collective experiences to emerge, enhancing the overall engagement.

Another way to bring these archives to life was through the efforts of schools, universities, and groups of young people, including activists and artists. They visited the exhibition and then took the concepts and information they learned and the emotions they experienced back to their own communities. During a

45 Orlando Fals Borda, *Double History of the Coast* (Bogotá: Universidad Nacional de Colombia, 1986); Orlando Fals Borda, *Una sociología sentipensante para América Latina*, compilado por Víctor Manuel Moncayo (Bogotá: Siglo del Hombre, 2009), http://biblioteca.clacso.edu.ar/ar/libros/coedicion/fborda/.

46 Fernanda Barbosa dos Santos, Clément Roux, Carolina Saldarriaga Cardona, and Eva Youkhana, "Una escena musical sentipensante en la transición posacuerdo en Colombia: El caso de la Casa de la Paz," *Cuadernos de Música, Artes Visuales y Artes Escénicas* 18, no. 2 (2023): 142–63, https://revistas.javeriana.edu.co/index.php/cma/article/view/37580

community meal at a school in western Bogotá, we started a conversation with teenagers about the issues they faced, including the disappearance of friends, relatives, and people from their neighborhoods. The taste of a familiar, shared meal activated the senses and helped connect participants to the information presented during the workshop and the subsequent discussions. This experience became a part of a collective memory that transcends rational understanding. It allowed the information to resonate with the attendees, moving from the published archive to each individual's archive, ultimately contributing to the collective construction of a living archive. Despite the different activities and efforts generated from the exhibition archives in Bogota, we faced some challenges and difficulties in expanding its dissemination to other platforms. Due to the institution's decisions, the planned travelling exhibitions in other Banco de la República buildings and creating a virtual museum did not materialise.. The exhibition launched on September 15, 2022, at the Museo de Antioquia in Medellín did not reach the same attendance numbers recorded in Bogotá. This was due to several factors: the museum's location in an insecure area of the city centre, the layout of the exhibition hall, insufficient promotion, and the lack of a comprehensive mediation and educational strategy to engage youth groups and communities.

From late 2023 to June 2024, the exhibition was hosted at the La Tertulia Museum in Cali to promote dialogue in the Valle del Cauca department regarding issues of forced disappearance, land dispossession, and their impact on indigenous peoples and their territories. One of the challenges in presenting these cases, which may seem distant to the residents of Cali, was to engage their interest and encourage public discussions and the sharing of experiences related to these same issues in the Valle del Cauca region. Fortunately, the results in this case were positive, largely due to an educational strategy that focused on attracting diverse population groups. Additionally, the establishment of a well-resourced didactic room facilitated in-depth discussions on various topics, drawing from the experiences of each group.[47] Over 10,000 people attended the exhibition, including the general public, guided tours, and educational activities.

These three different experiences in the country highlight the complexity and diversity of the contexts in which we decided to open and activate an archive of this kind. Beyond the disputes surrounding the truth in these sensitive issues, the key question that remains is how willing local, regional, and national societies are to engage in meaningful discussions about the structural problems that underlie human rights violations and the ongoing Colombian armed conflict. In summary, the various public expressions of "Traces of Disappearance" demonstrate that the challenges and efforts associated with the project are essential to creating this living archive. From this experience, we can

47 For a description of the didactic room of La Tertulia Museum see: https://museolatertulia.com/huellas-comun.

define a living archive as the interaction between the public and those familiar with it, actively engaging with its materials. This interaction broadens the archive's scope in different ways, from personal and intimate engagement to transmitting knowledge in collective spaces, where the archive is transformed or given deeper meaning. In other words, the archive takes on a life of its own.

Conclusions

"Traces of Disappearance" has built, developed, and published an innovative transitional justice archive. The search for, compilation of, and utilisation of other archives played a crucial role in this process. Access to conflict archives was integral to developing the research and the project's outcomes. While it was possible to access confidential information stored in public archives, such as the DAS report or declassified NSA documents, the state imposed limited access to documents not provided to the Truth Commission. Nevertheless, advancements in information technology and the extensive production of archives during periods of violence have enabled new opportunities for access to relevant information.

The project faced challenges due to both lack and abundance of archives. Thanks to the efforts of victims' families, human rights organisations, and subject matter experts, we gathered information from civil society and personal or collective archives. This collaboration helped us navigate through the vast number of available documents. Furthermore, the transnational and multidisciplinary team – comprising interns, research assistants, and researchers – contributed to a detailed and precise analysis of the information by effectively applying research methodologies. The gathered and analysed documents collectively formed a new archive, addressing many of the research questions posed. In instances where either a lack or an abundance of sources was encountered, this also formed part of the findings, as exemplified by the presentation of unanswered emails and the conceptualisation of the evidence as part of the "black boxes."

"Traces of Disappearance" has created new documents that help explain the violence and the context surrounding the cases studied. These collected and newly created pieces together formed a new archive, a puzzle that connected all aspects of the project's final narrative. The results were made accessible to the public through museum exhibitions and on the Truth Commission and Forensic Architecture websites. When we considered publicising the archive, we encountered the challenge of weighing the risks of exposing the collected information. The principle of maximum transparency regarding human rights violations – especially in the context of an ongoing armed conflict filled with threats and disputes over the truth – must always account for the potential risks to individuals who may be exposed. In "Traces of Disappearance," protecting the integrity of the people involved was our top priority.

The publication of the new transitional justice archive in the form of an art exhibition featuring audiovisual and artistic works has had a significant impact on the public. We have transformed the exhibition into a living archive through mediation, pedagogical preparation, and various activities developed around it. These efforts have helped create new platforms for understanding. On one hand, there is an intimate space where the information and emotions generated are absorbed individually. On the other hand, there are collective spaces inside and outside the exhibition where knowledge is built and shared emotional experiences are fostered. Not everything was accomplished. The exhibition's itinerancy and virtual dissemination faced various institutional and contextual challenges. However, the research's outcomes, extensive dissemination and activation, and some degree of criticism and silencing surrounding the project contribute to the lessons learned and legacy left by "Traces of Disappearance."

Bibliography

Balcells, Laia, and Christopher M. Sullivan. "New Findings from Conflict Archives: An Introduction and Methodological Framework." *Journal of Peace Research* (2018): 1–10. https://doi.org/10.1177/0022343317750217.

Banco de la República de Colombia. "Huellas de desaparición, Estrategias de mediación." 2021. https://www.banrepcultural.org/exposiciones/huellas-de-desaparicion/estrategias-de-mediacion.

Barbosa Dos Santos, Fernanda, Clément Roux, Carolina Saldarriaga Cardona, and Eva Youkhana. "Una escena musical sentipensante en la transición posacuerdo en Colombia: El caso de la Casa de la Paz." *Cuadernos de Música, Artes Visuales y Artes Escénicas* 18, no. 2 (2023): 142–63. https://doi.org/10.11144/javeriana.mavae18-2.emsp.

Centro Nacional de Memoria Histórica. *Política pública de archivos de derechos humanos, memoria histórica y conflicto armado*, 2017.

Comisión de la Verdad. "Las cinco peticiones de la Comisión de la Verdad ante la CIDH para facilitar el acceso a la información." 2020. https://web.comisiondelaverdad.co/actualidad/noticias/cinco-peticiones-comision-verdad-a-cidh-para-facilitar-acceso-informacion.

Comisión de la Verdad and Forensic Architecture. "Despojo y memoria de la tierra." 2022. https://www.comisiondelaverdad.co/violacion-derechos-humanos-y-derecho-internacional-humanitario/despojo-y-memoria-de-la-tierra.

Comisión de la Verdad and Forensic Architecture. "Experiencias de la exposición." 2022. https://www.comisiondelaverdad.co/violaciones-de-derechos-humanos-infracciones-al-derecho-internacional-humanitario-y/experiencias-de.

Comisión de la Verdad and Forensic Architecture. "Huellas de desaparición." 2022. https://www.comisiondelaverdad.co/violaciones-de-derechos-humanos-infracciones-al-derecho-internacional-humanitario-y/huellas-de.

Comisión de la Verdad and Forensic Architecture. "La selva detectada." 2022. https://www.comisiondelaverdad.co/violacion-derechos-humanos-y-derecho-internacional-humanitario/la-selva-detectada.

Comisión de la Verdad and Forensic Architecture. "Las cajas negras de la desaparición forzada." 2022. https://www.comisiondelaverdad.co/violacion-derechos-humanos-y-derecho-internacional-humanitario/las-cajas-negras-de-la-desaparicion.

Congress of the Republic of Colombia. *Law 1712*, March 6, 2014.

Constitutional Court of Colombia. *Judgment C-017/18*, 2018.

Constitutional Court of Colombia. *Judgment SU355/22*, 2022.

Cox, Richard. "Archives, War, and Memory: Building a Framework." *Library & Archival Security* 25, no. 1 (2012): 21–57. https://doi.org/10.1080/01960075.2012.657945.

Fals Borda, Orlando. *Double History of the Coast.* Bogotá: Universidad Nacional de Colombia, 1986.

Fals Borda, Orlando. *Una sociología sentipensante para América Latina*, compiled by Víctor Manuel Moncayo. Bogotá: Siglo del Hombre, 2009. http://biblioteca.clacso.edu.ar/ar/libros/coedicion/fborda/.

Forensic Architecture. "Data Mining." https://forensic-architecture.org/methodology/data-mining-2.

International Coalition of Sites of Conscience. "Live Archives: Introductory Guide for Civil Society Organizations in the Creation of Oral Human Rights Archives and the Organization of Their Documentation." 2020. https://gijtr.org/wp-content/uploads/2021/12/Living-Archives-Toolkit-6x9-EN-final.pdf.

Mbembe, Achille. "The Power of the Archive and Its Limits." In *Refiguring the Archive*, edited by Carolyn Hamilton, Verne Harris, Jane Taylor, Michele Pickover, Graeme Reid, and Razia Saleh. Cape Town: David Philip Publishers, 2002.

Meszaros Martín, Hannah, and Oscar Pedraza. "The Memory of Earth and Land Dispossession in Urabá." *Planning Theory* (2022). https://journals.sagepub.com/doi/10.1177/14704129211072651.

OpenSociety Justice Initiative. *Global Principles on National Security and the Right to Information.* New York: Open Society Justice Initiative, October 23, 2013. https://www.justiceinitiative.org/uploads/bd50b729-d427-4fbb-8da2-1943ef2a3423/global-principles-national-security-10232013.pdf.

Osuna Currea, Francisco Javier. "Proceso de Cambio y Memoria Histórica: Los Archivos Como Testimonio." In *Memorias: Seminario Internacional Desafíos para la Reparación Integral a las Víctimas del Conflicto Armado Interno en Colombia*, edited by Dary Luz Nieto Sua. Bogotá: Alcaldía Mayor de Bogotá, 2012.

Quintero Díaz, D. "La masacre de Punta Coquitos que se hundió con el Mar." *El Espectador*, 2023. https://www.elespectador.com/investigacion/la-masacre-en-punta-coquitos-que-se-hundio-con-el-mar/.

United Nations. *Basic Principles and Guidelines on the Right to a Remedy and Reparation for Victims of Gross Violations of International Human Rights Law and Serious Violations of International Humanitarian Law.* Geneva: United Nations, 2005, para. 10.

United Nations. *Question of the Impunity of Perpetrators of Human Rights Violations (Civil and Political): Revised Final Report Prepared by Mr. Joinet Pursuant to Sub-Commission Decision 1996/119*, UN Doc. E/CN.4/Sub.2/1997/20/Rev.1. Geneva: United Nations, 1997, 6–7. https://documents.un.org/doc/undoc/gen/g97/141/42/pdf/g9714142.pdf.

United Nations, Office of the High Commissioner for Human Rights. *Instruments of the Rule of Law for Societies Emerging from Conflict: Archives.* Geneva: United Nations, 2015, 36.

Weizman, Eyal. "Open Verification." *e-flux Architecture*, Becoming Digital, 2019. https://www.e-flux.com/architecture/becoming-digital/248062/open-verification/.

Index